COMPLETE IDIOT GUIDE TO

Canoeing and Kayaking

by the editors of *Canoe & Kayak* Magazine
and Dennis O. Stuhaug

ALPHA

A member of Penguin Group (USA) Inc

Dennis O. Stuhaug: It's been my good fortune, over many years and in many waters, to tag along with some of the best paddlers in the world. The good things I've learned come from them, the mistakes and flaws I carry with me are all of my own doing. Paramount among them is Suzanne, a delight with whom to share the river and the sea.

International Standard Book Number: 1-59257-239-1
Library of Congress Catalog Card Number: 2004103237

06   05   04   8   7   6   5   4   3   2   1

Interpretation of the printing code: The rightmost number of the first series of numbers is the year of the book's printing; the rightmost number of the second series of numbers is the number of the book's printing. For example, a printing code of 04-1 shows that the first printing occurred in 2004.

Printed in the United States of America

Note: This publication contains the opinions and ideas of its authors. It is intended to provide helpful and informative material on the subject matter covered. It is sold with the understanding that the authors and publisher are not engaged in rendering professional services in the book. If the reader requires personal assistance or advice, a competent professional should be consulted.

The authors and publisher specifically disclaim any responsibility for any liability, loss, or risk, personal or otherwise, which is incurred as a consequence, directly or indirectly, of the use and application of any of the contents of this book.

Most Alpha books are available at special quantity discounts for bulk purchases for sales promotions, premiums, fund-raising, or educational use. Special books, or book excerpts, can also be created to fit specific needs.

For details, write: Special Markets, Alpha Books, 375 Hudson Street, New York, NY 10014.

Publisher: *Marie Butler-Knight*
Product Manager: *Phil Kitchel*
Senior Managing Editor: *Jennifer Chisholm*
Acquisitions Editor: *Mikal Belicove*
Development Editor: *Jennifer Moore*
Production Editor: *Megan Douglass*
Copy Editor: *Jan Zoya*
Illustrator: *Richard King*
Cover/Book Designer: *Trina Wurst*
Indexer: *Angie Bess*
Layout/Proofreading: *Angela Calvert, Mary Hunt*

Contents at a Glance

Contents

Foreword

Imagine the quiet hiss of your canoe's bow cleaving the mirror-smooth surface of a remote northern lake at the end of a perfect day, the only other sound the wild laughter of a loon flitting away into the twilight. Feel the rise and fall of the sea, almost like breathing, as you skirt the shore of a lush island. Dance—there is no better word for it—in the twisting currents as you descend through a spray-filled rapid. Imagine? You don't have to imagine, you can experience it first-hand with the skills you'll quickly learn in these pages.

The world of paddling, whether you choose a canoe or a kayak, is a very large world indeed. You can cross oceans (it's been done) or poke around the lily pads in a small pond. You can venture out into the wilderness carrying all your possessions, or find close to home paddling adventures with your friends and family. You can paddle your canoe or kayak for recreation, competition, or exercise. Or, you can say "I'm a fisherman, I'm a photographer, I'm a …" and use your canoe or kayak as the vehicle that carries you deeper into your own endeavor. All this with boats that don't cost a fortune, that can be stored in your back yard, and that can be easily carried to water anywhere.

Canoes and kayaks are easy to paddle. They're safe. And they are just plain flat-out fun!

Complete Idiot's Guides serve you up the cream, the vital core, without swamping you in detail. This one is no exception. You'll find all the important topics, arranged in a logical sequence so that each leads you effortlessly to the next. You'll discover the essential differences between a canoe and a kayak (along with the advantages of each), practice getting in and on board each, and learn the paddle strokes that will propel you efficiently along your desired path. You'll acquire the basics of cruising down a river or across a bay. Most important, you'll learn how to do all these things safely. What should you wear (or not wear)? What's a guided trip? How can you plan an extended trip? Are you up for paddling with children? Page by page, here's the info you need to answer those questions for yourself. You'll paddle this course swiftly, gracefully, and with style. That's the whole point of the *Complete Idiot's Guides*— to put the information you need in your hands as easily and enjoyably as possible.

Is everything there is to know about paddling contained in these pages? Not by a long shot! It covers the basics, enough to get you out on the water safely. That's enough for some folks. If you're like me, and want more, check out some of the resources listed at the end of this book. From casual cruising to high-adrenalin competition, from conservation to boat construction, there's a welcoming harbor in the paddling world beckoning your particular interests. Come, launch your canoe or kayak, and let's go discover it. Let's go paddling!

—Glen Bernard, Publisher, *Canoe & Kayak* Magazine

Glen Bernard, publisher of *Canoe & Kayak* Magazine, has been a leading paddle-sports industry figure since joining *Canoe & Kayak* in 1986. Since then he has been dedicated to responsibly promoting and growing the sport while working toward preserving paddling resources for future generations. Glen has 26 years of publishing and marketing experience and has been a paddler for more than 30 years. He's married and lives just 3 minutes from the local put-in in the Seattle area. His 11-year-old daughter and 7-year-old son have been in boats their entire lives. Glen's boat quiver consists of 2 touring kayaks, 2 canoes, a white-water kayak, a wave ski, 2 sit-on-tops, a rec boat and an inflatable kayak. When not paddling throughout the Northwest, he enjoys skiing, hiking, camping, and photography.

Introduction

The basic skills of paddling a canoe or kayak are about the simplest thing imaginable to learn. Within five minutes of picking up a paddle, most of us can splash around more or less in the direction we want to go. We can also spend a lifetime exploring the nuances and subtleties of making our canoe or kayak glide elegantly and efficiently through the water.

The Complete Idiot's Guide to Canoeing and Kayaking is your guide to getting into your canoe or kayak for the first time, and starting on the voyage to becoming an expert paddler. We lay the keel (boating talk for the first step in building a boat) with the essential difference between a kayak and a canoe. You'll see why canoes and kayaks come in all those shapes, and what shapes work better for paddling on rivers or paddling on lakes, bays, and oceans. Along the way, you'll discover what kind of paddle will work best for you, as well as how to dress yourself and your boat for success in the paddling world.

By the time you turn the last page of this book, you'll have a good grasp of the paddling skills you need to move your canoe or kayak in the direction you want, easily and efficiently. You'll also discover the techniques you'll need for paddling rivers or on flatwater, where you can hone your paddling skills, what you really have to know about guided trips, and even how fun it can be paddling with children.

You don't have to read every chapter to make this book useful. If you only want to paddle a cruising kayak, just skim through the parts on canoes. Truth be known, most who paddle one also enjoy paddling the other, but take your time and savor those parts of the paddling experience that most appeal to you. Just don't dismiss the others out of hand.

We've organized this book so that you can easily locate the information you want—and need—whether you're just figuring out how to get into a canoe or kayak for the first time, or want to learn how to plan a voyage down a river or along a distant coastline. We've done our best to make paddling jargon understandable, to warn you about the hazards, and to pass along the little tips and tricks that have made our paddling easier over the years.

Canoeing and kayaking are as easy as they look, and a skilled paddler makes them look very easy indeed. First, learn the basic strokes. Explore how to combine strokes to maneuver your canoe or kayak. Discover how to adapt your maneuvers to the conditions you encounter. It becomes a combination of easily learned techniques leavened with common sense and the willingness to enjoy a new experience.

You shouldn't paddle alone. That's just common-sense safety. Paddling with more experienced fellow club members, in a school or class, or in the wake of a professional guide (all things you'll read about in these pages) will also enable you to practice your paddling skills and techniques and to develop those skills much, much faster. You'll have more fun paddling, you'll have more fun learning, and, in your time off the water, I hope you'll have fun reading this book.

This book is the put-in (paddling talk for the place that you launch your canoe or kayak into the water) to help you …

- ♦ Learn the difference between a canoe and a kayak, and learn the characteristics of each that allow them to perform so well on rivers and on lakes and salt water.

- ♦ Discover the accessories and equipment you should have, both for you and for your canoe or kayak, to increase your pleasure and safety while out on the water.

- ♦ Learn the basic paddle strokes that enable you to efficiently propel and precisely maneuver your canoe.

- ♦ Practice the techniques of getting in (and out of) your canoe or kayak.

- ♦ Discover the rhythm of paddling your canoe or kayak down a river, while understanding the techniques that make river-paddling fun and safe.

- ♦ Explore the delights of cruising a canoe or a kayak on lakes, bays, and the ocean itself, while examining the skills you need to paddle in wind, waves, and currents (as well as how to extricate yourself from challenging situations).

- ♦ Consider the options you have in honing your basic canoeing and kayaking skills, ranging from paddling with fellow club members to elite paddling schools.

- ♦ How to share the fun while paddling with the world's greatest paddlers—kids.

- ♦ Build the very kayak or canoe that you dream about.

How to Use This Book

The Complete Idiot's Guide to Canoeing and Kayaking portages all the information you need to get started in canoeing or kayaking right to your launching site. Read this book to learn the basics, and then take it with you as you explore the amazing variety of paddling experiences opening to you all across North America. The important details are covered in six parts:

Part 1, "Let's Go Paddling," opens up the wonderful world of paddling, from family picnics to high-adrenalin competition. It walks you through the differences between canoes and kayaks as well as the differences between a river boat and a flat-water boat (who ever thought to call the ocean flat water?), and you'll begin to see just why certain canoes and kayaks work better in certain kinds of paddling environments. You'll also see the materials canoes and kayaks are made from, and perhaps why one is the best for you.

Part 2, "You and Your Paddle," brings you up close and personal to the transmission, the wheels, the brakes, and the steering in your canoe or kayak. We'll unlock the mystery of how you can find a paddle that fits you, your paddling, and your boat. You'll see why paddles come in so many shapes and lengths, and will learn how to find the one that will work best for you.

Part 3, "Gearing Up," reviews the accessories and gear you need for your canoe or your kayak, from mooring lines (called painters) to flotation bags (that keep a swamped boat afloat). You'll examine the gear you really need, and why. You'll also try on the clothing that will make your day on the water a lot more comfortable, whether you'll be drifting along a tropical beach or swooping down a chilly river. The most important piece of gear for your canoe or kayak is your life jacket, your personal flotation device (PFD), and you'll learn what you want to have and what you must carry.

Part 4, "At the Water's Edge," takes your canoe or kayak out of the backyard and puts it in the water where it belongs. You'll practice getting into and out of your canoe or kayak on the beach (sometimes your boat should point straight out from the beach, and sometimes be parallel to the water's edge). Once in your canoe or kayak, we'll share the basic paddle strokes that move you ahead, backward, will turn you, or will move you directly to the side.

Part 5, "On the Water," puts you, the paddling skills you've learned, and your boat on the water. Whether you paddle a canoe or a kayak, you'll discover how to make your new-found skills work as we head down a river. You'll learn to watch the marks of the current, and discover how to safely move down the ever-exciting and changing world of the river. Then we'll move over to flatwater—lakes, ponds, bays, and the broad reaches of the ocean. You'll find the techniques you'll need for paddling in wind, waves, and currents, and to predict the state of the tide and the speed of currents.

Part 6, "Go Paddling," shares the nitty-gritty on buffing up your paddling skills and expanding your paddling horizons. You'll discover the great range of paddling instruction available to you, from basic to post-graduate. You'll enjoy the luxury of a guided trip in the waters as well as the off-water fun of planning your own voyage. Share the fun as well as ease the strangeness of a day on the water with young children. And, not the least, on your days away from the water, explore your options in building the canoe or kayak of your dreams.

Extras

Sometimes the best information comes in little pieces, a flash that resonated with what you've been thinking or what you've been wondering about. Just the facts, stripped to their bare bones. *The Complete Idiot's Guide to Canoeing and Kayaking* comes through with plenty of these little bite-sized nuggets that both satisfy your taste for knowledge and whet your appetite for more study. Look for these compact, easy-to-find, and easy-to-read tips throughout the book:

In the Wake

Everyone has an unlabeled drawer in the kitchen where all the miscellaneous stuff that you just can't live without and yet can't find a logical place to put gets stored. In these pages, In the Wake is that drawer, and the hints and tips come from all over the paddling spectrum.

Rocks and Shoals

There are hazards when you go out on the water with your paddle in your hands. Rocks and Shoals, the ancient hazards facing all who are afloat, tell you exactly what to watch for when a situation can turn nasty or challenging.

The Old Paddler Says

Look for the Old Paddler to pass along the tips and advice that make canoeing or kayaking easier, safer, or just plain more fun. Some will make you a better canoeist or kayaker, some will prevent you from heading into bad water, and some will show you different ways to approach the task at hand.

Paddlin' Talk

These are the canoeing and kayaking terms that precisely and exactly illuminate the language of the river and the sea. Read them, and you'll understand what the paddle-wielders are talking about on the beach.

Acknowledgments

There are many slips between the thought and the word. Jennifer Moore's patient and unerring eye picked up the lapses, the inadvertent transpositions, and the trains of thought gone astray and carefully redirected all back on track. Everyone should have the good fortune to work with an editor like her. Any mistakes herein are simply those I managed to slip by her, and I take full responsibility for them.

Almost every person I have met with a paddle in his or her hand gave me bits of information appearing in these pages. The foundation for all of it came from paddling master Werner Furrer who insisted that the single most important part of paddling was to have fun while doing it. That's a fine, fine thought to paddle by.

Trademarks

All terms mentioned in this book that are known to be or are suspected of being trademarks or service marks have been appropriately capitalized. Alpha Books and Penguin Group (USA) Inc. cannot attest to the accuracy of this information. Use of a term in this book should not be regarded as affecting the validity of any trademark or service mark.

Part 1

Let's Go Paddling

Help! Kayaks and canoes, rivers and flatwater, solo paddling and tandem, competition and relaxation. With all these choices, where do you find out what canoe or kayak is best for you?

Right here! Part 1 offers you a look across the wide, wide world of paddling. You'll learn the difference between a canoe and a kayak, between a river boat and a flatwater boat (who ever thought to call the ocean flat water?), and you'll begin to see just why certain canoes and certain kayaks work better in certain kinds of paddling environments. We'll also look at the materials canoes and kayaks are made from, and perhaps why one is the best for you.

Will we tell you what canoe or kayak to buy? Nope. But we will lay out the guidelines so that you can make a better informed decision when choosing your favorite boat.

Just What Is Paddlesports?

In This Chapter

- Exploring your paddlesports options
- The ins and outs of kayaks and canoes
- Discovering the thrill of competition
- Adapting your boat to your hobby

Paddlesports is an umbrella term, a word used to describe a huge range of activities involving canoes and kayaks. It's a name big enough to encompass international kayaking and canoeing competitions and Sunday afternoon lolls on the lake. It's searching for a safe beach on a surf-battered remote Arctic Island, cavorting down a whitewater river, and bobbing just off the surf line in a search of red snapper.

Getting a Handle on Paddlesports

Paddlesports can also mean spending the morning teaching a kid the discipline involved in commanding a touring kayak, and then taking the afternoon to daydream on a quiet float on a winding river to get away from all that discipline and responsibility.

You can work on your physical conditioning as you power ahead with a high stroke-per-minute paddle stroke, or you can work on your mental well-being by contemplating the oranges and reds of a sunset filtering through high-rise buildings and splashed on an urban lake. You don't have to be in the wilderness to enjoy paddlesports.

There are boats for every level of ability, and for people with any combination of abilities. You can sail or paddle. You can sit, kneel, or stand. You can be the captain, cook, and crew of your own solo vessel, or you can work as a carefully meshed member of a smoothly synchronized team. Canoes and kayaks are truly the people's yachts.

The line between canoe and kayak blurs as their forms are shaped by their functions. For practical purposes, a kayak is a vessel that you sit in or upon and propel yourself with a double-bladed paddle—a paddle with a blade on each end. A canoe is a vessel in which you sit, kneel, or stand, and propel yourself with a single-bladed paddle or a pole. Either can be propelled by sail.

Not only are they boats that can serve multiple purposes, canoes and kayaks can also morph from one to the other to increase their flexibility.

The Clean, Green Low-Impact Sport

The wake trailing out behind your canoe or kayak dissipates in seconds, the small waves vanish in the surface, and even the sounds of water drops falling from your paddle are inaudible just a few feet away. You leave no mark—not even footsteps—of your passing. In a world with increasing population and decreasing recreational outlets, that's a major benefit.

In the Wake

Paddlesports competitions usually take place on existing waters, though a few artificial venues have cropped up. The Olympic slalom course in Barcelona, Spain, was built for competition. For the Atlanta Olympics, a slalom course was constructed in a usually dry river channel. Other artificial courses have been built at Wausau, Wisconsin; Washington, D.C.; and South Bend, Indiana.

Paddlesports requires little in the way of facilities. A path down to a narrow beach launches voyages on rivers, lakes, or oceans.

You don't use up a waterway by paddling over it. You don't beat down a groove in a lake, in a river, or in the ocean in your passage. You don't swill down gallons of fuel every hour and spew out its fumes as you enjoy the beauty of a river. (The peanut-butter sandwiches you eat to give yourself energy don't count—they are made from totally renewable resources.)

Canoes and kayaks are, admittedly, manufactured items. So are paddles and PFDs, the life jackets all paddlers must wear. But compared to almost any other activity that re-creates and refreshes us, the equipment of the paddler is minimal. Canoes have long been called the people's yacht, because they are within the financial reach of the vast majority of us. A canoe costs less than a mid-range bicycle, costs less than a lot of snow skis, and comes without the on-going burden of expensive lift tickets. With even just a smidgen of care and maintenance, the usable life of a canoe or kayak can stretch over generations of paddlers. Even plastic, popular in so many hulls, is recyclable.

If you paddle, you're going to be healthier. Your heart will be more alive, and your blood will run freer in your veins. You'll discover that stress and a paddle are not com-patible, and that the paddle will win every time. You'll breathe easier, and you'll be less susceptible to colds and other bugs. Maybe you'll see a huge improvement, or maybe it will be miniscule, but it will be there. If you want a more scientific approach, talk to your doctor about the benefits of light-to-moderate exercise, and you'll get an earful. We also know that those without sight,
those with twisted bodies or injuries that deprive them of full mobility, and those who disease has slowed find the comfort of a canoe or kayak most enjoyable.

Oh, one more thing: The paddlers we know tend to smile far more than those nonpaddlers we know.

The Old Paddler Says

Join a paddling club first off. You'll find good used boats and paddling gear as well as the knowledge of how to eval-uate the state of repair.

Fun for the Whole Family

Canoeing and kayaking are a great solo sport. You can go by yourself. Common sense and Mother Nature strongly advise that you paddle in a group of at least three boats, but with the active nature of paddling clubs all across North America, the only time you won't find two friends to paddle with will be during the winter solstice on the shores of the Great Slave Lake; the ice is a little thick. But you will find a friendly gathering around a warm stove to discuss trips after the ice breaks up, the merits of new equipment, and the advantages of a just-learned stroke.

Paddling is great for a pair. On the most basic level, it gives you company in the boat, to share the sights and savor the day. Learning to paddle in unison, anticipating the moves and power of your partner, tremendously increases the pleasure of a day's paddle on

Rocks and Shoals

Remember the 20/20 rule of paddling: If the tempera-ture is below 20°F or the wind is over 20 mph, stay ashore.

flatwater or down a river. It's like dancing, only with a paddle in your hand. At the same time, it enables people of different fitness and skill levels to share a sport together. No one is left behind, no one has to wait: Both ends of the boat arrive at your destination at just about the same time.

Children start out as great boaters. We know families (admittedly, the folks were outstanding paddlers before they had their first child) who rocked their pretoddlers to sleep in the easy motion of a canoe on protected waters. A three-year-old loves to splash at the water with a paddle sized to fit him or her. The inside of a canoe or touring kayak is perfect for driving toy cars or coloring, for stories and songs, and watching for birds. A boat is an exciting way to embark on a two-hour voyage after pirates, to sneak up on a turtle, to impart a little bit of paddling skill and technique while exchanging a broad range of confidences and concepts across the generations. A child can venture into what he or she perceives as an adult world (with adult responsibilities) with a single dip of a paddle—and at the same time remain safe within a harbor of family and childhood.

Your canoe or kayak is a magic carpet that can move you across time, enabling you to share in the world of your children, and giving both of you a new vocabulary with which to communicate. In your house, in your child's school, communication is from the authority of an adult. In a canoe, communication morphs into conversation.

Paddlin' Talk

When paddlers talk about **flatwater,** they mean water without rapids, such as a slow-moving river, a lake, or a sheltered bay. It's also sometimes *flat water* (two words).

Rocks and Shoals

For some unknown reason, the dominant (or louder) person in any pair likes to jump in the rear seat of a canoe or kayak on the river and then bellow orders. The paddler in the front, on a river, controls where the boat goes.

High-Level Competition for the Adrenalin Set

Does pushing "the wall" with your muscles and maxing your cardiovascular system ring your bell? Is crashing through the finish line the meat and potatoes of your existence? Then grab a paddle and come on, because canoeing and kayaking kick out every imaginable level of competition in a range of venues unparalleled in any other sport.

Dragon boats push the envelope of what most people think of as a canoe. They're big—as long as a city bus—and with 20 paddlers, a steersman, and a drummer for cadence, they're fast enough to tow a water skier. In the fourth century B.C.E., a Chinese poet and scholar named Qu Yuan became so angry over rampant corruption within the Chu Dynasty that he threw himself into the Mi Lo River. Local fishermen saw the beloved poet sinking and paddled furiously from shore in an unsuccessful attempt to save him. That incident inspired top-level Dragon-boat competitions in Hong Kong, Vancouver (Canada), New York, London, Cape Town, and Wellington (New Zealand) as well as in almost every city with a stretch of water long enough for the race. Dragons race in assigned lanes from 250 to 1,000 meters, with races lasting anywhere from three to six minutes, and first to the finish line wins the heat. It's more than likely the fastest-growing water-sports competition around the globe. Sweden alone has nearly 500 teams.

Needle-thin and wicked-fast sprint canoes and kayaks, solo to four paddlers, rocket down lanes on a flatwater course. Men compete in single and double canoes and kayaks at distances of 500 and 1,000 meters and in four-man kayaks at 1,000 meters. Women compete in single, double, and four-woman kayaks at 500 meters. Single kayaks are 17 feet long and weigh only 26.4 pounds. The four-person kayaks stretch out 36 feet and weigh 66 pounds.

> ### In the Wake
>
> Flatwater sprint racing was introduced into the Olympics in the 1924 Games. The XI Olympiad, in Berlin in 1936, saw classes for one- and two-person folding kayaks, one- and two-person rigid kayaks, and solo Canadian canoe.

The Old Paddler Says

In early June 1790, during his epic exploration of the West Coast of North America, Captain George Vancouver watched sprint canoe races on what is now known as Puget Sound. The Captain and his men watched, amazed, as crews of eight Native American youths competed in 45- to 50-foot canoes hewn out of individual cedar logs. Similar races, and ceremonial visits between the coast tribal communities, continue to the present day.

How fierce can the competition get?

Imagine a series of 25 narrow gates suspended over a foaming whitewater river, snaking along a convoluted 300- to 600-meter course that severely tests the skills of any paddler attempting to pass through each in sequence without so much as a touch. That's whitewater slalom, occasionally included in the Olympic Games, with a huge international following and a closely fought World Championship decided by World-Cup races held around the world. It is very similar to the snow ski slalom races you've seen on television, other than that the route through the gates is far more complex. Some of the gates must be passed through heading downstream, while others must be looped around and run heading back upstream. All the while racers battle the clock.

Wildwater racing is an all-out three- to five-mile sprint down a rapid-filled river. The goal is to find the fastest foot-and-a-half-wide strip of river current leading through each rapid, to stay on that ribbon, and to drive the boat as fast as muscles will allow.

Marathons take grueling to an entirely new level. These solo and tandem open canoe races, run in ultra-sleek competition cruisers, often extend from 5 to 15 miles on river and occasional flatwater courses. A typical race is between one and three hours long. Some races can extend over hundreds of miles, taking days to complete. Portages are just part of the course, with the canoes carried at a run. Many of the races (held in 50-odd countries and on every continent except Antarctica) begin with an exciting LeMans start, in which the paddlers hoist their boats up over their heads and run through city streets on their way to the first put-in.

Outrigger canoe racing attracts solo paddlers as well as teams of up to eight paddlers, both men and women. An outrigger canoe is made of three pieces: the main hull itself in which the paddlers sit; the akas, or crosspieces, extending out from the hull on one or both sides of the main hull; and the amas, or secondary hulls, providing stability. The outriggers may sprint at pulse-building paddle cadences over short distances on a sheltered lake, or may settle down into a muscle-tormenting 30 miles or more open-ocean crossing between tropical islands. The races, built on the long tradition of Polynesian sea paddling, are very popular from the West Coast of North America to all across the island-dotted Pacific to Australia and New Zealand.

The Old Paddler Says

One of the most famous of the big outrigger races is across the wave-swept 30-mile-wide Molokai Channel in Hawaii. If you question the seaworthiness of canoes, reflect on that long open ocean crossing.

Closely allied to outrigger racing are the needle-slim surf skis rocketing across the open ocean as well as on furious sprints in more protected waters. Surf skis are long, 19 feet and more, and are barely hip-width wide. Shallow divots hold your fanny and heels. While most of these marine rockets are for single paddlers, tandems and up to four-paddler models also exist. They are exceedingly popular all over the world.

Surf skis go best in the long waves of the open ocean while wave skis are built for the foam and crash of breaking surf. Confusing as the names may be, that's just the way it is. Think of a wave ski as an eight-foot-long pumpkinseed, with a divot for your fanny, and toestraps for your feet. These solo kayaks play like traditional board surfers within the curl of the waves crashing onto exposed beaches, with even more control and moves than the stand-up surfers. They're sometimes called "butt-boarders" because of their sit-down style. Judges grade their performance on the difficulty, grace, and duration of the tricks they perform on their wild ride into the beach. Surf kayaks are sit-inside versions of wave skis.

Rodeo kayakers are minimal-flotation river versions of wave skis. The paddler gyrates through loops, spins, and on-end stands during a timed ride in a single hole on a whitewater river. A boater may spin in a lazy pirouette balanced on the tip of a bow, only to plunge deep underwater to bounce off currents and explode back to the surface a half minute or more away.

Freestyle canoeing is like ice dancing on water. Its graceful moves are timed to beautiful music. This is a flatwater competition, in which spins, glides, and turns are performed to the notes floating over the lake.

You don't even need a paddle to compete in paddlesports! Polers stand up in their open canoes, using canoe-length poles to precisely move themselves up and down whitewater rapids. Poling off the bottom has been a canoe technique since the first paddler had to head upstream. Today's poling competitors quickly and precisely move themselves in a battle against the clock, one competitor on the course at a time.

If you just want to lean back without the effort of paddling, canoe sailing is a long-established sport with its own regional and national champions. Canoe sailing regattas are like any other sailing competitions, with upwind and downwind legs, and all boats on the course during the race. It evolves into a taut battle of strategies, snagging each puff of wind.

The Old Paddler Says

Dr. Hannes Lindemann sailed his Klepper folding kayak across the Atlantic Ocean. The astounding voyage of this great humanitarian is told in *Alone at Sea*, (Menasha Ridge Press, 1999).

The racing styles listed here are just the beginning of the formalized competitive world of canoe and kayak competition. Touring kayaks, definitely not designed to a single rigid standard, race over a stunning variety of distances. We've caromed down snow-covered slopes in open aluminum canoes, attempting to skid across a pool of half-melted snow water at the bottom. Some made it; some slewed to the side and waded out. We recollect a sit-on-top "race" in which paddlers merely carefully paddled out 50 meters or so from a dock, around a buoy, and returned. The competitive side came on each lap, as you added yet another square flotation cushion to your seat. It took about seven laps before the last paddler, and winner, flopped over.

Great Exercise, Lily-Dipping Leisure

The paddler out to cover miles in the gray early-morning light is a common sight on many shorelines. Expanding rings of ripples mark each paddle stroke and a long vee of wake stretches back from the stern to mark direction and distance.

Rocks and Shoals

Most paddling injuries come about because of improper technique. A paddler may, for instance, improperly lift his arms well above his head while doing a high brace, and the leverage inflicted may painfully twist or even damage a shoulder joint. Learn to do the strokes properly to avoid injury.

The Old Paddler Says

A few years back, *Canoe & Kayak* Magazine loaded up its 26-foot voyageur canoe with marathon and Olympic sprint paddlers and, with all that horsepower, towed a water skier around an urban lake near its office.

In the Wake

The popular hydration packs, used by runners, cyclists, and other endurance athletes, came from outrigger canoe racing. You just can't put down a paddle and grab a water bottle, as much as you need to, when you're part of a synchronized team keeping a boat moving for hours and miles. But you can suck on a tube for water.

It's an interior voyage, more involved with the sound of blood flowing through arteries and the flex and lubrication of muscles growing stronger. The paddler returns from the morning workout wet with sweat—that was part of the purpose—but at the same time, physically and mentally rejuvenated. Paddling defines low-impact exercise. You don't stress joints or muscles. By merely slacking off on the paddle cadence, you can rest as you choose.

Most paddlers will find that their arms and torsos will tire long before they achieve an anaerobic exercise level, and that's for the good. If you want, or believe you need, to bulk up your muscle mass, then paddle with a large blade. That's exactly like using heavy weights, or turning the exercise machine up to a high number. If you want to tone up your cardiovascular system with little stress on your joints, paddle with a small blade.

How much energy will you burn paddling? A better question is to ask how much energy you're going to throw into the paddling mix. In either case, the answer is strictly up to you. As a rule of thumb, eat (an energy bar is fine) before you are hungry, and drink before you get thirsty. By the time you feel hunger or thirst, you're already well into food or water debt.

Lily-dipping refers to the paddler(s) preferring to poke along the edges of the lily pads in a smallish pond. It is low-energy, short-distance, high-fun paddling, as often as not with a ukulele and a picnic hamper. You can launch your canoe on Monday for two hours of sweaty exercise, and launch again on Tuesday afternoon for a friendly drift across a mirror-smooth pond. Same boat, same paddle.

The Ultimate Fishing Machine

Your basic canoe or kayak is among the most versatile craft ever created. Whether sailing, hauling cargo, playing in white water, racing long distance, traveling to the remote corners of the world … these amazingly efficient small boats can do it all with a crew ranging from a solo paddler up into the dozens. What's even better is that each can be modified into a specialty machine that serves your particular needs to a tee.

Rocks and Shoals _____

Consider renting a canoe or kayak your first few times on the water, and wangle rides with more experienced paddlers in your club to experience the widest range of boats possible. That will help channel you in the right direction when you purchase your first boat. A used boat from a fellow club member can be a smart buy, especially since you'll have the chance to see it perform in your own paddling waters.

Take fishing, for example. If you've limited yourself to partyboat charters, you go where others want to go on their schedules and with a fairly hefty outlay of cash every time you head out for a few hours of fishing. And that's fishing shoulder to shoulder on a crowded deck, by and large with heavy gear more suited to winching fish out of the depths rather than to a contest between fish and fisherman.

Instead, consider a sit-on-top kayak. The boat will probably cost you less than a few trips on a partyboat. Lash a watertight hamper for fishing gear onto the rear deck, mount fishing rod holders on each side, add in a self-contained fishfinder/depthfinder for checking out bottom structure, and fasten a fish box or bucket on the fore deck ahead of your feet. Install a cleat on each gunwale (side of the boat) at the mid-point to secure a small sea anchor. A sea anchor looks like a small parachute, and it floats just under the surface of the water. It will hold you in one place on the water, despite the wind. A cell phone in a waterproof housing ($20 or less for the housing) keeps you in contact with the world.

With this simple rig you can launch off almost any beach, paddle to great near-shore fishing grounds, and come and go as you please. You're not subject to the schedule of other passengers or a paid skipper and boat.

Rocks and Shoals _____

Remember the fish box! Dropping a few pounds of slimy fish into your cockpit when you're wearing shorts is a delight you can afford to pass up.

That's about as close to the ideal fishing machine as you're likely to find. It will work in salt water, sneaking through freshwater lily pads after bass, or slipping down a stream after salmon.

If birding or its cousin wildlife photography is your bag, look at a beamy—wide—canoe. A wide canoe will be more stable than a narrow one, and is a better camera platform. Lash together a simple framework over the open hull and cover it with a mesh camouflage fabric and you have a portable, comfortable hide. You can drift up amazingly close to most animals (know the law, some, like whales, you're not supposed to approach too closely) for great photos.

These are but a few examples out of a million possibilities. If your second hobby (we assume the first is paddling!) is concentrated in or around the water, you can modify your canoe or kayak to carry you to participate in it. Woodworking? Build a boat. Sewing? Paddle jackets, spray covers, or tents. Cooking? You'll be invited on every overnight trip within 100 miles of your home. Just assemble a lightweight, portable kitchen that will stow in a boat and you have it made. Painting? Jokes about *water*-colors aside, think of the *plein aire* (outside in the real world) vista you may capture along any shore.

The Least You Need to Know

- Canoes and kayaks offer an incredible amount of paddling variety—and your pleasure is among the choices.

- Paddling competition comes in an almost-unbelievable range of boats and venues.

- Canoes and kayaks were called "the people's yacht" for good reason—they are the ideal way of taking a family on the water.

- You can (and should) modify your canoe or kayak to mesh with your hobbies and interests.

Chapter 2

What's the Best Boat for Me?

In This Chapter

- ◆ Matching your boat to your dreams
- ◆ White water versus touring
- ◆ Paddling alone versus paddling in tandem
- ◆ Storing your canoe or kayak
- ◆ Boating vocabulary

What's the best boat? There's a simple answer—the one you're paddling right now. Like most simple answers, it contains both a grain of truth and a bit of a fib. If you're paddling and enjoying it, that's good. It is also possible, by looking at the options available to you, that there is a boat that can afford you more paddling pleasure, and quite possibly you're not in it.

What Kind of Paddling Do You Dream Of?

Land the boat you're paddling, for a moment, and come sit on the beach and daydream. Just what has attracted you to paddling? Do you want to play in a foaming rapid, spinning about and dancing on the waves and currents? That can lift your adrenaline level, big time, in a sport that's both technically demanding and superbly fun.

Do you have visions of trekking through the wilderness for days, for weeks, on end? Would your perfect day involve picking your way carefully through a maze of small channels—even carrying your boat over a small rise of land to find the next watercourse? Do you long for the lift of a wave and the sight of whale flukes rising against the setting sun? Do you see yourself as a member of a closely knit team functioning with machinelike precision as you drive a boat at maximum speed against equally matched competitors?

The Old Paddler Says

Expand the range of your dreams by linking up with the paddling clubs in your area. You may discover that you enjoy a type of paddling you never contemplated. Equally, you may discover that a type of paddling you dreamed about has little attraction for you.

These aren't rhetorical questions. The greatest featherlight flatwater sprint racing canoe, as you've likely seen in the Olympics, is a pig when it comes to camping along a winding stream. A touring kayak may get wedged sideways in a narrow whitewater steep creek, and the best of paddlers will labor, vainly attempting to keep a whitewater canoe moving in a straight line across a windy bay.

So what's a paddler to do? On Apollo's Temple, at Delphi, "Know thyself" is inscribed in the white marble. Thomas Carlyle, a couple of thousand years later, wrote: "The folly of that impossible precept 'Know Thyself' till it be translated into this partially possible one, 'Know what thou canst work at'."

In the Wake

Touring boats, both canoes and kayaks, are designed to paddle and glide in a straight line, requiring few course-correcting strokes. White-water boats are designed to be nimble, turning on a dime and handing you back change.

They're both saying the same thing. Find the kind of paddling you want to do, and, from that, select the tools—the type of boat and paddle—that are most efficient under the conditions you're most likely to encounter.

There's a problem with those wise words. Your words. As you say, "But I want to do it all: I want to cruise and tour; I want to paddle white water (maybe not really huge whitewater) and little streams; I want to camp in the wilderness and explore big lakes and the ocean."

For the Person Who Wants to Do It All

How can you be expected to discover your paddling forte when you've only just been bitten by the paddling bug? Fortunately, it's easy.

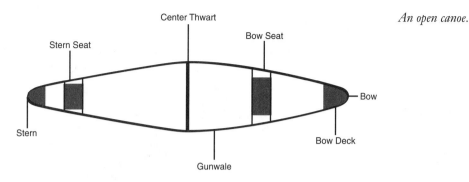

An open canoe.

The ideal paddling boat exists. From bow to stern it measures 16 feet long, and at its widest point it's 33 inches broad. At its middle, its sides rise between 11 and 13 inches from the water to the upper edge, and the sharp point atop the pointed front and back are perhaps 4 inches higher than that. The bottom is very slightly vee'd—meaning the left and right sides of the bottom meet in the middle and form a very broad vee shape. The sides slant outward from the waterline to the upper edge of the hull just a bit, with the outward flare accentuated a bit at the front and back. There are two seats. A generation or so ago, it probably would have been made of aluminum, a century ago of thin wood planks covered with painted canvas, but today is most likely a plastic called Royalex or one of its derivatives.

It has a name. It's a general recreational canoe, and it has looked pretty much the same for 150 years. You can poke around little streams in it all day—enjoying the paddling, watching wildlife, fishing, or playing a ukulele. Add a few accessories and it safely handles some fairly turbulent white water. It will carry two paddlers and all their gear for two weeks in the wilderness. With care, you can explore the edges of big lakes and oceans. You can compete against similar boats over measured flatwater distances, or attempt to beat the clock while twisting and turning down a slalom course on a river. You can sail it, or you can stand up and push it along with a pole.

It's a ball to paddle with two people, and that's one of its strengths. One paddler can be as strong as an ox, and the other far less physical, and yet they can paddle together without one being left far behind in the wake. A solo paddler finds it responsive, light on the water, and easy to push on for the entire day.

It is a truly phenomenal boat, this recreational canoe.

The Old Paddler Says

The seats in a recreational canoe are usually a flat bench. The canoe may be paddled in either direction, with a paddler simply turning around on the bench seat. Competition cruiser or marathon canoes have molded seats that look like old-fashioned tractor seats, and the paddler may only face forward.

The Drawbacks of a General-Purpose Boat

Our general purpose canoe has a drawback. Because it is called upon to do so many different things, it is not specialized enough to any one thing extraordinarily well. You may follow your nose into big white-water paddling, and partway up the ladder of rapid difficulty you'll push beyond the capabilities of the recreational canoe. You might plunge into a month-long exploration of the wilderness, and the recreational canoe won't carry the gear and supplies you'll need for such a long trip. You might fall deeply in love with the breath and long inhalations of the sea, and that can lead you into waters unsuitable for this generalized canoe.

> **Rocks and Shoals**
>
> Today's canoes and kayaks are amazingly well designed, and that's a problem. The boats handle so well that a less-than-cautious paddler can imperceptibly edge into waters over his or her head.

Canoe or Kayak: What Suits You?

Choosing between a canoe and a kayak isn't easy. It's possible, if you just divide it on functional lines, but unfortunately you'll collide with aesthetics, preconceptions, and a tad bit of physics.

You first must decide where you like to paddle. If you paddle on a network of small streams and lakes, linked by trails or portages over which you'll have to carry your boat, you'll probably prefer a lightweight open canoe. You can flip a canoe over and carry it on your shoulders, which is far easier than attempting to manhandle the slick shape of a decked—a solid cover over the open space of the hull—kayak. It's also easier to load and unload, no small matter when you've beached at one end of a tough portage and camp is planned at the other end of the trail.

If you want to venture out onto the big swells and long distances of big-water touring, you're going to tilt toward a touring kayak. There are long, sleek touring canoes but you'll find a much narrower choice of craft available to you. Generally speaking (and we're hiding under a lightning rod as we write this, lest we be struck), most beginning paddlers will find a touring kayak a more efficient and easier boat to paddle than a decked touring canoe. A double-bladed paddle enables you to use more energy in forward-paddling and less in corrective strokes than its single-bladed cousin. Newcomers to the sport may well find that the higher center of gravity in a canoe feels less stable and thus less comfortable than the low seat of a kayak. This impression changes with experience.

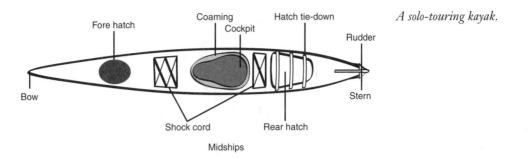

A solo-touring kayak.

In all fairness, we must point out that a canoe's single-bladed paddle drips less water on your hands and douses you with less spray than does a kayak's double-bladed paddle.

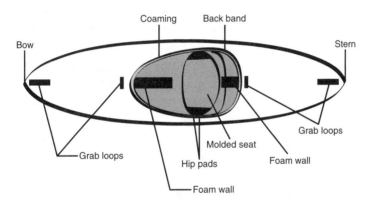

A white-water-river kayak.

In *white water*, solo kayaks probably outnumber decked solo canoes by 20 or more to 1. They are more popular because they are easier to learn to paddle (the balance of a double blade versus the off-center stroke in a decked solo canoe). Because so many more kayaks are manufactured than solo decked canoes, in actual numbers as well as in the variety of models, the price of individual kayaks may be a bit less.

Decked tandem canoes, on the other hand, are a bit easier to paddle than decked *tandem* white-water kayaks. Canoeists have developed a wider range of paddle strokes and techniques than their double-bladed tandem kayaking friends, crossing over from the versatility and performance of open canoes. Again, white-water K-2s (K for kayak, 2 for the number of paddlers) are relatively rare and will command a higher price tag because of that.

Paddlin' Talk

White water literally means water that is white and foaming as it cascades through a rapid. Often it is used to describe turbulent and frothy water.

Paddlin' Talk

A **tandem** is a canoe or kayak paddled by two people. Also called a "double."

The letter **C-** indicates the paddler capacity of a canoe, most often a decked canoe, followed by 1 for a single paddler, 2 for a tandem, etc.

The letter **K-** indicates the paddler capacity of a kayak, most often a decked kayak, followed by 1 for a single paddler, 2 for a tandem, and so on.

Open white-water canoes are a different breed of cat. They are stuffed with so many inflated air bags that they might as well be decked. They are a superb rough-water craft, and for the paddler evolving into a whitewater specialist they are an exhilarating choice. Like decked white-water canoes, they come in solo and tandem models.

Our standby recreational canoe is quite willing to go both ways. With two paddlers aboard, the stern paddler sits on a seat tucked way in the back of the boat, and the bow paddler sits on a seat well back from the bow to leave room for long legs. This keeps the canoe level. When used as a solo boat, the lone paddler plops down on what would have been the front seat, but faces the other end of the boat and, in effect, paddles stern (back) first. By sitting on the back edge of the "front" seat, the paddler's weight is near the center of the canoe and the boat is balanced.

Flatwater Touring or White-Water Play?

River paddling is reflexive. The paddler responds instantly to changes in the river flow and the obstacles that create those changes. Everything takes place in the flow of the immediate now.

An inflatable white-water kayak.

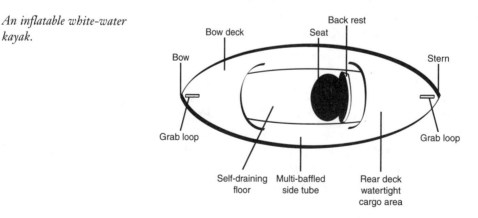

Touring is contemplative. The paddler reasons out a step-by-step plan for the next few strokes, for the next few minutes, for the next few hours, and then follows the plan.

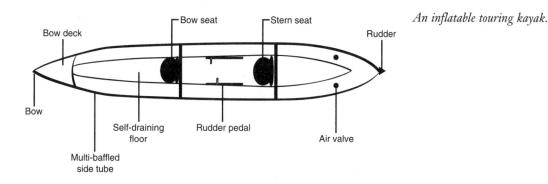

An inflatable touring kayak.

Although these descriptions are generalizations, they do illustrate the differences in approach between the two ends of the paddling spectrum.

It is also true to say that river paddling, canoe or kayak, calls for high-energy bursts of activity, followed by periods of relaxation. That burst of activity may extend over a l-o-n-g rapid or a closely linked set of several white-water sections, so we're not talking about mere seconds. In almost all cases, though, the paddler has the option of slipping into an eddy for a breather, or even landing on a convenient shore to mop out a boat and grab a bite to eat.

The touring paddler is tuned to a long-haul, efficient paddling style that puts miles in his wake at a relatively constant speed. A saltwater touring paddler will chart out the ebb and flow of the tides, the predicted speed of currents through the entire tidal cycle, and the expected duration and strength of wind and waves in planning a course for a day. His or her chart will be strapped to the foredeck in a waterproof case, and or he or she will mark off distances and times on the outside of the plastic as he or she compares predicted times and his or her course. The wilderness tripper pushing down placid rivers and across remote lakes will do the same.

Both paddling disciplines call upon the same paddling techniques and skills, but put a *little* different emphasis on how those skills are used. The touring paddler concentrates on going ahead smoothly and efficiently with a constant speed. The white-water paddler emphasizes quick maneuverability and turning, with rapid changes in speed.

One of the great pleasures in paddlesports is that you don't have to choose one kind of paddling to the exclusion of the other. You can enjoy a hard workout in white-water froth one weekend, and leave for a week-long paddling camping trip the next. You'll find that you'll choose different boats for the two styles of trip, and somewhat different paddles. The strokes will be remarkably the same.

Paddle Solo or with a Partner

Choosing between canoe or kayak for a solo paddler versus a tandem designed for a pair of paddlers is about as easy as learning to tickle a porcupine behind the ears. It can be done, but it's definitely a prickly situation.

If you're truly misanthropic, the problem doesn't exist. Most of us are more social creatures, enjoying the company of our friends on the water and on the beach. We're also concerned with safety, and we've learned that companions create a safety net when we miscalculate as well as a standard against which we learn and grow.

If you're a solitary person by nature, a solo boat—canoe or kayak—may well be the best choice for you. You won't have to scramble for a paddling partner to fill the other end of your double when a friend calls with an invitation for a trip the next morning.

Paddlin' Talk

Gunkhole is the act of exploring the little out-of-the-way places along your route.

The Old Paddler Says

We always like to have at least one double canoe or kayak on our own trips. The advantage of having a seat for an ill or exhausted paddler is tremendous.

You can play a rapid as hard as you want, or you can leisurely drift down the current without any conflict of desires with the other person in your boat.

You can sprint across a bay, outracing your friends if you desire (and can!), or you can poke and *gunkhole* in little bays and openings to your heart's content. On a multi-day camping trip you can be packed and on the water at the crack of dawn, or at the crack of noon. You won't feel held back by a partner sleeping in, nor hurried by a partner with all his or her gear packed in the boat well before you finish brushing your teeth.

A solo boat is all about doing your own thing. Sure, you work within the group's dynamics and rules, but you are the master and commander of your own vessel.

A double touring kayak.

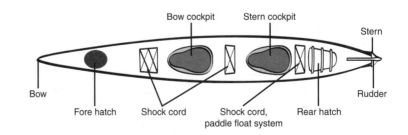

A double canoe or kayak is all about teamwork. You paddle together in a locked rhythm, you maneuver with coordinated shifts of your balance, you agree (wordlessly or not) on goals, pace, and distance. Some would call it compromise, but a good doubles team goes beyond that to a union of shared objectives. A skilled doubles team also divides its functions. On a river, for example, the person in the front of the boat has a much better view of the water, the currents, and the obstacles, and because of that, decides where the boat should head and when. The paddler in the stern applies power, aligns the boat, with the *bow paddler's* heading, and applies bracing strokes—keeping the boat balanced and upright—at the bow's lead. That doesn't mean the bow is more important than the stern. It merely reinforces the reality of who can do what most effectively. You don't have to assume tasks in the most logical manner. For that matter, you don't have to agree with gravity, but that's more your problem than the earth's.

The bow paddler in a kayak, touring or river, normally sets the paddling cadence. The *stern paddler* can watch the action and go along with it, while the bow paddler can't see what's happening in the back. The stern paddler in a touring kayak normally operates the rudder pedals and sets the direction.

The double boat, canoe or kayak, gives each paddler a tremendous freedom to follow an individual passion. If one paddler wants to frame a great photo, that person can concentrate on the camera and let the other balance and align the boat. If one paddler is reeling in a fish, the other controls the relative position of the boat during the battle. If one paddler wants to bury his or her face in a map and determine their position, the other maintains course, speed, and control. These, and a lot of other activities you can well imagine, are darned difficult in a solo boat.

 Paddlin' Talk

The **bow paddler** is the front paddler in a canoe or kayak with more than one paddler.

The **stern paddler** is the rear paddler in a canoe or kayak with more than one paddler.

The double has another, impossible-to-quantify but easy-to-identify virtue: You can immediately share any experience.

In the Wake

A solo kayak, river or touring, is quite easy to flip right side up if accidentally capsized. That's an Eskimo Roll, and it's a combination of bracing your paddle and shifting your weight and balance. It is also easy to Eskimo Roll an open solo canoe, especially if you've filled the boat with flotation bags. It is far more difficult (but still possible) to roll a double kayak or canoe upright.

A double touring kayak is faster than a solo touring kayak. That's partially because of length, because a longer boat is faster than a shorter one. The double also has twice the horsepower of the solo, with only a small increase in frontal area, which is one of the main factors in how difficult it is to push a boat through the water.

Speed is a tricky concept. You can go more quickly and cover a greater distance with a more efficient, faster boat. More important, you can paddle for a shorter distance and at a slower speed but in doing so use far less paddling effort. One boat can cover, for example, 12 miles at near its maximum potential speed and the paddler(s) will be tired. A boat with a potentially higher speed may cover that same 12 miles in exactly the same time, but the paddler(s) will arrive fresh and filled with energy.

A solo marathon canoe.

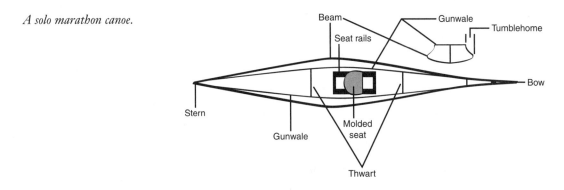

The Old Paddler Says

You can cram the contents of about three big rucksacks under the decks of a typical solo touring kayak. Before you start loading the kitchen sink to top off your load, remember that you'll have to move all of it through the water as well as from the beach to the campsite every day. Less really is more, when the less is gear and the more is fun.

Two single touring kayaks can carry more gear and supplies than one double touring kayak. As a rule of thumb, the double can carry about one and a half times the weight that a solo kayak can carry. Looking at it the other way around, the double can pack about three quarters of the amount carried by two single kayaks.

This becomes a performance issue. If you load up a canoe or kayak to the very edge of its carrying capacity, it will tend to wallow sluggishly along and require a lot of paddling effort. If you give yourself a comfortable margin between what you are carrying and what you could cram in, the boat will feel lively and will glide for great distances with an easy stroke. That's why two lightly loaded single kayaks will paddle more easily than one very heavily loaded double—even though the actual weight carried by the two is the same as that in the double.

CAUTION

Rocks and Shoals _____

Three canoes or kayaks are the minimum needed for a group's safety. That provides the muscle and hands for a rescue in the event of an upset. One boat may stay with a rescued paddler on the beach if necessary while the other races for assistance. If the rescued paddler doesn't need assistance but is unable to continue because of damaged equipment, the other two boats may support each other on their way for further assistance. Five boats—the damaged boat, a partner staying on the beach with the damaged craft, and three going for aid—make a better-balanced party.

Two single boats provide a slim but slightly larger safety net compared to one double. In the event of trouble, one boat can rescue the other, can tow a boat or a swimmer to shore, or once having brought the swimmer to shore, can go for more help or assistance.

A double provides a slim but slightly larger safety net compared to two solo boats? Does that sound contradictory? Imagine a situation with an ill, injured, or exhausted paddler. In a double, that paddler becomes a passenger, and the other paddler becomes the power moving the boat to shelter. With two singles, the option is for one to tow the other. That's difficult at best, and leaves the paddler being towed still having to cope with balance and steering.

Where Can I Store It?

If you have a very large, very empty garage, you can accumulate as many kinds and sizes of canoes and kayaks as you wish. Few of us have that luxury.

If you can store your boats under cover, they will be better off. They will stay cleaner, they'll be less likely to become habitat for little crawly things, and they will be protected from the damaging rays of the sun. You can get sunburned, and so can fiberglass, plastic, wood, and most other fabrics.

Store your canoe(s) upside down, supported on two horizontal braces spanning the gunwales—the upper edges of the hull—a quarter to a third of the way toward the middle from the bow and the stern.

Touring kayaks do best stored right side up, resting on cradles, padded supports, or broad slings. Deflate flotation bags, empty all the removable gear, and snap a plastic dust cover over the coaming to keep debris from filtering in through your cockpit.

White-water decked boats, like touring kayaks, are happier right side up on cradles or padded supports conforming to the hull cross section. You can also stack them on edge, tied down to prevent them from tumbling down.

Rocks and Shoals

Dirt and direct sunlight are the major enemies of most canoes and kayaks. Keep them clean and covered for a long and trouble-free life.

Frame and fabric skin take-apart boats should be disassembled and have all the sand and grit cleaned out from the skin. Clean (and perhaps varnish) the frames and stringers—the long pieces from the bow to stern around the frames, clean and wax any metal parts, and lay the skin out as flat as possible. In most cases, the frames and stringers will fit in a closet, while the skins can be laid out over storage cupboards in your garage and covered to keep off dust and dirt.

An inflatable canoe.

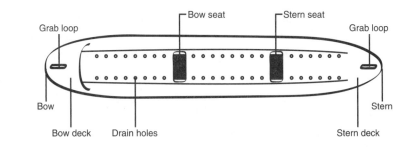

Inflatable canoes and kayaks do great with just a little care. Rinse your boat thoroughly with clean water and lean it up on edge to dry. Once completely dry, wipe off any residual dirt. Remove any wet ropes. Semi-deflate the boat (or semi-inflate it, depending on your viewpoint) so that it has just enough air to maintain its shape. A partially inflated boat is less likely to suffer fabric stresses or delamination. Belaboring the obvious, keep it away from direct sunlight, excess heat, or sharp objects.

Making Your Way Around a Boat

By now you've probably figured out that canoes and kayaks come with their own vocabulary. If you catch on to a few simple terms you'll find these boats—and this book—a lot easier to understand. Length refers to the distance from the very front of the bow (the front of the boat) to the very back of the stern (the back part of the boat). Beam is the measurement from side to side across the widest part of the boat. Depth measures the vertical height from the floor (that's the inside bottom of the hull) to the deck if it is a covered boat or to the gunwales (the uppermost edge of the side of the boat) if it is an open boat. Freeboard measures the distance from the waterline (where the water comes to when the boat is floating and with a normal weight inside) to the lowest portion of the gunwale.

Other terms you'll run across in this book are ...

◆ **aft.** The stern, or rear part of a canoe or kayak.

◆ **amidships.** The middle part of the canoe or kayak.

◆ **bow.** The front or leading edge of a canoe or kayak.

◆ **chine.** The juncture of the side and bottom of a canoe or kayak.

◆ **cockpit.** A hole through the deck, in which a paddler sits or kneels.

◆ **deck.** A surface extending from one gunwale to the other of a canoe or kayak, enclosing part of the interior of the boat.

◆ **fore.** The front part of a canoe or kayak.

◆ **gunwale.** The top edge of the sides of a canoe; the top edge of the hull sides where the hull and deck join in a decked boat.

◆ **hull.** The body of a canoe or kayak, including the bottom and the two sides as well as the front and back where the sides meet.

◆ **keel.** The bottom of a canoe or kayak, where the left and right sides meet.

◆ **rocker.** The curve of the bottom of a canoe or kayak from bow to stern, as seen from the side.

◆ **stem.** The sharp edge at the front of a canoe or kayak, that first cuts into the water.

◆ **stern.** The very back of a canoe or kayak.

◆ **thwart.** The seat in a canoe, or the crosspiece extending from gunwale to gunwale in a canoe against which a kneeling paddler braces his weight.

The Least You Need to Know

◆ All-purpose boats are available, but more specialized river and touring boats offer more paddling pleasure.

◆ Solo versus tandem: Each type of boat has advantages.

◆ White water or touring: You can match your boat to your paddling personality.

◆ Boats can sunburn, too—store them under cover.

Chapter 3

Just What Makes a Canoe?

In This Chapter

- ◆ The many kinds of canoes
- ◆ How shape determines function
- ◆ How the parts work together
- ◆ Choosing the right canoe for you

We each hold the vision of a perfect canoe in our minds, carving a line across a remote lake, dancing in foaming rapids, or nudging across a tiny current on a placid stream. We know the graceful curves, the arc of the bow, and the gentle burble of water in its wake. We've seen it in the movies, read about it in histories and adventure stories, and admired it in paintings. It is even engraved on the back of one of the new U.S. quarters.

Most of the cities in the United States and Canada were founded along the canoe routes. Inhabitants of this continent have splashed along in summer camps and in the Scouts with them, played ukuleles and courted in them, and raced in the Olympics and between islands over the wave-swept oceans in them. Canoes are the foundation of our North American heritage.

The canoe's distinctive shape defines what it is and what it does. If we look at the parts that make up the whole of these graceful boats, we can discover how and why they perform the way they do. Over the years, designers have juggled the parts to create boats for a variety of conditions and paddling styles.

A canoe is a boat in which you can sit, kneel, or stand facing forward, propelling yourself with a single-bladed paddle or pole. It may accommodate one or many paddlers. It may be open or covered with a deck. That's a rather open-ended definition, but it is necessary because canoeing is a very wide-ranging activity.

Many Shapes of Canoeing

To understand just how a canoe works, first we ought to divide the entire family of canoe shapes into five related but distinct categories. Really, there's a continuous spectrum of canoe shapes, and, like colors in a rainbow, they blend seamlessly from one into the next. Also like colors, most of us can easily differentiate between the different categories of canoes. Let's look at each in turn.

The Recreational Canoe

In the middle floats the recreational or casual recreation canoe, a canoe that easily spans the middle of the casual calm water voyage and the mild river trip. If the lake or bay you're crossing is protected and the weather is fine, you'll be safe and comfortable. If the river is placid with no more than a few small waves and an occasional splash (with no need for quick maneuvers) you'll enjoy the ride.

The recreational canoe tends to be pretty stable and somewhat maneuverable, but it does not track (glide in a straight line) as well as canoes aimed at more efficient flat-water paddling. They tend to be owner-friendly craft, normally constructed of fairly durable materials requiring a minimum of maintenance. As such, recreational canoes are good starter boats. They'll carry two adults plus a child on a day trip, or can pack the gear needed for a weekend camping trip without bogging down. A solo paddler can sit on the front seat facing the stern and maneuver the boat on his or her own. Because of their stability, they're a good platform for fishing, bird-watching, or photography.

The casual recreation canoe can be used to paddle rivers, lakes, as well as protected salt water. It is the jack-of-all-trades, without the specialization to completely master any.

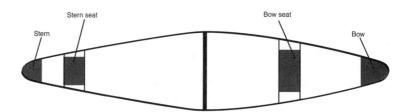

A typical recreational canoe is about 16 feet long, 33 to 34 inches wide across the *beam*, 14 inches deep (measured from the gunwale to the floor, vertically, at the centerline amidships), and 21 inches deep at the bow and stern. It has a shallow vee-shape bottom, a slight bit of what's called a rocker, meaning that if you look at the canoe from the side, you'd see that the keel (bottom edge) is slightly arched (kind of like a rocker from an old wooden rocking chair) rather than being absolutely straight. It also has a relatively sharp bow and stern. It weighs about 70 pounds, which means that one person can pack it over a *portage*, but you wouldn't want to fight through brush and bugs for any great distance.

It is equipped with two bench-type seats, usually made of molded plastic, along with a center thwart. A very limited amount of flotation, such as foam or an air-tight space, may be placed in the bow and stern, to aid in keeping a canoe afloat if filled with water.

Most of these types of boats are made of Royalex (a sandwich of different kinds of plastic) or one of its cousins, but they are also available in fiberglass, thermo-molded plastic, aluminum, and, up at the pricier end of the scale, wood strips covered with epoxy or thin wood planking over steam-bent ribs, covered by canvas (for more on canoe materials, see Chapter 5).

Recreational canoes are maneuverable enough to run relatively easy rivers. Wind won't spin them around, and they tend to go in a straight line once you get them moving.

Paddlin' Talk

Portage is carrying a canoe or kayak, or gear, from one paddleable water to another, around an obstruction. The term "portage" also refers to the path used to carry the canoe.

The Tripper or Touring Canoe

The tripper is the "let's head for the back country" canoe. They are a bigger, beamier, beefier version of the traditional canoe. Some people call them touring canoes.

They have a greater carrying capacity than recreational canoes, usually are a little fuller in the bow and stern for additional buoyancy (and the ability to ride over a wave), and glide farther and straighter with equal paddle strokes. Touring boats are also longer—17 feet is not out of line, and 18½ feet is a good size. Instead of flared sides, the sides are actually narrower at the gunwale than at the waterline—this is called a tumblehome design, and you'll learn more about it later in this chapter. While it might trim away some of the stability when you aggressively lean the tripper, the tumblehome allows for a more efficient paddling stroke because you're less likely to bang your lower hand or paddle shaft on the gunwale during the stroke, and you can sit or kneel in a more comfortable, relaxed, and centered position.

Trippers are usually made out of a fabric-and-resin composite, with the very light and very strong Kevlar being the fabric of choice in the mix. Trippers should be as strong, durable, and light as possible and the hull materials (Chapter 5 discusses the different materials) take these needs into consideration.

The Old Paddler Says _____

When a canoe is still relatively wide close to the bow and the stern, and the sides are both high and flared out, it is referred to as having *full ends*. Full ends make it possible for a canoe to easily ride up on a wave while keeping the paddler(s) dry. Canoes with fine ends are narrow close to the bow and stern and their sides are vertical. Water is more likely to splash aboard a canoe with fine ends. Canoes with full ends are normally a bit slower to paddle. Canoes with fine ends cannot carry as much weight as their full-ended cousins.

White-Water Playboats

White-water playboats are short, often no more than 7 to 9 feet for a solo canoe, and in profile they look like someone braced the bow and stern on sawhorses and jumped up and down in the middle of it until it resembled a banana. These boats are designed to turn very quickly and to respond instantaneously to the slightest paddle command or change in current. They also accelerate incredibly well. On the other hand, such playboats have no inclination to go in a straight line, a breeze will make them spin, and their carrying capacity is essentially limited to the paddler(s), some flotation devices, and about two energy bars. With a boat like this, you can play all day at one rapid, at one hole.

Most are made from one or another kind of molded plastic and are designed to suffer the knocks and dings of white-water play.

The Competition Cruiser

The opposite of the white-water boat is the cruiser, or marathon, canoe—elongated, sharp, narrow, efficient, and fast. Its keel is straight as a ruler's edge, its bow and stern are sharp, in order to cut through the water with little fuss, and it will glide a great distance in a straight line with a single stroke. Everything is sacrificed to speed: They resist turning, they are tippy, their carrying capacity is severely limited, and their very narrow bow and stern mean that they won't rise over a series of waves.

Seen from above, a cruiser canoe is shaped like an elongated diamond, 34 inches wide at the widest part of the waterline and a couple of inches narrower at the gunwales. The bow and stern thin out rapidly, until, at the thwarts, they are only as wide as the paddler. Many have molded seats that look strangely like old tractor seats, which can be adjusted forward and backward to balance the boat.

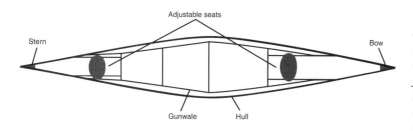

Stern · Adjustable seats · Bow · Gunwale · Hull

The competition cruiser is stripped of all inessentials in the quest for maximum speed over many miles of river and flatwater. The hull is shaped like an elongated diamond, with its bow shaved to a sharp edge to slash effortlessly through the water.

In the Wake

Balancing a canoe involves adjusting the weight in the bow and the stern so that the boat floats as nearly as possible on its designed water line. Moving the bow paddler ahead (fore) or back (aft) works just like moving the weight on a balance-beam scale in a doctor's office. Moving the stern paddler ahead or back, sometimes only fractions of an inch, does the same.

Most cruisers are built to rigorous competition-class standards and offer superb racing possibilities. A competitive 18½-foot double (two paddlers) may weigh in the very low 30-pound range. These are occasionally made with fiberglass cloth, but more often are made with Kevlar or carbon-fiber fabric to reduce weight. (See Chapter 5 for more information about hull materials).

Paddlin' Talk

Double or **tandem** refers to a canoe paddled by two people. **Single** or **solo** refers to a canoe paddled by a single person.

Cruiser canoe races typically cover 15 to 25 miles, a three- to five-hour course, but ultra-marathon events cover hundreds of miles of waterway.

Design Characteristics

By now you've probably figured out that the shape of a canoe defines how it will respond. Length, beam, cross section, keel profile, even the shape of the bow and stern all have significant effects on how a canoe handles in any given set of circumstances. The challenge to designers and builders, as well as to paddlers, is that changing any single shape affects all the others. The possible combinations are almost limitless.

The Canoe Bottom

Let's start at the bottom. Imagine that you've just cut a canoe in half at the mid-point, from one side to the other at right angles to the keel. You're then looking at what is called the cross section. The profile of the bottom edge of this cross section will fall into one of three broad categories: flat, arch, or vee.

The bottom profile of the cross section of a flat-bottomed canoe is, as the name implies, flat. This type of hull feels initially very stable.

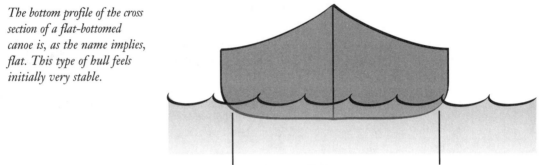

Flat bottom

The broad center section of a flat-bottomed canoe is totally flat. If you place it on the floor, it will touch the floor from one side to the other. A flat-bottomed canoe feels very stable (not at all wiggly) when you first get aboard it. This *stability* comes at the expense of speed, however, as it is the slowest shape to push through the water. But it is the easiest shape to push sideways through the water, and therefore, the easiest shape to turn.

Paddlin' Talk

Stability is the tendency of a canoe or kayak to remain in one position without wiggling or feeling tippy. **Initial stability** is the tendency of a canoe or kayak to not wiggle or feel tippy when it is flat (or level) on the water. **Secondary stability** is the tendency of a canoe or kayak to become more stable (less wiggly or tippy) when it is tilted to the side.

With an arch hull, the profile of the bottom of the cross section is a gentle curve. The canoe feels a little more tippy when you first get in. This hull design has less *initial stability* than the flat-bottomed hull, which means that it wiggles a bit more when you first get in. You might remember from geometry that a circle has the smallest surface compared to the enclosed volume, so an arch hull has less drag, or friction, when you move it through the water. The ultimate arch hull would be a true half-circle. This would be the potentially fastest or most efficient hull shape, but it would have no stability whatsoever.

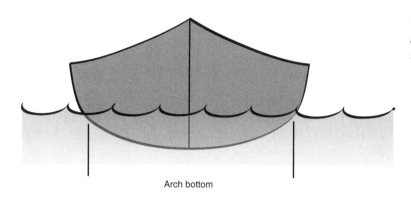

The bottom cross section of an arch hull is shaped in a gentle curve from side to side.

Arch bottom

A vee hull is shaped like a squashed letter V. Two more or less flat surfaces descend from the chine—the area joining the bottom and sides—to a defined edge at the keel. This vee shape works like the blade of an ice skate or sled and keeps the canoe heading in a straight line. The sharper the vee, the straighter and faster the canoe will go, but it will also decrease the canoe's initial stability.

Vee-bottom canoes feel wiggly or tippy when you first board them. However, they feel much steadier as you begin to paddle and increase the speed of the canoe. They also feel much more stable and steady when leaned to one side or the other for making turns.

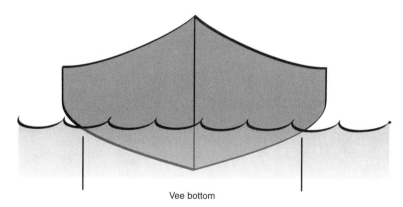

The vee-bottom hull feels more tippy initially, but becomes more stable when paddled or when leaned.

Vee bottom

A line drawn along the bottom of a canoe from the sharp edge of the bow to the sharp edge of the stern marks the keel of a canoe. The bottom may be smooth, as in a flat or arched bottom, or with a slight edge as in a vee bottom. Some canoes have a ridge running down the outside of the hull along the center of the bottom, also called a keel. This increases the canoe's ability to track—to glide in a straight line—but reduces its ability to turn quickly.

The Sides

Canoes' vertical sides also come in one of three shapes: flaring out, straight up and down, or curving in.

If the sides of the canoe flare out, the *secondary stability* of the canoe increases—because as you lean your boat to the side you increase the amount of canoe that is in the water. Your canoe becomes effectively wider. Flaring sides also deflect spray and waves away from the canoe, offering a drier ride, and they lift the canoe when you push into a wave. On the other hand, flared sides mean that your canoe is wider at the gunwales than the waterline, forcing the paddler(s) to stretch farther to the side to make an efficient paddle stroke and avoid banging the paddle or hands on the gunwale.

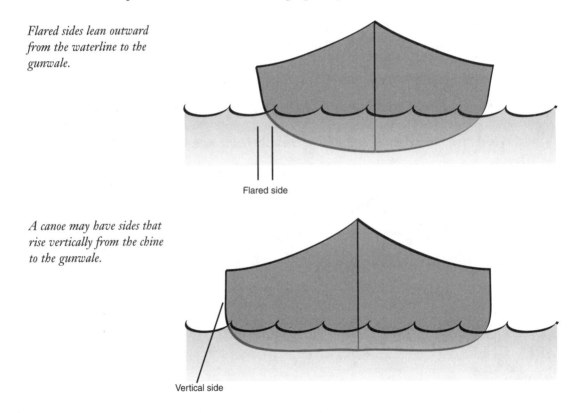

Flared sides lean outward from the waterline to the gunwale.

Flared side

A canoe may have sides that rise vertically from the chine to the gunwale.

Vertical side

Vertical sides offer none of the advantages of the other two shapes. They don't create the additional stability nor the dry ride of a canoe with flared sides. They don't offer the paddling ease of a canoe with tumblehome, or inward-leaning sides.

The Old Paddler Says

The most efficient possible paddle stroke would be with the paddle inserted right at the keel line of the canoe. That's impossible, considering that the paddle would have to be forced through the bottom of the canoe. Tumblehome enables you to place the paddle as close to the keel line as possible, increasing the efficiency of the stroke.

If the sides of the canoe bend in from the waterline to the gunwales, a design called *tumblehome*, you won't have to reach so far out for an efficient paddle stroke. However, waves will more easily splash aboard with this design. This hull will feel more stable when you first board, but will be less stable when you lean it to the side.

Tumblehome

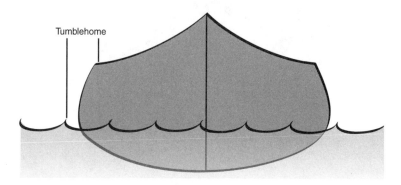

Paddling becomes easier and more efficient when the canoe sides bend inward from the waterline to the gunwale.

As noted previously, the line at which the side and bottom of any canoe meet is called the chine (rhymes with chime). (If they don't meet, then you have a gap and your canoe is now a submarine.) If the bottom and side meet at a sharp, defined angle, it is called a hard chine. A canoe with a hard chine tends to be more stable initially, and is well suited for flatwater. It's a good choice for photography, fishing, wildlife watching, and other activities requiring stability. A soft chine is when the side and bottom merge in a smooth curve. With no sharp edge for the current to grab, this is a better choice for moving water.

Paddlin' Talk

Tumblehome is a design in which the sides of the canoe curve inward from the waterline to the gunwales.

The bottom and the side of the canoe meet with a sharp and distinct angle.

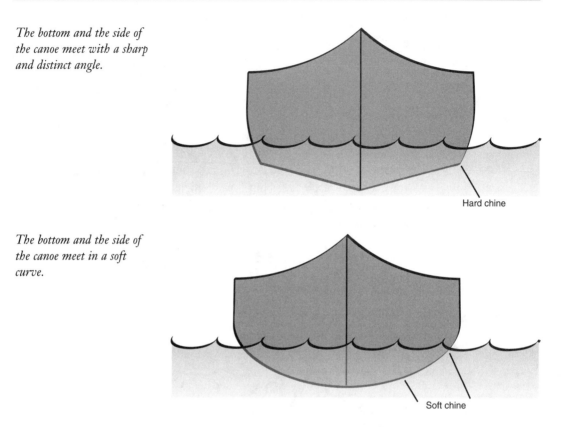

Hard chine

The bottom and the side of the canoe meet in a soft curve.

Soft chine

The very front end of your canoe, the bow, from the foremost point to the water, may be plumb (vertical), raked (slanted back to the canoe), or recurved (the traditional circular shape arcing back at both the top and bottom).

A plumb bow has the longest possible waterline length when compared to the overall canoe length, and is thus the potentially fastest (or more efficient) design. The longer waterline also increases tracking and reduces the ease of turning. At the same time, a plumb bow often is the wettest.

A plumb bow provides the longest waterline and best tracking.

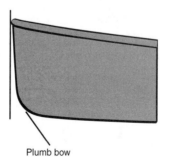

Plumb bow

Raking the stem back from the upper point of the bow to the water line creates a shape that deflects splash and waves away from the canoe and also can provide additional lift (because of the flared sides of the canoe) when the bow is shoved into a wave. A raked bow may offer a little easier turning than a plumb-bowed canoe of similar length.

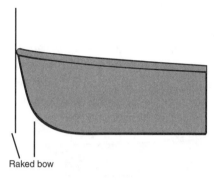

Raked bow

A bow raked back from the leading point of the canoe to the waterline offers the driest ride and the best lift into a wave.

A recurved bow is pretty, but with modern hull materials, it is more decoration than function. A minor problem is that the higher bow area may catch a bit more wind.

Recurved bow

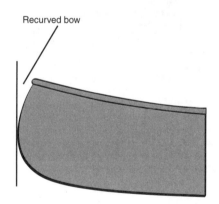

The pretty recurved bow recalls Native birchbark canoes.

Keel Line

Place your canoe right side up on the ground and look at it from the side. The shape of the bottom from bow to stern is called the keel line. If the entire bottom, from bow to stern, rests on the ground, then the hull is said to have no rocker (think of a rocking chair), and the boat will go straight and fast. Marathon or cruising boats, with their need for speed, have this keel line design.

The canoe is straight from bow to stern.

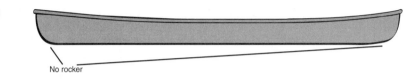

No rocker

If the canoe balances on just the middle of a gentle curve from bow to stern, then the hull is said to be rockered. Increase the rocker, the amount of curve along the line of the keel, and the easier the canoe turns. That's because the ends of the canoe, the bow and stern, will sit higher in the water and offer less resistance when you push one or the other sideways. Canoes with more rocker are great for small streams, slalom racing, and areas requiring great maneuverability.

The canoe forms a slight, smooth arc from bow to stern.

The keel line is curved in a very noticeable arc, allowing quick turns.

The canoe shaped for aggressive white-water play is deeply curved from bow to stern, permitting near-instant turns and spins.

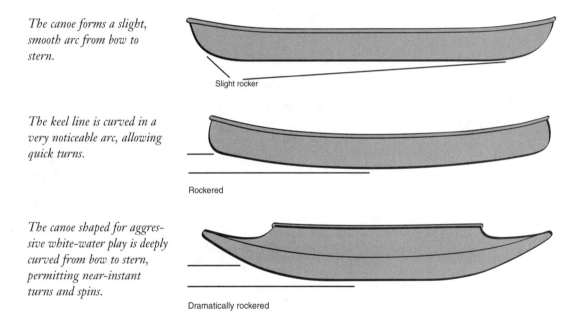

Slight rocker

Rockered

Dramatically rockered

Symmetrical vs. Asymmetrical

If you chop most canoes in half crossways at the middle, the two halves will be mirror images. They are symmetrical. Symmetrical hulls tend to turn better with less effort. As such, they work well in small streams or in white water where maneuverability is at a premium.

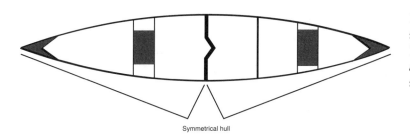

The bow and stern halves are mirror images of each other. This shape is maneuverable, and good for paddling in moving water.

Symmetrical hull

Canoes with asymmetrical hulls have lengthened and streamlined bows. This sharper edge cuts through the water more easily. It also makes turning more difficult. Asymmetrical hulls are found in flatwater racing and marathon canoes.

The Old Paddler Says

A symmetrical hull doesn't care which way it moves through the water, forward or backward.

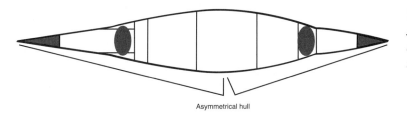

The bow of this hull has been stretched and thinned, enabling it to carve easily through the water.

Asymmetrical hull

Draw imaginary lines connecting the bow of the canoe to the outside edge of the midpoint. The actual shape of the bow will likely bulge outside of these imaginary lines. If the bulge is far outside the imaginary line, the bow is said to be full or have full ends. This volume creates buoyancy, which lifts the bow up over a wave, and also increases the carrying capacity of the canoe. If the bulge is closer to the imaginary line, then the bow is fine or thin, also called a fine bow or fine ends. It has much less buoyancy, and is less able to rise up and over a wave. With less volume it cannot carry the weight or cargo of the wider canoe. However, its streamlined shape will easily cut through the water resulting in a canoe that will go faster with less effort than its more full cousin.

Pictured are the front halves of two canoes, each the same length and close to the same beam—width—at their midpoints. The upper canoe carries its width well forward toward the bow, creating a lot of volume or enclosed space—called full or full ends. The lower canoe is very narrow behind the bow, like the sharp edge of a knife—called a fine bow or fine ends.

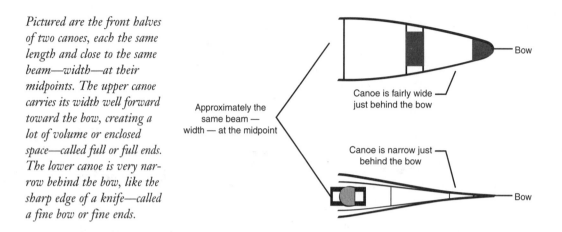

Approximately the same beam — width — at the midpoint

Canoe is fairly wide just behind the bow

Bow

Canoe is narrow just behind the bow

Bow

Length, Beam, and Depth

The final design characteristics that you need to know about involve a canoe's length, width, and depth. Let's consider each in turn.

The Long and Short of It

There are good reasons to go with a longer canoe, and equally good reasons to paddle a shorter boat. It depends entirely upon the type of water you want to paddle.

Longer canoes tend to be easier to paddle, are more stable than shorter canoes with the same amount of weight aboard, and can carry heavier loads without bogging down and shedding performance. They will go farther faster and with less effort than shorter boats. They are less affected by wind, and you'll need to make fewer energy-robbing corrective strokes to keep them going in a straight line.

Longer canoes tend to be more sea-kind. They cope with waves, on a river or on a lake, more easily than their shorter brethren.

Before you rush out to buy a longer canoe, remember that one of the prime virtues of a shorter boat is maneuverability. You can turn and twist down a narrow stream, or pop from eddy to eddy while playing in a rapid. The shorter canoe will be lighter, probably a bit less expensive, likely a little stronger, and easier to transport.

In the Wake

Longer canoes will go farther faster and with less effort than shorter boats only up to a certain point. As the wetted surface—the amount of hull that is in the water—increases, friction increases as well. In addition, when you add length, you also add weight, and it takes power to move each ounce of added weight. You have to trade off the efficiency of a longer hull against the friction and weight of a longer hull.

This trade-off becomes a concern only if you're a fast paddler and can push your canoe at close to the maximum efficient hull speed. If you're a number cruncher, the maximum efficient speed of a displacement hull (one that sits in the water rather than planes over it) is roughly 1.4 times the square root of the waterline length. The total wetted surface area is of more significance in determining a canoe's efficiency than theoretical maximum hull speed. A very wide canoe will have more surface area in the water than a narrow canoe, and will create more friction with the water. That means it will take more energy to paddle the same distance as the narrower boat.

A shorter boat may be easier to paddle than a longer canoe at the typical pace of most recreational paddlers, 30 to 40 strokes per minute. The shorter canoe, even if it is the same width as the longer canoe, has less surface area and creates less friction while moving through the water. Don't overload a canoe, of any size, and expect it to paddle easily.

If you need a maneuverable boat, or if you paddle narrow streams, a long hull is a disadvantage. Put a one-foot ruler on edge in a sinkful of water and it requires effort to turn, with a great deal of burbling water. Twist a six-inch ruler in the same sink and the effort is far less. Shorter canoes simply turn easier than similar but longer canoes.

How Wide?

Width affects a canoe's performance in two primary ways. A wider boat has to push more water aside in order to move forward than does a narrower canoe. A wider boat is also more stable than a narrower canoe. If you're fishing, taking pictures, or carrying small children, that might be an important factor.

A narrower canoe is easier to paddle than a wider one. That's because it enables you to place the paddle in the water closer to the keel line of the canoe, and that makes the stroke more effective.

The Old Paddler Says

There are two ways to consider the width of a canoe. *Beam* measures the widest part of the top edges (the gunwales) of the canoe. That will affect how you paddle. The waterline width is the maximum width of the canoe at the waterline when the canoe is at rest and floating. This establishes how streamlined the hull is in (or through) the water.

How Deep?

Depth is the vertical distance measured at the center of the canoe from the gunwales to the floor. It is often measured amidships (at the middle of the canoe) and at the bow. Greater depth often means greater carrying capacity and a potentially drier boat with less water splashed or washed aboard. It also means a boat with more surface exposed to the wind, and may mean a less efficient paddling position.

Shallower boats may be easier to paddle (it becomes easier to reach the water) and less affected by wind. They also tend to get wetter than deeper canoes.

Choosing the Right Canoe for You

With all these design factors to consider, how can you choose a canoe for yourself? Any canoe ever made, from Ogg's prehistoric log to tomorrow's Olympic flatwater sprint canoe, is a compromise between a huge number of variables. The following tips should help you to narrow down the choices to a couple of different kinds:

◆ Ask yourself what kind of paddling you want do. Flatwater or river, casual recreation, competition, or wilderness exploration? Will you paddle alone, always with the same partner, or with a mix of partners and activities?

◆ Visit every demonstration day, canoe symposium, and paddling shop in your area. Study the canoes that potentially fit your needs.

◆ Paddle as many different canoes in a class as you can find. Check with your local paddling club (join one!) as well as neighboring clubs for the dates and places of swap meets to inspect used canoes.

◆ Hang out after a club meeting or paddling trip, listening to what other paddlers think of their boats. More important, find out why they have that opinion.

◆ When you find the canoe you think you want, one that performs as you hope in the waters you want to paddle, take the plunge and buy it. You might end up offering it at next year's boat swap if you outgrow its capabilities, or it might be a lifetime friend. That's okay. You'll know how much you enjoy paddling it, and that's the only thing that really counts.

As you fall deeper in love with paddling, you'll find new paddling experiences to explore, and you'll want a more specialized canoe with which to explore them.

The Least You Need to Know

- The shape of a canoe determines its performance.

- Flatter-bottomed canoes offer the most initial stability and are easiest to turn, but they are less efficient than arched or vee-bottom boats.

- Canoes with rockered keels are more maneuverable than canoes with no rocker. White-water playboats have extremely rockered keels.

- Longer canoes will go farther faster and with less effort than shorter boats, but they are more difficult to maneuver.

- When deciding what kind of canoe to buy, think about the kind of conditions you'll be paddling in, try as many different kinds of canoes as you can, and talk to people who do the same kind of paddling as you want to do. Then go ahead and take the plunge!

Chapter 4

Just What Makes a Kayak?

In This Chapter

- ◆ The differences between touring and river kayaks
- ◆ Understanding basic kayak characteristics
- ◆ Balancing your kayak and keeping it on course
- ◆ Keeping the water on the outside

Show a Chihuahua and a Saint Bernard to someone who's never seen a dog before, and they'll argue that those two creatures couldn't possibly belong to the same species. Show that same person a sculpted and form-fitting extreme river playboat beached next to a surf ski, and they'll argue from now until dark that those two boats can't possibly both be kayaks.

Back in prehistory most dogs looked pretty much the same, until selective breeding and specialization began emphasizing desired characteristics. Kayaking prehistory was only about a half century ago, when most kayaks looked pretty much the same. Then designers and paddlers started tweaking their boats to increase performance and efficiency in a specific water environment. The resulting extended family of kayaks today floats in a bewildering array of shapes, sizes, and materials. That's the best news possible for a paddler.

Best? Yeah. Because, without compromise, today you can find that kayak that fits you, fits the waters you want to paddle, and fits the style of paddling you want to enjoy. Not long ago, you had a choice when buying coffee: It came in a 1-pound or a 3-pound can. Today grocery stores display a whole wall of coffees: dozens of roasts, beans from around the world, and a variety of grinds to suit the way you like to make it. You did a little research, a little experimentation, and you found your coffee of choice.

That's what you're going to do when you go paddling.

Kayaking's Parallel Universes

Function divides kayaking into two parallel universes: river kayaks and touring kayaks. At their most fundamental, touring kayaks are designed to go straight while river kayaks are designed to turn. In both, you sit and apply the power to the water with a double-bladed paddle (a paddle with blades on either end of it). The touring kayak cruises in an environment dominated by wind, while the river kayak moves in an environment dominated by current.

Actually, you sit *in* traditional kayaks, you sit *on* open-top or wash-deck kayaks. Both traditional enclosed kayaks and the sit-on-top open-top or wash-deck kayaks are used for touring and for white-water play. How you sit is a matter of personal choice, how the hull is shaped defines the kayak's paddling abilities.

Most kayaks, touring or river, are designed to be used by a single person. These are dubbed K-1, with "K" indicating "kayak" and the "1" the number of paddlers. A significant number of touring kayaks are set up for two paddlers, K-2, as are rare two-person white-water kayaks. Up to four paddlers power the swift flatwater racing K-4 kayaks.

Why did kayaking split into two such different families? Let's take an all-purpose kayak from 40 or 50 years ago (and one that still exists today) and launch it into the two paddling environments.

Paddlin' Talk

The **cockpit** is the hole through the deck in which the paddler sits.

The **deck** is the upper surface of a canoe or kayak.

The Standard Kayak Shape

Our prototype kayak is about 15 feet long, 24 inches wide at the *cockpit*, about 15 inches deep from the floor to the *deck* at the front edge of the cockpit, and has a gently arced bottom in cross section and a slight rise in the keel at the bow and stern. The bow and stern are slightly lower than the cockpit coaming (the raised edge or lip around the cockpit).

Reach over to the fruit bowl and pluck out a banana. From the side, with the stem curved up, it looks just like a kayak with an upturned front end or bow. The very bottom edge of the banana is the shape of the keel, or bottom edge of the kayak. The deck is the upper surface of the banana. If you cut an egg-shaped hole through the top surface (the deck), you'd create a cockpit. The inside surface of the peel below the cockpit you just cut is the floor, and that's where the paddler would sit. If you cut the banana cross-wise in half, you'd create a cross section and you'd see that the bottom edge of the banana's cross section is kind of rounded.

Just from its shape we know some good things about our prototype kayak. It will paddle and *glide* in a straight line without constant attention. When you want to change course, it will turn predictably and at the degree you want. It will feel pretty stable as you board it. You can also stow enough gear for a reasonable camping trip under its decks. You could paddle a placid river or work your way through easy rapids, although you'll be heading downstream rather than carving quick turns from eddy to eddy. You'll also feel comfortable on reasonable lakes or protected bays. Don't expect sparkling performance, but it will be serviceable.

Paddlin' Talk

The ability of a kayak to coast (hopefully in a straight line) between paddle strokes is called **glide**. Glide is important for a touring or racing kayak, but not nearly so important for a whitewater play boat.

The shape of our kayak determines how it's going to respond to our paddling and how it will react to the wind and the water as we paddle. By adjusting the shape, we can change how the kayak responds so that it moves more efficiently—paddles more easily—in the particular paddling universe we'd like to explore.

What Makes a Kayak Turn?

The ability to turn is one of the key differences between touring kayaks and river kayaks. Touring kayaks are designed to go straight, while river kayaks have to be able to turn quickly. The profile of the keel and the parts of the kayak that touch the water help establish how easily a kayak turns.

Keel Profile

Visualize an old wooden rocking chair. The curved pieces of wood on which the legs rest and that allow the chair to move back and forth are called rockers. The keel

CAUTION

Rocks and Shoals

What if the rocker is reversed, and arcs up instead of down? Walk away from that boat! When a kayak has this shape, it is said to be hogged (like the shape of a hog's back) and whether it was designed that way or was bent later, it results in a kayak that will never paddle easily, never go straight, and will never turn as desired.

line of a kayak has that same shape, and that curve determines how easily any kayak can turn.

Place our prototype kayak on a level floor and look at it from the side. Most of its keel (the bottom of the hull) touches the floor from just behind the bow to just in front of the stern. There is no rocker shape. If there was a slight rise in the profile of the keel line from its low point amidships to the bow and stern, then the kayak would be slightly rockered. If the kayak balances on a tiny patch under the cockpit with the bow and stern high in the air, then the kayak is highly rockered. Other factors come into play as well, but the more rocker—or arch—in the keel line, the more easily the kayak will turn.

Keel is flat from bow to stern

If the line of the keel from the bottom of the bow to the bottom of the stern is straight, then there is no rocker. This results in a kayak that will go in a straight line but will resist turning.

Slight upturn from midpoint to bow and stern

If the arc from front to rear is slight, then the keel is slightly rockered. This results in a kayak that will go in a straight line with only a little need for correction paddle strokes, and one which will turn with some encouragement.

Exaggerated upturn from midpoint to bow and stern

If the line of the keel from the bottom of the bow to the bottom of the stern is deeply curved, then it is extremely rockered. This kayak will turn very easily, but will require constant attention and correction strokes to be paddled in a straight line.

Lateral Resistance

The other component in turning ease is a kayak's lateral resistance. Lateral resistance is simply the resistance to pushing (or pulling) a canoe or kayak sideways through the water. If you push hard enough at your kayak's midpoint, you'll move the entire boat sideways. If you push on one side of the stern, the stern will move away from your push and the bow will move toward the side of your push as the kayak pivots around its midpoint. If there is a lot of resistance to sideways movement, you'll have to work harder to make the kayak turn. If there is little resistance, the kayak will turn quite easily.

The size of the kayak's footprint in the water—the part of the kayak that touches the water—determines its lateral resistance. A kayak, from overhead, looks like a pair of joined parentheses: (). By leaning your kayak to the side, you submerge that side and lift the other side (you're supporting more of your weight on the side of the kayak, rather than just the bottom). As the lean increases, the rocker of the keel lifts the bow and stern from the water, making a much smaller footprint. This shortens the effective waterline and dramatically reduces the lateral resistance at the ends. You can lean your kayak and spin like a top.

Touring Kayaks

The touring world demands a kayak that will track—that will continue to go straight without energy-wasting corrective strokes. The kayak should be fast, to cover distance with the least expenditure of precious energy. It needs the inertia to keep that speed when slapped around by waves or wind. It needs the capacity to carry gear for extended cruises.

What changes can we make to turn our prototype kayak into an efficient touring kayak? First, let's stretch our kayak to 17 or 18 feet, measured from the front-most part of the kayak to the rear-most. As we do that, we'll flatten the keel line to eliminate most of the rocker. The bow and stern are now farther apart, increasing the lateral resistance (the size of the footprint) at the ends. We'll change the smooth arc of the bottom into a slight vee, exaggerated at the bow and stern, which also increases tracking ability. We'll reshape the cone-shaped bow and stern into vertical knife edges, enabling us to cut through rather than bash across the waves.

> ### In the Wake
>
> Touring kayaks are sometimes called sea kayaks, even though they're just as much fun on fresh water as salt.

We've made the kayak bigger and more buoyant, and we're bobbing on the surface and being blown all over by any breeze. We can hunker down out of the wind by lowering the deck height from bow to stern, trimming 2 to 3 inches. We'll also narrow the hull from the cockpit to the ends. We'll keep the bow higher and flared a bit, allowing the kayak to rise into a wave and to deflect splash and waves from the deck and, ultimately, from us.

A beam of 23 to 24 inches will give us plenty of stability, but we can reduce the waterline beam and then flare the hull out to the deck for extra stability. A narrower kayak, within reason, will be faster and more efficient than a wider kayak.

With these changes, we're now paddling a kayak that is deeper in the water, less subject to being buffeted by wind, faster, drier, more stable, and with at least the same carrying capacity as our prototype kayak. We can paddle farther with less effort and in greater safety than we could with our original boat.

We've just built a kayak that works very well in the wind-tossed world of oceans and big lakes, a boat that will carry us swiftly to the farthest shore in comfort and with the gear and goodies we desire for a comfortable camp. If we don't have a spare couple of months for a major expedition to Cape Horn, that same kayak will provide us with an exhilarating workout on a neighborhood pond.

River Kayaks

On the river, though, our touring kayak would be a wallowing disaster! The river environment demands a kayak that can turn on a dime and hand you back change. Top speed is not nearly as important as quick acceleration. All you'll carry is a water bottle and a couple of energy bars. These are the same characteristics we eliminated from the touring kayak! We'll have to change the shape of the basic kayak again, to come up with a kayak that is maneuverable, that changes speed quickly, and that isn't required to carry a large amount of gear and equipment.

Paddlin' Talk

Put-in is the beginning point of a trip, where you launch the kayak or canoe into the water.

Take-out is the end point of a trip, where you take the kayak or canoe out of the water.

North American paddlers approach rivers with two completely different (and to each other, incomprehensible) attitudes. One, perhaps because of their experience with the less-maneuverable kayaks of the past, calls for "running" the river right down the middle of the current from the *put-in* to the *take-out*. The underlying idea is to bypass or skirt the hazards encountered on the downstream run.

The other breed of river paddler doesn't view the challenges of the rapids and obstructions as "hazards"—instead, he or she views them as opportunities for good clean fun. They see every rock, obstruction, and wave as a place to play. The playing paddler can spend all day in the few meters of a single *rock garden*. Many will take out at the same beach from which they launched hours before.

Our prototype kayak might work to run a section of river, but we have a lot of changes to make if we want to play in those rapids. When the water is white, when the currents collide, or when rocks comb the river's flow into braided vees, the ideal kayak must be able to turn and twist at the paddle's most subtle command. The flick of a blade instantly accelerates your kayak from the shelter of an eddy into the churning flow of the main current.

Paddlin' Talk

A **rock garden** is a rapid in a river with a bunch of rocks. It offers a delightful variety of waves, currents, and eddies in which to play. You can quickly develop your river paddling skills by playing in a rock garden.

A word of caution here: Don't confuse speed and acceleration. We're not after blistering top speed—we abandoned that when we clambered out of the cockpit of the touring boat in search of the ability to quickly change speed.

Start by squishing our prototype kayak down to no more than 13 feet 2 inches—that's the maximum length for an Olympic slalom kayak—and perhaps as short at 7 feet for an aggressive playboat.

The longer kayaks will have a rounded bottom and chines coupled with a slight amount of rocker, a combination that enables them to carve a turn, surf, or easily ferry across a current. That boat, with a rounded deck, offers you a great big water ride. Flatten out the deck in the front and back by lowering the height and you reduce the interior volume, which in turn reduces the tendency of the kayak to bob about like a balloon. With less kayak to push around, the force you put into each paddle stroke becomes more subtle and more precise. We've splayed the sides of the kayak out wider, 33 inches or so, with a bottom that enables us to slide sideways as we wish and with an aggressively curved edge that lets us carve a precise turn.

To play in the foaming waters of steep creeks, you'll need more buoyancy, so increase the volume by raising the deck a bit as well as increasing the rocker of the keel. Now your kayak will seemingly react to your thoughts of a change in balance or stroke and will turn in the blink of an eye.

Rodeo and play boats work best as short boats, between a mere 7 and 8 feet long, with flat bottoms and steep squared-off sides. All those flat surfaces mean that they surf like a dream on steep waves and fast currents. The hard chines are a huge plus while carving extreme moves, and the flat surfaces—bottom, sides, and deck—are great surfaces with which to play the currents. With their flat decks and relatively broad beams, the cockpits appear to be raised well above the decks.

Ends of playboats and rodeo boats are sharply turned up, again aiding you in grabbing every ounce of energy out of a surface or subsurface current as well as opening the door to spectacular cartwheels.

The Old Paddler Says

Paddlers seem to become one with today's low-volume and highly responsive river kayaks, carving tight turns with a shift of weight as much as a paddle stroke.

When sliding into the cockpit of a touring boat, or even an Olympic slalom kayak, paddlers prefer a snug fit. Many paddlers go beyond that, adding hip and thigh pads to the cockpit to give them even more grip on the boat. Aggressive white-water boats go in the other direction, increasing the size of the cockpit both lengthwise and across the beam for easy (and safer) access and exit.

The Kayak Spectrum

Every kayak is a balance between maneuverability, stability, and speed, designed to paddle well under a particular set of circumstances. No sharp lines divide one from another, and the basic design morphs continuously as you move from one end of the paddling spectrum to the other.

At one end of the spectrum are the kayaks that go very fast in a straight line, such as the 1- to 4-person Olympic racing-class sprint kayaks or the needlelike surf skis. Touring kayaks are also capable of packing a big load through exposed waters at a fair rate of speed, but in doing so, sacrifice quick maneuverability. With the touring kayaks are the downriver or wildwater racing kayaks, speedburners capable of flashing down the current while dodging every eddy or backwater.

The Old Paddler Says

You can take an extended trip in a slalom kayak, and you can go picnicking in an Olympic flatwater sprint boat. But you'll be more comfortable in a kayak with capabilities more closely matching the kind of environment you'll be paddling in.

In the middle of the spectrum are the general-purpose or casual-recreation kayaks, more maneuverable but less speedy than their pure touring cousins. Although they give up some long-distance voyaging efficiency, they can venture out on easy rivers with a certain aplomb. Similarly, slalom kayaks maintain good forward speed for sprinting from gate to gate, yet they are capable of carving precise turns. Close to the slalom kayaks are surf kayaks, "sit-inside" craft built for riding the falling face of big surf.

Play boats and rodeo kayaks are the pinwheels of the river environment, carving incredible turns combined with dazzling vertical stands and cartwheels. Matching them are pumpkinseed-shaped waveskis, dancing through long sets of precise acrobatics while riding a breaking wave in to the beach.

There's a kayak for every paddling desire somewhere along that paddling continuum!

Design Characteristics

Boat builders don't consciously sit down to develop pretty boats, or floating works of art, if you prefer. Instead, they mine thousands of years of hard-won experience in an attempt to meld together those characteristics proven to have worked well in a particular water environment. Sometimes they succeed. Sometimes, with the best of intentions and the best of concepts, they fail.

What they have learned, and passed along to other paddlers, is that certain characteristics yield consistent and predictable results. If you know what kinds of water you want to paddle and the skills you're willing to bring to the paddle, you can evaluate how a particular kayak (or canoe, for that matter) will perform for you in that environment.

Efficiency

Efficiency while paddling is a simple concept: it means getting the most results for the least effort. A peanut butter sandwich will provide only so much fuel for your muscles. A touring kayak that glides straight through the water, without correction paddle strokes, and that glides for a long distance with each paddle stroke, can cover a greater distance on the energy from that sandwich than a kayak requiring more correction strokes and more power strokes.

The river kayak that turns almost effortlessly, or changes speed at the flick of a paddle, requires less energy than a kayak resisting each turn and opposing each change of speed.

Efficiency hinges on the kind of paddling you do. The efficient kayak allows you to make better use of the energy in your muscles. That lets you paddle farther, if that is your plan, allows you to paddle faster if you wish, and allows you to be fresher or less tired when you reach your destination.

All other things being equal, a longer kayak will be more efficient through the water and thus faster than a shorter boat. You can turn that upside down by truthfully saying that it takes less effort to paddle a longer and more-efficient kayak than a shorter and less-efficient kayak. The first 10 minutes you paddle either one won't make that seem all that important. The last 10 minutes of a 22-mile, six-hour crossing will convince you of the value.

The maximum efficient speed of a displacement hull, which is a way to describe a boat body that moves through the water rather than skids over the top of it, is about 1.4 times the square root of the hull's waterline length. However, length has its limitations. At somewhere around 24 feet, the friction of the water and hull becomes greater than the efficiency of the longer hull, and simply buries the limited muscle power you bring to the party. In the real world, this limits single touring kayaks to around 17 or 18 feet, and brings doubles (two-person kayaks) to a maximum of 21 to 23 feet.

The Old Paddler Says

Maximum efficient speed is a way of looking at how easily a kayak will move through the water. In the real world, few touring kayakers hold a flatwater speed of more than three or four knots roughly $3^1/_2$ to $4^1/_2$ miles per hour ... One nautical mile equals 1.15 statute or land miles.

Efficiency is hampered at each end of the kayak. At the bow end, you have to part the water to let the bow through. At the stern, the passing hull creates turbulent water, which in turn drags at the aft end of the kayak, slowing it down. Designers have attempted three solutions to these problems: the Swedeform, fishform, and the symmetrical kayak.

In Swedeform kayaks, the widest part of the hull is behind the cockpit. This gives the boat a long and narrow bow section that quite easily and efficiently parts the water. The downside is that it also makes the stern section more bulbous, which causes greater turbulence in its wake.

In a Swedeform hull, the greatest beam (the widest part) of the hull is behind the cockpit.

In *fishform* kayaks, the widest part of the hull is located ahead of the cockpit. Their wide bows generate more energy-sucking splashes and greater waves, in turn diminishing efficiency. However, the narrow and tapering stern allows such kayaks to slip by with very little energy-robbing turbulence in their wake.

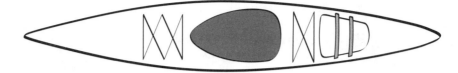

In a fishform hull, the greatest beam (the widest part) of the hull is in front of the cockpit.

The Old Paddler Says

Design symmetry is the waterline shape of the kayak floating empty in a placid pool or pond. If you put all the weight in the back of a kayak and twist from side to side as you paddle, you'll change the floating shape, which will in turn change the design symmetry!

A symmetrical kayak is a compromise between the Swedeform and the fishform shapes. The widest point of a symmetrical kayak is at the cockpit, which is located halfway between the bow and stern ends. The bow end isn't quite as efficient as a Swedeform, but is more so than a fishform kayak. The stern is more efficient than the Swedeform, but less so than the fishform.

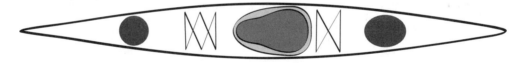

In a symmetrical hull, the front half and the rear half of the kayak are mirror images of each other.

What's the best design? Sorry, but that's up to you to decide. The efficiency of a kayak moving through the water is at least the sum of all its parts, and is, in truth, a compromise among the attributes of all its parts. Go paddle a boat and you'll know by its feel if it is the right boat for you in any given paddling environment. The more you learn about how the kayak reacts to a particular environment, the better grasp you'll have of how closely that particular design will fit into your paddling plans.

Rocks and Shoals

Remember that each of these descriptions is for the footprint of the kayak at the waterline, and not at the deck. Flared sides, tumblehomes, and overhangs may distort your perception of the actual footprint.

Keel Line

Place a ruler on edge on your rug. It will slide easily along the direction of its length, but will resist your attempts to turn it in a new direction. The long, straight *keel* line of a touring or flatwater racing kayak works just like that ruler. Most of your paddling effort is translated into forward motion with little need for corrective strokes to maintain your course.

Now put an egg on your rug. You can send it spinning with the flick of a finger. However, if you attempt to push it across the floor it will wobble and twist about erratically.

Paddlin' Talk

The **keel** is the profile of the kayak's bottom along a direct line from the stem (front) to the stern (rear) along the outside of the hull.

The short keel base and highly rockered ends of a playboat work just like the egg. It responds immediately to your turning efforts, but any sustained straight-ahead motion requires continuous corrective strokes.

Many other factors determine paddling efficiency, but your kayak's keel line establishes the foundation for the overall design.

Cross Section

The first thing you notice when you slide into the cockpit of a kayak is the cross-section profile of the bottom. You might not think of it that way, but your comfort as you wiggle into the seat is a direct reflection of the cross section of that particular kayak.

From a purely mechanical viewpoint, a totally round bottom proves extremely fast. It also feels as if you'll capsize if you look to the side and sneeze.

A flat-bottom profile, merging into vertical sides, initially feels extremely stable—as well as extremely slow. However, that stable feeling extends only so far, as you begin to lean your kayak. It goes from stable to upside down in the blink of an eye.

If a cross section of a kayak shows that the bottom is a straight, flat line connecting the chines (where the sides and bottom of the kayak meet), then the kayak is flat-bottomed. This kayak will feel very steady when you first board, but will be slow to paddle through the water.

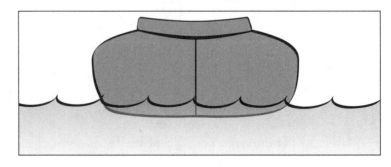

Cross section of hull bottom is flat from side to side

Paddlin' Talk

As noted in Chapter 3, **stability** refers to the kayak's ability to stay deck-side dry. **Initial stability** refers to that balance when the kayak is floating flat on the water. **Secondary stability** refers to the kayak's balance as it is leaned further and further from the horizontal.

To increase the stability, designers flare the sides out from the waterline to the gunwale. As you tilt the hull, more of the flared side goes into the water, which offers more buoyancy and more support (which is simply another way of saying that it provides more *secondary stability*).

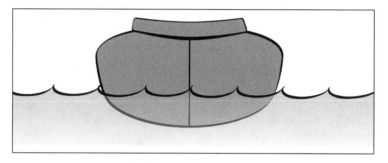

Sides flared outward from waterline to gunwale

When the vertical sides of your kayak slope outward from the waterline to the deck, its called flared-sided. Flared sides give a boat a narrower waterline, which increases paddling efficiency and provides secondary stability as the kayak is leaned to the side.

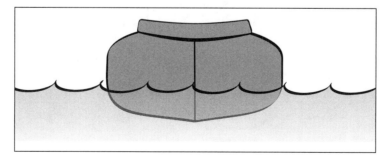

Sides vertical from waterline to gunwale

When the sides of a kayak are vertical from the chine to the gunwale, it's called straight-sided. When coupled with a flat bottom, this design creates a kayak that feels initially very stable but that becomes less stable as the kayak is leaned sideways.

In a tumblehome design, the sides slope inward from the waterline to the gunwale. This design offers the stability of a broader beam at the waterline and makes paddling easier (especially in a wider kayak), as you're less likely to bang your knuckles on the deck.

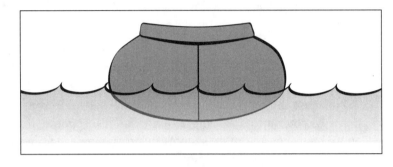

Sides slope inward from waterline to gunwale

A gently arced bottom cross section isn't quite as wiggly as a true round-bottom cross section, but nor is it quite as fast—make that efficient—through the water. It is, however, a quantum step up from the performance of a flat-bottomed cross section.

If the shape of the bottom, from chine to chine, is rounded, then the kayak is round-bottomed. A round-bottom kayak feels quite unstable but is fast and efficient. Few kayaks are truly round-bottomed, but instead are more or less arced.

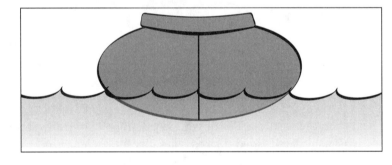

Cross section of hull bottom is rounded from side to side

Weighing all the alternatives, a vee-bottom kayak combines most of the speed and efficiency of a round-bottom hull with most of the stability of a flat-bottom hull. Add fairly sharp chines and a moderate amount of flare, and the kayak feels quite stable. That's true even if the bottom of the kayak is quite narrow from the keel line to the chines.

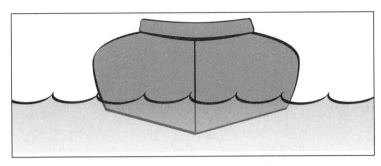

Cross section of hull bottom forms a V-shape

If the shape of the bottom, from chine to chine, forms a vee, then the kayak is vee-bottom. A vee-bottom kayak feels stable and at the same time is fairly fast. The vee at the keel line helps the kayak track along a straight line, and offers structural strength to the kayak hull.

Typically, in a touring kayak, the hull will have a rather shallow vee cross section at the cockpit, turning into a sharper vee when approaching the ends. This increases the structural rigidity of the hull, with the point of the vee working like a knife edge and adding to the hull's tracking ability.

Kayaks with more rounded bottom panels meeting at the keel vee, and with sharply angled chines joining slightly flared sides, will retain their hull speed and efficiency as well as the tracking ability with only a slight loss of initial stability. While an empty hull may wiggle a bit more under you, it will quickly firm up when camping gear is loaded aboard.

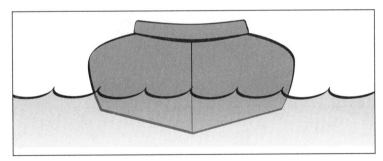

Side and bottom surfaces meet in a sharp edge

The area where the bottom of the kayak merges into the side of the kayak is called the chine. A hard chine is when the transition from bottom to side is abrupt, forming an angle.

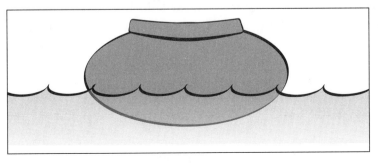

Bottom and sides meet in a smooth curve

When the bottom of a kayak merges into the side with a gentle, rounded curve, the result is known as a soft chine.

Width

All other things equal (are they ever?), a wider kayak will tend to be more stable than a narrower kayak. At the same time, a narrower kayak will make more efficient use of your paddling power because you're pushing a narrower and more streamlined cross section through unyielding water than if you were paddling a wider kayak.

The Old Paddler Says

If you can paddle a narrow kayak, one with less initial stability, then you can switch comfortably into a wider and more stable kayak. If you learn to paddle a wider, more stable kayak, you'll have to spend a few hours of practice in order to swap into a narrower kayak.

Generally speaking, most touring kayakers will be happy with a 23- to 24-inch beam kayak. They find that a 19-inch beam kayak feels more unsteady in the water and requires many hours of paddling practice to feel secure.

Width is relative. If you use a 220-centimeter paddle, not unusual in a touring kayak, you can reach out 5 feet on either side to brace the paddle blade against the water (you'll learn bracing paddle strokes in Chapter 13). Essentially, your narrow kayak has an effective width of 10 feet—5 feet on each side.

Rudders and Skegs

Any boat, whether an aircraft carrier or a kayak, exhibits one of the following three steering characteristics in a wind:

- A weather helm means the boat wants to turn its bow (or weathercock) into the weather, or wind.

- A lee helm means the boat wants to turn its bow away from the wind and point downwind.

- A neutral helm means the boat doesn't attempt to turn.

The type of helm a boat has varies with the angle between the boat and the wind, and the trim of the boat (the distribution of weight). If you have all your weight in the stern of your kayak with the bow sticking high into the air, the pressure of the wind will shove your bow downwind. This tendency may be increased if you have a high, flared bow. Conversely, if your bow is heavily loaded and your stern bobs along the surface, a side wind will shove your stern away from the direction of the wind and leave your bow pointing into the wind.

The Paddle Solution

The instinctive solution is simply to paddle a little harder on one side of the boat, thus correcting the slewing motion. This is a great short-term solution but can get tiring in a strong wind. The next solution is to lean your kayak as you paddle, changing the underwater shape and letting the altered shape correct your course.

Trimming Up with a Skeg

The next level of solution, in terms of complexity, is to hang an adjustable skeg (sort of a rudder fixed in the straight-ahead position) or a controllable rudder off the stern of your touring kayak. Emphasize *touring*. Skegs and rudders have little space in a quick-current world. The rudder or skeg is not used to steer the boat but to counter the variable effects of the wind. How can an "adjustable" skeg be "fixed"? Because we can adjust the amount of the skeg that is lowered into the water, and thus the amount of lateral resistance at that end of the boat.

How does this work? Imagine that you're paddling your kayak about 45 degrees into a brisk wind, with your skeg fully retracted, and you're making a lot of corrective strokes to keep your boat from weathercocking or turning directly into the wind. What's happening is that your stern is being pushed downwind and pivoting your kayak to face directly upwind. If you lower your skeg a bit into the water (trial and error is the best teacher for determining how much), it will increase the lateral resistance at the stern and hold your kayak to your desired heading. If the wind pushes your bow downwind, lift your skeg a bit to reduce lateral resistance and, by doing so, keep on your heading.

Rocks and Shoals

Every piece of equipment will fail at some point, and both skegs and rudders are very exposed pieces of equipment. You should learn to paddle your kayak without these aids in all kinds of weather and conditions before taking advantage of them.

You're not stopping the wind from pushing your kayak sideways. What you are doing is balancing the total effect of the wind on the length of your kayak so that while you're being edged to leeward—downwind—your kayak is not being pivoted away from your desired course.

Turning to Go Straight

A rudder does the same thing, but in a slightly different way. If weather conditions are turning your bow to the left, turn your rudder so that it turns your bow to the right. The two turning motions, left from the weather and right from your rudder, will cancel each other out and you'll maintain your desired heading. If the weather turns you to the right, apply a bit of left-turn rudder.

The downside of a rudder correction is that you're adding drag as you rotate the rudder to one side or the other. You'll work harder to cover the same distance or to maintain the same speed.

Keeping the Water *Outside* Your Kayak

Face it: The materials used in today's kayaks simply don't float. If you don't want to see your kayak, and you by default, slowly heading for the bottom of the lake or river, you have to find some way to keep the water on the outside of the boat where it belongs.

We're not talking about ruptured hulls or disintegrating seams. We're talking about the upsetting circumstances that every paddler experiences. You test the very edge of balance, discover that your skills don't quite measure up to your expectations, and end up in the water. You can discover the true weight of falling water as you miscalculate the curl of a breaking wave. That'll pop your spray deck (a flexible material that fastens snugly around your waist and the lip of the cockpit coaming to cover the cockpit opening) right off your coaming. Heck, you could even be changing the film in your camera with an open cockpit when you get washed down by the wake of a passing powerboat. These examples are not meant to frighten you, but only to point out why you should be prepared for taking on water.

Rocks and Shoals

At some point you will get water inside your kayak. The handiest way to send it back home is with a pump, and that's something you should carry from day one. Some paddlers like the flexibility of a portable hand pump, some like a foot-powered pump, and others like a pump permanently mounted through the deck.

The Air Defense

What's the easiest way of keeping water out of the interior of your kayak? Fill it with the lightest thing you can think of—air. Cram an air bag into the ends of your kayak, inflate it, lash it into place, and you've successfully kept water out of that much of your kayak. An air bag, like its name implies, is an airtight bag with a tube and/or valve, which enables you to fill the bag with air. Simple, elegant, and effective.

Want to carry a change of clothes, a lunch, or other items that must remain dry to remain serviceable? Consider the gear bag. That's a waterproof bag with a watertight and usually airtight sealable opening in which you can stow your prized possessions before you stow the bag into the end of your kayak. Unless you're carrying your prized collection of lead fishing sinkers, the bag will displace more water than it weighs and you'll have positive flotation in your boat.

The goal is to keep the most water possible out of the interior of your kayak. A combo air bag/gear bag will hold your possessions, and will enable you to fill the rest of the bag with air to displace the maximum possible amount of water.

Few river kayakers opt for bulkheads and hatches as air chambers, having little (justi-fied) faith in the integrity of the system. Hatches are a touring thing, with their use extending over to the prototype little-bit-of-everything kayak.

What if your kayak has a center foam wall between the deck and the keel line for addi-tional strength and rigidity? No problem. Use two half-width bags, one on each side of the wall.

> **Rocks and Shoals**
>
> Waterproof bags not only keep your gear safe, they also displace empty space that could be filled with water follow-ing an upset. Every drop of water you keep from inside your kayak means less water you'll have to remove in case of a damp incident.

Sock It to Me

A sea sock looks like a giant anklet sock, made from a watertight material. You stick the toe of the sock (and the heel) inside the cockpit of your touring kayak and snap the elastic top of the sock around the cockpit coaming. Your spray deck snaps down over the sock edge, with you sitting in the sock within your kayak. The amount of water that can work its way under your spray deck is limited to the volume of the sock. Fall out of your kayak, and you can invert the sock to empty the water.

Walling Off the Water

You can always install bulkheads—form-fitting walls spanning the width and depth of your kayak—behind your seat and in front of your feet. In theory, this creates air chambers in the bows and the entire aft end of your kayak. On the reality side of things, bulkheads leak, walls

> **The Old Paddler Says**
>
> Some kayaks will be con-structed with bulkheads in place. Other builders feel that if you want bulkheads you can install them your-self, just where you want them. Kayaks with bulkheads in place normally also have hatches installed. Hatches can also be added later, when and if you choose to add bulkheads.

sweat, and hulls ooze water—all of which carry the potential of filling these chambers with water. Not only that, but you've effectively sealed off most of the stowage space within your kayak.

What's the alternative? Install the bulkheads, because they work. At the same time, install hatches through the decks giving you access to the spaces behind the bulkheads you installed. A hatch is just a door, usually with a gasket to make it as watertight as possible. Sure, all hatches leak, but this can be kept to a manageable trickle. Some people prefer a plastic screw-in round hatch, some like a rubber hatch that seals over a coaming lip much like a spray deck; others like a solid hatch cover that is strapped over a seal around the opening. Remember that the largest object you can insert into a sealed-off chamber behind a bulkhead must be smaller than the hatch opening itself.

> **CAUTION**
>
> **Rocks and Shoals**
>
> If it's important to keep something dry, double-wrap it. Put it into a waterproof bag (or into a waterproof case and then in a waterproof bag) before stowing it behind that watertight hatch.

Will your gear remain dry? Probably not. Plan ahead by placing each item into a dry bag that will fit through the hatch opening, and make certain that the dry bag is sealed before letting drips of water probe your handiwork.

Careless sit-on-top, open-top, or wash-deck paddlers blissfully assume that the entire interior of their hull is a sealed, watertight chamber. Not! Remember that even a sit-on-top kayak can pop a hatch cover, crack a seam, or even spit up the drain plug in the ends. Any of these can dampen—literally!—the pleasure of a day on the water. Cram some air bags into the hull or stow your "keep dry" possessions in dry bags, and you'll keep the water at bay.

The Least You Need to Know

- To enjoy paddling on lakes or ocean waters with their winds, or upon rivers with their currents, you should know what makes a kayak maneuverable, stable, and efficient, and what combination of characteristics are needed for each.

- A kayak's length, rocker, and cross section are key indicators of its capabilities.

- Rudders and skegs alter a kayak's balance, and thus its paddling efficiency.

- Paddling is a wet sport, but with the right combination of dry storage spaces and waterproof bags you can keep your possessions and gear dry and safe.

What's It Made Of?

In This Chapter

- ◆ Matching function to materials
- ◆ Riding the plastics revolution
- ◆ Wood—the miracle material
- ◆ Boats with a skeleton

Function, unless you're talking to a high-style shoe salesperson, defines form. To a great extent, function and form define the materials used to build today's kayaks and canoes. Some materials simply offer advantages that others can't match. Plastics can be mass-produced. Composites made with fiberglass, Kevlar, carbon fiber, or other fabric, sculpt incredibly sharp and clean hulls. Wood is light, strong, and beautiful. Inflatables as well as take-apart frame-and-fabric boats can be moored in the back of a closet when you're not paddling. Frame-and-fabric boats give and flex in bouncy water, giving a smooth and efficient ride.

Some materials transcend utility to coddle a paddler's psyche. One person may fall in love with the give and flex of a wood-frame touring kayak with a fabric skin (outer layer), knowing in some unspoken part of his or her mind why early Native kayakers said they were *riding* their kayaks. Another might recreate part of Polynesian history aboard a dugout outrigger canoe voyaging between islands. Still a third might paddle around in a marred and scuffed plastic river boat, as comfortable and reliable as an old slipper. Why a person prefers one hull material to another and why a second person really doesn't care what molecules are keeping him out of the water are inarguable questions of taste.

Common Kayak and Canoe Materials

Is there a best all-around material? Nope. There may be a most appropriate material considering a paddler's skills, waters to be explored, cost, and paddling efficiency. That's a choice beginning with the boat designer, filtered through the manufacturer, and clarified by a dealer. Oh, yeah, and influenced by your fellow paddlers. But the final decision is up to you, and you alone. Here's a quick look at the most common materials.

Plastic

Plastic—and I'm not talking about credit cards—grabbed paddlesports and turned it on its head. The development of molded polyethylene as a hull material reinvented the way boats are made, and in doing so, made doggone good boats far more accessible to far more paddlers.

Boatbuilding Before Plastic

Not all that long ago, every boat was an active partnership between the designer, with carefully drawn plans, and the craftsman, using all his or her skills to bend and shape his or her materials into an approximation of that desired shape. Hand-crafted? You bet!

Consider fiberglass, in which the ultimate shape of the boat is determined by the mold in which the hull is built. I'll discuss the process of laying fiberglass in detail later in this chapter, but let's consider it briefly here to see what role the boatbuilder plays in a nonplastic boat's construction. The artisan applying the colored resin of the gel coat—the visible exterior of the hull—varies the coat's thickness depending on where he or she believes the wear areas will be as well as his or her own skill in laying down a smooth coat. The process of placing each layer of fiberglass cloth into the mold can be modified endlessly to create slightly different angles, and the amount of resin used in each layer can vary significantly. Similarly, the amount of overlap of the layers and the number of pieces of 'glass cloth can vary. Conditions—including the temperature and

The Old Paddler Says

Arguments over the best material miss the point. The debate is really over which material works best for a particular paddler in a particular type of water at a particular cost.

humidity—in the shop also affect the final product, resulting in variations from boat to boat. As a result of these (and other) factors, boats built using the same frame may have slightly different weights, shapes, and degrees of resiliency and rigidity.

These would be great boats, built to exacting standards, but each would bear the unmistakable and unique stamp of a craftsperson.

The Old Paddler Says

Plastic kayaks put well-designed boats in the hands of a lot of paddlers by turning output into a manufacturing process. It trimmed away "grunt" work and enabled designers to concentrate on creating better boats.

Enter Plastic

And then came plastics. All the designer's skills and visions take shape in a single mold. Plastic pellets are poured into the mold, heated, and a stream of identical boats is churned out of the molding machine.

That's not to demean the skill and hard work of the people running the molding machines. What's happened, though, is that boat-building moved out of the artisan's shop and into the factory. The challenges and expense of fabricating great molds means longer production runs of each model. Couple low materials costs with long production runs, and you end up with more affordable manufactured boats.

You'll hear five phrases bandied about when talking of plastic boats. Polyethylene is the first, and it is just the most common type of plastic used in boat manufacturing. Polyethylene most often comes in either linear or cross-linked. Linear is shaped as long strands, which stick to adjacent stands. Cross-linked strands are shorter, and chemically bonded to adjacent strands. Linear is the heavier of the two (for the same strength) and is easier to repair. Cross-linked is a bit lighter.

The two most common ways of shaping a plastic boat are roto-molding and blow-molding. During roto-molding, the mold is spun and tilted to place a coating of molten polyethylene on the inside, which in a few minutes becomes a boat. During blow-molding, the molten polyethylene is injected or blown into the mold cavities.

Any combination of these materials and techniques, in the hands of a skilled builder, can result in a great boat.

Plastic boats are heavier than their composite cousins, less expensive, and less efficient. Because of the manufacturing process, bows and sterns are more rounded than sharp. This makes them a little less streamlined and a little more difficult to push through the water. On the other hand, plastic will take a heck of a whack without marring. You won't wince at the thought of nudging up against a rock.

All told, for most of us in most paddling situations, plastic can be a good and satisfying choice. It's used for touring and river kayaks with great results, and for some canoes. Some canoe manufacturers counter plastics' flexibility with internal frameworks, such as from aluminum tubing.

ABS

ABS, the initials of acrylonitrile butadiene styrene (don't worry: no one is expected to remember, or even less to pronounce, the scientific name), burst onto the canoeing scene in the early '70s and revolutionized river paddling. In short, ABS is a sandwich of foamed plastic between two layers of vinyl. Its most common form is Royalex, which has evolved into a family of products all built on the same technology but each with slightly different characteristics. What makes it so neat is that it has a heat-activated memory. Place a sheet of this sandwich in a mold and, with heat and pressure, shape it into a canoe hull, and the hull will "remember" what it is supposed to look like. Drop it off a building and it will bounce. Wrap it around a rock in a river, and once you pry it free it will spring back into shape, though you might have to replace broken gunwales. Hit it with a 2 × 4 and it will boom and bounce the board back at you.

With all those nifty features, it's not a wonder material. You can't shape it into a knife-edge stem or stern. The material flexes a bit, so to prevent oil-canning (flexing or popping a small amount in and out), surfaces have to be slightly arched or vee'd. And it's possible to cut the vinyl exterior on a sharp rock or other protrusion. With that said, anyone looking for a good material for river-running or lake exploration should take a close look at faithful ABS.

Like polyethylene plastics, ABS is shaped in an expensive, heated mold. Because of this, ABS canoes tend to have long production runs before changing basic designs.

ABS is most commonly used for open canoes. An open canoe is formed from a single sheet of ABS. A second sheet would be needed to form the upper deck of a kayak or an enclosed canoe, and the two would have to be joined together, not an easy process.

Composite

Composite is a sort of generic term, describing a material made of a hard-setting resin and layers of fabric placed carefully into a smooth mold. A *fiberglass* canoe or kayak really means a hull constructed of resin and woven fiberglass cloth or fabric. Fiberglass was the first widely used composite, and some older builders and paddlers still differentiate between fiberglass and other cloth or fabrics used in making a composite hull.

Kevlar, used to make military helmets and bulletproof vests, can be woven into a lightweight and super-strong alternative to fiberglass. Carbon fiber is another space-age alternative to fiberglass. There are many others, some developed for a specific builder. Builders can also combine different fabrics in the layers within the composite.

Paddlin' Talk

Fiberglass is a synthetic material shaped into strands and woven into cloth. When a boat has a fiberglass hull, it means that the hull is a composite of resin and fiberglass cloth.

However you think of them, the process of laying up fabric in a mold and wetting out each with a resin results in a wonderful hull. It is relatively light, super strong, and capable of forming the most demanding shapes.

I've already discussed the downside, if you want to call it that, of this process. It's under the control of an artisan and, as such, each hull is slightly different. Cloth overlaps at the stem and stern or around support structures may be just slightly different. The gel coat, the smooth exterior layer of (usually) colored resin, is sprayed in place, and the hand of the craftsperson may allow slight variations in thickness. The amount of resin left in the cloth rather than being squeezed out and discarded before setting up differs from boat to boat, and from craftsperson to craftsperson. All told, there are a host of small differences in each lay-up that result in boats of differing weights, hull resiliency, and balance.

The negatives are totally overwhelmed by the consistent shape, low maintenance, and easily repairable hull. If you want an efficient canoe or kayak that will easily slip through the water, composites are the way to go. That's why composites dominate the international racing community.

You'll pay a hefty price for this efficiency. A fiberglass hull is moderately priced. Change that to an Kevlar fabric and a more esoteric resin and the prices ratchet up quickly—almost as fast as the weight goes down. Kevlar is used in bulletproof vests and military helmets, giving some indication of its strength and resistance to penetration. Go to a carbon fiber hull, and you would get little change back from a $5,000 bill for a flatwater sprint C-1, or solo canoe.

Rocks and Shoals

Don't confuse price and value. Higher prices usually reflect correspondingly lighter materials. Most paddlers don't need Olympic-level performance, and would do better to pay a lower price for a heavier and more durable boat.

Not all composite materials are deserving of such high praise, however. Some boats have what's called a *chopper gun fiberglass hull*, which is made by squirting a mixture of short fiberglass strands and resin into a mold. The resulting hull is heavy and relatively weak.

Composites are used to lay up both kayaks and canoes, generally ones where clean lines, lightness, and rigidity are at a premium. Chopper gun fiberglass is used in lower-end canoes.

Wood

Wood is an elegant material, so versatile that one scientist commented that if it didn't occur naturally, whoever invented it would have received the Nobel Prize. It can be manipulated into fabulous shapes, it's strong, it's light, it's durable, and it is pretty.

What kind of canoes and kayaks can it build?

On the traditional side, one outrigger canoe racing class to this day uses *koa* dugout hulls carved from single logs, much like the Polynesians who used similar outrigger canoes to explore the vast reaches of the Pacific. Native Americans in the Pacific Northwest and First Peoples in western Canada still hollow out great cedar logs for their traditional "war" canoes used in ceremonies and in competition. Birchbark canoes are still built in the Upper Midwest and the Northeastern United States.

Planked Wood

Graceful canoes with closely-spaced wooden ribs supporting an outer skin of thin wooden boards covered with painted canvas draw a crowd anytime they're launched, and a handful of dedicated builders still craft them. These are among the most pricy and fragile of wooden canoes or kayaks, but are also among the nicest to paddle. Some manufacturers now line the inside of their fiberglass composites hulls with bent ribs to replicate the look of the traditional canoe.

The Old Paddler Says

A reasonably competent craftsperson working at home with a bit of help can build a strip-built or "stitch and glue" canoe or kayak in a month of steady work. Most will take twice that, with all the interruptions of today's world.

It is not common, but a scattering of touring kayaks, with ³/₄-inch solid-wood sides, a thick wooden board bottom, and arched decks, poke and pry around the water world.

Strip-Built

Strip-built canoes and kayaks are formed by bending thin cedar strips along formers, or frames, which will be removed, and by gluing the strips into shape. Most of these are covered with resin and fiberglass cloth, a structure that is fantastically light and strong.

Stitch-and-Glue

Some plywood canoes and kayaks are built over frames. The new technology, though, dispenses with frames altogether. Instead, shaped plywood planks are "sewn" together with wire and then glued. The wire stitches are removed, and the resulting hull is strong and light. These hulls are normally covered with resin and a layer of fiberglass.

The downside of wood is that it is a craftsperson's medium, requiring care and skill to fabricate a stunning boat. The upside of wood is that it is a craftsperson's medium that, with care and skill, can fabricate a stunning boat.

Both canoes and kayaks are fabricated from plywood, edge-glued strips, and solid wood. Wooden canoes and kayaks range from high-technology ultra-modern hulls to classic works of art. Prices tend to be high, reflecting the craftsmanship involved in building them.

In the Wake
Wood-strip canoes and kayaks are the easiest and least-complicated boats for the amateur builder, because they don't require molds or the precisely shaped panels of a stitch-and-glue hull. They do require patience, precise measurements and assembly, and a moderate amount of woodworking skill and equipment.

Frame with Fabric Skin

Frame-and-fabric kayaks (and a few canoes) are lineal descendants of the classic boats of the Arctic. A series of frames set along a keel define the cross section of the boat, with stringers (thin pieces of wood or other strong and light material) stretched from the bow to the stern over the frames supporting a fabric exterior. Within that broad definition, there are two extended families of frame with fabric skin boats: folding, which means that the frame can be removed and disassembled, and rigid, which means that the craft doesn't come apart.

Don't dismiss frame-and-fabric kayaks and canoes as toys. In recent years, they've crossed the Atlantic Ocean westbound, pushed around stormy Cape Horn, paddled the entire north shore of Australia, and bumped around the ice at both poles of the world. Those were all take-aparts. Rigid-frame boats routinely voyaged from western Alaska to San Francisco during the Russian fur trade, paddled all across the Northwest Passage between the Atlantic and Pacific in the Canadian Arctic, roamed from somewhere around Labrador all the way north to the land of solid ice, and, in addition to hopping from fjord to fjord in Greenland, in at least one case crossed from Greenland to Ireland!

Framing It Up

Traditional builders use wood for their frameworks, often multi-ply Baltic birch ply-wood for frames and spruce for stringers. In a way, they are copying the earliest builders who had sought out curved pieces of driftwood that could be cut and shaped into naturally bent frames. Plywood allows for larger frame pieces, making the frame easier to design and build as well as far easier to snap together.

Some builders opt for multi-piece frames, bolted or riveted together. These are more material-efficient but at the same time more labor intensive. Yet others use fewer pieces in each frame, manually bending parts into the shapes—vees or arches—needed for the cross sections.

> **In the Wake**
>
> The first time you paddle a frame-and-fabric kayak in waves can be unnerving. The kayak flexes and twists, almost as if it were alive, and it takes you a while to realize that it is seeking the easiest path through the chop rather than smashing against the power of the waves.

Wood is still a popular frame material, but cost and the availability of craftspeople have sent builders on a search for alternatives. Aluminum is an increasingly popular frame choice because it is an easily shaped and lightweight material that lends itself to machine fabrication. Paddlers can make emergency field repairs on critical aluminum parts almost as easily as you once could have with wood.

Wrapping It Up

No one, not even the most dedicated traditionalist, uses hide as a skin any more. Instead, a wide variety of waterproofed fabrics are used to encase the frame. Woven fabrics with a waterproof coating tend to be the rule. Although cotton was once the preferred fabric, polyester fabrics have replaced cotton in popularity. Rubberlike Hypalon is one of the most popular and durable waterproof finishes, but some boatbuilders apply vinyl coating, which is less expensive and lighter than Hypalon. Urethane-coated nylon is also less expensive than Hypalon.

You'll also see, primarily on rigid hull boats, canvas skins waterproofed with a few coats of paint. This is about the least expensive material, particularly for those designing and building their own boats, but it also require more maintenance.

Keeping It Tight

The basic skin on frame model calls for a very snug skin that barely fits over the framework. A form-fitting, sleek skin is going to be easier to paddle than a loose and bulging skin. How can you keep it tight?

One solution is to install air bladders (long, thin balloons) within a pocket sewn into the fabric skin the length of the hull from near the bow to the stern. Once the snug skin is fitted around the frame, the air bladders are inflated to tighten up the hull.

Another option is to have shoelacelike lashing on the hull skin. Insert the frame into the skin, and then lace up the adjustments until all is taut.

Some rigid-frame builders use a heat-sensitive synthetic material that is sewn in place over the frame as snugly as possible. Then the skin is heated, and "shrink-wrapped" into a drumhead-taut skin.

Proponents of each skin material and each hull material will argue passionately about the virtues of their particular favorite and how it is obviously superior in all regards. Most likely they are all correct.

Inflatable

When space is at a premium and easy transportation a priority, plain old air is of worthy consideration. Inflatable kayaks work, and work well. Simply pump up their multiple air chambers and you're set to go.

Technology changes faster than writing, but at the time of this writing, the hull of an inflatable kayak or canoe begins with a base of either polyester (woven or knitted) or nylon threads. Polyester is less stretchy but not as strong, while nylon is more stretchy but stronger.

Each of these base fabrics can be coated with either a rubberized coating, such as Hypalon or neoprene, or substances called plastomers, which include reinforced vinyl, PVC, and urethane. Some inflatables have a solid floor connected directly to the inflatable sides. These are the least expensive to build, and perfectly satisfactory for placid rivers and calm waters. On the downside, any water splashed into the passenger compartment stays with you until you bail it out. At best, that's uncomfortable. At worst, that's a significant weight of water you're trying to move until such time as you can bail it out. Self-bailing inflatables have buoyant foam-filled or air-supported floors with scuppers (drain holes) that allow any water splashed aboard to quickly drain out. The foam offers your backside more protection from the hazards of the water. The inflatable floor can be deflated and rolled tightly for more compact storage.

 Rocks and Shoals

If an inflatable canoe or kayak has but a single continuous air chamber and you puncture it, you're going to become a swimmer. If each tube is divided into several separate air chambers, a puncture becomes an inconvenience and not a disaster.

The Pros and the Cons

Here's a subjective list of popular canoe and kayak hull materials, comparing some of the following attributes of each:

♦ **Cost** refers to the hull material itself.

♦ **Impact** refers to that material's ability to resist damage from an impact.

♦ **Abrasion** refers to the material's resistance to wear or cutting.

♦ **Slipperiness** refers to how well (relatively speaking) the material will slide over rocks.

♦ **Weight** refers to a hull's approximate weight in comparison to the average of all other equal hulls.

♦ **Repairs** refers to the ease of making repairs to that material.

Canoe and Kayak Materials

Material	Cost	Impact	Abrasion	Slipperines	Weight	Repairs
Aluminum	Low-mod.	Fair	Good	Poor	Moderate	Difficult
Polyethylene (Linear)	Low	Good	Fair	Good	Heavy	Hard
Polyethylene (Cross-Linked)	Moderate	Good	Fair	Good	Heavy	Difficult
Fiberglass Chopper gun	Low	Poor	Poor	Good/fair	Very heavy	Easy
Fiberglass Cloth	Moderate	Good	Good	Good	Moderate	Easy
Kevlar	High	V. Good	Good	Good	Light	Easy
Composites	Very High	Good	Good	Good	Light	Moderate
Wood	High	Good	Good	Good	Light	Varies
ABS	Moderate	Excellent	Fair	Good	Moderate	Moderate
Rubber-coated inflatables	Moderate	V. Good	Good	Good	Light	Easy
Plastomer-coated inflatables	Moderate	V. Good	Good	Good	Light	Easy

Concrete?

It's not a joke. You can build a canoe or kayak from virtually any material, including concrete. Civil engineering schools from universities around North America compete to build the best possible concrete canoe, and then race their canoes against each other on a flatwater course. A good grade, we suspect, includes completing the course without sinking.

The Least You Need to Know

- The best hull construction material depends on where and how you want to paddle.

- Plastic has reshaped the way canoes and kayaks can be built, putting more good boats in the hands of paddlers at affordable prices.

- Craftsperson-built composite canoes and kayaks produce sleek and efficient hulls.

- Frame-and-fabric kayaks established their seaworthiness, with voyages across the Atlantic Ocean, around Cape Horn, and through the ice-clogged waters of Canada's Northwest Passage.

- When storage space is at a premium and performance is a requirement, today's well-designed and well-built inflatable canoes and kayaks can be a super choice.

Part 2

You and Your Paddle

A paddle, they say, is a stick with water on one end and a person on the other. That's true. It's also true that a paddle is an amazingly technical piece of work, which works just like the transmission, the wheels, the brakes, and the steering in your car. Not to mention its role in keeping you upright and dry.

In this part, we'll look at the parts of both canoe and kayak paddles and show just why each is shaped the way it is, and how that shape defines the overall performance of your canoe or kayak. You'll see how to fit a paddle shaft to your hand (they do come in different sizes) as well as choosing the right paddle length for you and for your boat. You'll also see why so many kayak paddles have their blades twisted at an angle from each other while logic says they should be in line.

Chapter 6

What Shapes a Canoe Paddle?

In This Chapter

- ◆ Learning your way around your canoe paddle
- ◆ Finding the right shaft length
- ◆ How blade shape determines function
- ◆ What canoe paddles are made of
- ◆ The four families of canoe paddles

Your canoe paddle is the transmission and drive wheels of your canoe, your steering wheel, and the extendable arm that makes your boat effectively 10 feet wide and incredibly stable. That's a tall order for a simple little stick with a wide spot on one end and a paddler on the other. Fortunately, those tasks are well within the little stick's capabilities.

The Multifaceted, Multitalented Paddle

You are the engine in your canoe, but you can't make your canoe move by itself. You transmit your power through your paddle. You reach forward, stick the blade into the water, and pull yourself and your canoe toward the paddle. You only thought you were pulling the paddle blade through the water—the blade provides so much resistance and friction that it's easier for your canoe to slide toward it than for it to slide toward you.

You also use your paddle to pull or push one end of your canoe sideways to aim your bow in the direction you want to go. A twitch of your paddle, a turn of the blade in the current, and you and your canoe carve a subtle arc over the water's surface.

The Old Paddler Says

It is incredibly tiring to move even a good canoe with a heavy, dead-feeling paddle. Swinging a good, light-weight, and lively paddle, even aboard a slug of a canoe, leaves you far more refreshed at the end of the day. Opt for the best paddle you can afford, and upgrade your canoe to match it.

A canoe 10 feet wide? Absolutely—if you can reach out 5 feet to each side, the effective beam of your canoe is 10 feet! With a little practice you can slap the blade of your paddle flat against the surface of the water 5 or more feet out from the centerline of your canoe. The pressure of that blade can right an overturned canoe or stabilize a shaky one. Just as easily, you can reach with your paddle and pull yourself back into an erect and balanced position (this is called a high brace, and you'll learn about it in Chapter 12).

Parts of a Canoe Paddle

Your basic canoe paddle is a pretty simple device. It's composed of a round or oval stick, called a shaft, into which a flattened blade—the part that pushes through the water—has been inserted. The place on the paddle where the blade and shaft merge together is called the throat. Most paddles today have a fitted handhold at the upper end of the shaft, called a top, or upper, grip. The lower grip is on the shaft a few inches above the throat. The very end of the paddle blade is called the tip. The rim around the paddle blade is called the blade edge.

The parts of a standard canoe paddle

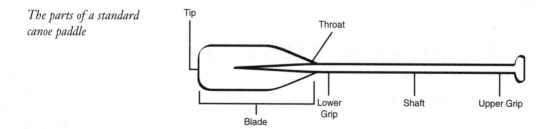

Characteristics of a Well-Built Paddle

It's easier to describe a good paddle than it is to build one. Developing a pound-and-a-half tool that will stand up to the stresses of a day's paddling is a major accomplishment. All paddles weaken over time, and paddle makers must attempt to balance a long product life against an overly massive structure.

In addition, well-built paddles must be properly balanced. The blade of a paddle is much like a child perched way out on the end of a teeter-totter. The blade (or the child) is a long way from the fulcrum—which, on a teeter-totter, is the center balance on which the board teeters and totters; on a paddle, the fulcrum is the lower grip where your hand pulls the blade through the water. The heavier the blade, the more effort needed to keep the paddle (or the teeter-totter) moving. But it's not a simple matter of making the paddle blade lighter. Reducing weight in the paddle blade means removing structural material, and at some point the blade will be catastrophically weakened. That's not an easy compromise.

Blades Shape Paddling Performance

There is no single right paddle. Just like with canoes, different paddles—and, in particular, different paddle blades—work better in different environments. The tripper moves a load over distance, the flatwater racer sacrifices all else for speed over a projected distance, and white-water player demands control and durability. To excel at their respective paddling styles, they each need a different kind of blade.

Think of blade size much like bicycle gears. You can shift into the biggest bike gear, and it will take all your effort just to turn the cranks slowly. Shift into a lower gear and you'll find it far easier to turn the cranks, and you'll probably pick up speed.

Grab the paddle with the biggest blade and you'll exhaust yourself with a few strokes. Go to a smaller blade and, like with bicycle gears, you'll take more strokes but you'll expend far less energy on each one. You could, if you'd rather, imagine lifting 500 pounds of flour from a pallet on the floor to a shelf. You could lift 5 100-pound sacks, with a lot of effort. You could lift 10 50-pound sacks with just a few grunts. Or you could move 50 10-pound bags without breaking a sweat.

Racers like a small blade and a high paddle-stroke cadence. That's super-efficient and keeps their canoe moving smoothly and quickly. Wilderness trippers prefer a small blade and a quick paddle stroke for the same reason. This combination puts the least strain and effort on your muscles.

White-water paddlers need a quick and secure grip on the water and the current. That means a wider (and bigger) blade.

Casual recreational paddlers rarely put in the time and effort to learn how to paddle with a high cadence. Instead, they tend to rely on a larger paddle blade to move them through the water. That's one reason a recreational paddler will be more tired after a short day on the water than a proficient paddler after a long day. It isn't all physical fitness, but a big part of paddling pleasure is fitting your physical ability to the demands of the paddling experience.

Getting a Grip on Your Paddle

Canoe paddles are designed to be held in two places: at the top, or the end opposite from the blade, and just above the throat, or about 8 inches above the place where the top of the blade merges into the shaft. How you grasp the paddle, at least at the top end, is determined by the type of water you choose to paddle.

> **In the Wake**
>
> You might decide that you like a particular handhold so much that you'll use it for all kinds of paddling. If you pick up a paddle with an open mind, however, you'll discover that certain grip shapes will work better for you in certain types of water.

The T-grip is the upper grip of choice for hardcore white-water paddlers. A short crossbar tops off the paddle shaft, at right angles to the shaft and parallel to the paddle blade. It looks just like a capital letter T, giving it the name. The top bar gives the paddler an immediate indication of the position of the blade in the water—the blade is the same angle as the crossbar—and provides excellent leverage to rotate the paddle shaft and the paddle blade. It offers the ultimate in paddling control.

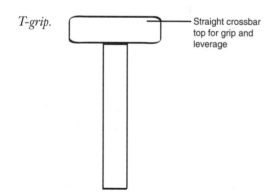

T-grip.

Straight crossbar top for grip and leverage

The soft T-grip provides the same leverage, but the top bar curves in a gentle and arguably more comfortable arc. It's pretty darn good for paddling white water, and reasonably comfortable for paddling flatwater.

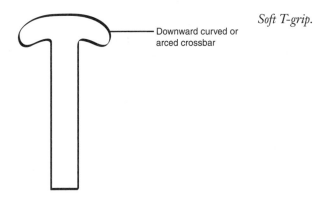

Soft T-grip.

Downward curved or
arced crossbar

If you have the need for speed, then make certain the top grip of your paddle is shaped a lot like a hollowed, flattened pear. This has nothing to do with your personal preference for fruit—the pear shape fits the shape of your hand as it grasps the paddle, with the ball of your thumb and the base of your palm nestled into the curved lower portion of the grip and the line of your knuckles at the top of your palm hooked over the top ridge of the pear grip. You can easily push against this shape with the full power of your arm and the big muscles of your torso without diverting any energy into rotating or correcting the paddle shaft.

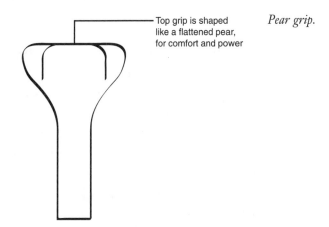

Top grip is shaped
like a flattened pear,
for comfort and power

Pear grip.

To paddle, you jab your paddle blade into the water and you pull yourself—with your lower hand—toward the paddle blade. The upper hand forces against the paddle to hold the shaft (or blade) as vertical as possible. The pear-shaped top grip puts the paddle into your palm at the most comfortable and effective angle for this maneuver.

Yet another type of grip is the offset grip, also called an offset pear grip. With the increasing use of bent-shaft paddles (more on them in the next section), the offset grip was the logical evolution of the pear grip. To picture the offset grip, think of a paddler so strong as to shove the top grip of a paddle forward an inch or so. This off-set grip aligns the center of the paddler's upper hand with the force exerted on the paddle. It also makes it more challenging and less efficient to use the back side of the paddle blade for low bracing strokes. The forward offset grip is only more efficient for bent shaft paddles.

Offset grip.

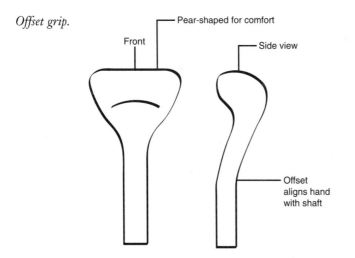

Appreciating the Shape of the Shaft

White-water paddling is a highly reflexive activity, with as much as 90 percent of the paddle strokes being instinctive reactions to what the current is doing to your boat and your paddle. You shift your weight and you adjust the angle of your paddle for its most effective interplay with the motion of the water. Which is another way of saying that unless you put the paddle blade the right way, there's a good chance you'll end up swimming.

You rarely have time to think about what to do. You always need to know which way your paddle blade is pointing, so that you can make quick adjustments as the conditions change. Luckily, you have two precise dials to indicate the direction of your paddle blade without having to stick your head in the water and look at it.

I've already told you about the first such indicator: It's at the very top of the paddle shaft. The crossbar on a T-grip paddle is exactly parallel to the paddle blade. With your thumb hooked around one horn of the T and your fingers folded over the top, you can feel precisely how the blade is aligned. The top crossbar and grip also give you more-than-adequate leverage to rotate the paddle shaft when you need to adjust the angle to the current.

The second can be the shape of the paddle shaft itself. Some paddle shafts are round while others are oval. You don't have to rely on your top hand to do all the work. The oval in an ovalized paddle shaft is set so that the long axis of the oval is at right angles to the paddle blade. While you only gain very little grip and torque while grasping the oval shape, it does indicate just how the paddle blade is oriented.

Rigid or Flexible?

A paddle maker can build a paddle shaft that bends or flexes a bit during the paddle stroke, creating a flexible paddle. It will not be like a piece of cooked spaghetti, but there will be a bit of spring or give to the paddle. The maker can also build a paddle that is very stiff or rigid, with no give or flex at all. The two paddles may weigh the same, be shaped the same, but will feel different in the hands of a paddler.

Whitewater paddling demands power, and you don't want to let any of your limited energy evaporate in the effort to merely bend your paddle shaft. For white-water paddling, you want a rigid shaft that will react instantly to any demands you place on it. Flatwater paddling is a different kettle of fish. You don't want to beat up your own joints by the repetitive impact of countless paddle strokes. A paddle shaft with a little bit of flex works just like the shock absorbers in your car and takes the thump out of the push you apply to the paddle.

Shaft Size

An inch on one ruler is the same as an inch on another ruler. Unfortunately, paddle-shaft sizes are more like clothing sizes than inches. Every paddle maker comes up with his or her own. Your only option is to experiment until you find a shaft size that fits your hand and to make note of it. Too large a shaft, and your hand tires. Too small, and your hands cramp. Measure the diameter of a good-feeling round shaft, or the long axis and the short axis of an oval shaft that you like, and compare that to the measurements of whatever new paddle you're considering.

Straight-Shaft and Bent-Shaft Paddles

To make the best use of your efforts, a paddle blade has to be absolutely vertical in the water. Any force applied to the paddle blade has to be at right angles to the blade itself. Unfortunately, our arms and joints make such maneuvers difficult. Because of the way we're shaped, we tend to insert the paddle blade in the water at an angle and sweep the paddle blade in a vertical arc through the stroke. We push down on the blade at the beginning of the stroke, which lifts the front of the canoe, and we pull up on the back part of the stroke, lifting a weight of water or forcing the stern of our canoe deep into the water. This is wasted effort.

To counteract this motion, paddlers have developed ways of cocking or bending their wrists and bodies to keep the paddle blades in the most efficient position. It isn't easy. Fortunately, paddle makers have developed more ergonomic paddles in recent years, thanks to one paddle maker who invented a new kind of paddle for his wife.

Paddle maker Brad Gillespie enjoyed boating with his wife. A few years back she was plagued by an injured wrist, and it hurt for her to paddle. Brad figured that he could mount a blade at an angle to the shaft. With this bent paddle she could keep the blade closer to vertical in the water throughout the stroke while reducing the amount of wrist strain and, consequently, wrist pain. It worked darned well. They paddled faster and her wrist healed.

That was quite possibly the first bent-shaft paddle ever developed. In a bent-shaft paddle, the blade is turned at an angle from the line of the shaft. By a process of trial and error, paddlers have discovered that the maximum usable bend is about 17 degrees, and that a bend of less than around $7^1/_2$ degrees doesn't seem to have any positive effect. Most contemporary bent-shaft paddles seem to be in the 12- to 14-degree range.

Before you rush out and buy a bent-shaft stick, you should know that there are drawbacks to this ergonomic design. The two faces of a straight paddle are identical. You can push or pull against either side of the blade, depending on the paddle stroke you perform. (More about canoe paddle strokes in Chapter 12). The bent shaft paddle is a little more complicated. You can only apply power to one face (or side) of the blade. You'll have to turn and twist the paddle more for some of the paddle strokes you'll use in controlling your canoe. You'll need more practice to be able to make the stroke movements second nature.

Rocks and Shoals

When it comes to paddling, learn the basic strokes and techniques. With those as a foundation, explore the high-efficiency world of bent-shaft paddling. If you start with bent-shaft paddle, you'll have to go back to paddling school and learn the basics anyway.

I suggest that beginning paddlers learn the basic strokes with a straight-shaft paddle. Keep the unique advantages of a bent-shaft for a future present to yourself.

Once you've paddled for a while with a straight-shaft paddle, and you're set on covering a lot of lake, ocean, or placid river miles with the most speed and least effort, you might want to invest a few days in learning the quirks of a bent-shaft paddle. For most people it pays off handsomely. If you're sporting in white water, you really will prefer the control and versatility of a straight-shaft paddle.

In the Wake

For good reasons not entirely connected to their crook, bent-shaft paddles tend to have shafts 4 to 6 inches shorter than their straight counterparts. First of all, they have been widely adopted by racers, who typically have a high-cadence paddling style calling for a shorter shaft. Racers tend to hang in low, sleek hulls such as cruiser or marathon boats, allowing for shorter paddle shafts. They also tend, with a lot of training and physical conditioning, toward a shorter and wider paddle blade. So it's hard to tell if bent-shaft paddles work better when shorter, or if the kind of powerful paddlers who are most likely to try bent-shaft paddles opt for a shorter stick.

Paddle Length

There are a number of myths still floating around paddle camps as to the proper paddle length. One of the enduring myths is that you should stand tall with your paddle vertical in front of you. The tip should be on the ground, and the upper grip should be between your chin and eyebrows. Another is that you should stretch your arms straight out to your sides, and hold your paddle horizontal across your chest. Your fingers should barely reach around the paddle tip and upper grip. Neither of these takes into consideration shaft length, which is the critical measurement.

For comfortable paddling (and for the most efficient use of your muscles) when you're in your paddling position in your canoe your upper hand (and upper grip) should be about chin-high and the paddle throat should be just in the water.

Why shouldn't you just use an overall length to find a paddle that fits? Because a 56-inch-long paddle may be effectively 3 inches longer than a 58-inch paddle. If you stand the two together, it is easy to tell which is longer. Now measure the parts. The 56-inch paddle could have a blade measuring 22 inches from tip to throat, and a shaft length of 34 inches. The 58-inch paddle may have a 27-inch blade from throat to tip, and a shaft length of 31 inches.

 Rocks and Shoals

The length of the paddle shaft, from grip to throat, is the critical measurement when finding a paddle that fits you.

The shorter (overall) paddle has the longer shaft length.

Finding the Best Shaft Length

The easiest and most accurate way of measuring for a good paddle shaft length is to sit upright in your accustomed position in your canoe. Make a perfect paddle stroke, but freeze the motion when the paddle is vertical in the water. Measure the vertical distance from your nose to the top of the paddle blade. That's a good basic shaft length for you.

If it's winter and the water is frozen, sit in your canoe and make believe you're in the middle of a great forward paddle stroke. Measure the vertical distance from your nose to the ground, and then subtract 2 inches. That 2 inches is close to the depth your canoe floats in the water. Once again, that's your basic paddle shaft length.

Rocks and Shoals _____

Are you normally on your knees, resting against a thwart when you paddle, rather than sitting on a seat? Then that's the position you want for figuring out your paddle length. Get into the position you actually use while paddling to determine the right shaft length for you.

It's essential that you sit in your canoe in your accustomed seat when figuring the proper shaft length. That's because the seats in a big tripper canoe can be 13 inches off the floor, putting the paddler high above the water line. A sleek and finely honed competition cruiser or a decked single-paddler slalom canoe can put the seat down a bare 7 inches from the floor.

If you don't own a canoe or don't have access to it when selecting your paddle, a quick rule-of-thumb way of guesstimating whether a paddle shaft will work for you is to squat down so that you're sitting on your heels and balancing on your toes with your back vertical. Put your paddle grip on the ground next to you and hold the paddle vertical. The throat of the paddle should come about mouth to chin height on you.

How Blades Measure Up

The Old Paddler Says ___

The sharper corners of a white-water blade can easily catch a stray current, which will twist the paddle in the hands of an unwary paddler. This can be an upsetting experience. The river can and will force its demands on you through your paddle, just as you use your paddle to force your demands on it.

Blade length will vary with the shape of the blade, but most will be somewhere between 14 and 28 inches from throat to tip. Generally speaking, white-water blades will be short and wide, either rectangular or with a wide tulip shape. A shorter blade is also preferred for shallow-water paddling. Tulip and rectangular white-water blades can be 8 to 10 inches wide, to better grip aerated water and currents. A tulip blade for white water or river use will have a relatively blunt tip with rounded corners, all reinforced. The rectangular blade will have a reinforced tip that's flat across the end, with square corners. Edges of both will be thick and reinforced.

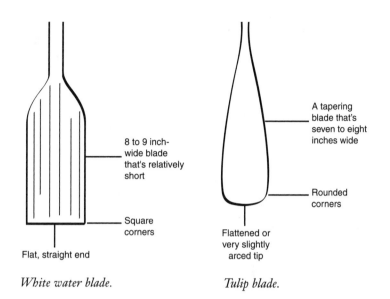

White water blade.

8 to 9 inch-wide blade that's relatively short

Square corners

Flat, straight end

A tapering blade that's seven to eight inches wide

Rounded corners

Flattened or very slightly arced tip

Tulip blade.

Paddles for flatwater or for touring tend to be longer and narrower, perhaps only 5 inches across the face. The beavertail, named because it's shaped like a beaver's tail, is all smooth curves and generally runs 5 to 7 inches wide and from 14 to 20 inches tip to throat. It's about the only design still made from a single piece of wood—Sitka spruce will work for a pond or other small and sheltered waters, while ash will stand up better to the knocks and dings of (shallow) river paddling.

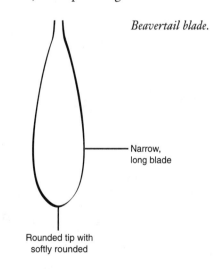

Beavertail blade.

Narrow, long blade

Rounded tip with softly rounded

Tulip-shaped blades for touring are both wider and longer than beavertails. Blades will run 8 inches or more across at the widest part of the blade, and can be 24 inches

In the Wake

Thin paddle edges slice sideways through the water easily and with little disturbance. The burble and splash of a thicker edge moving through the water indicates that you're wasting energy just moving water.

from tip to throat. The tulip-shaped blade is the most common and most popular among recreational paddlers. It performs adequately in both flatwater and moving-water environments.

Edges of both beavertail and tulip blades for flatwater use are shaved thin, and stout reinforcing along the tip and edge is uncommon. Blades are fabricated from fiberglass, other composite lay-ups, or laminated wood.

Tulip-shaped touring blade.

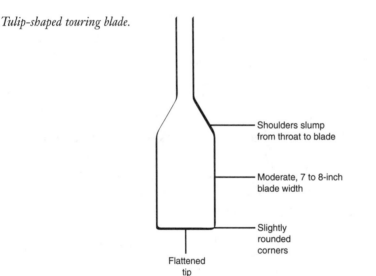

Shoulders slump from throat to blade

Moderate, 7 to 8-inch blade width

Slightly rounded corners

Flattened tip

A Quick Guide to Fitting You and Your Paddle

Rudyard Kipling could have been speaking for paddlers the world over when he summed up his "In The Neolithic Age" by wryly observing that:

> There are nine and sixty ways of constructing tribal lays,
> And every single one of them is right!

There are at least that many formulas for determining the "right" length of a paddle.

You've measured out the "ideal" shaft length, selected the blade shape best suited for your paddling waters, and you researched which paddle makers build the paddle of your dreams. Now you start the fiddling and fine-tuning to come up with the paddle you really want. To do so, ask yourself the following questions:

◆ **Will you be paddling solo or with another person in a tandem canoe?** Solo paddlers tend to like a paddle shaft a couple of inches longer than the formula I gave earlier in this chapter, so that they can carve quick turns as well as hold a straight line with a proper J-stroke (see Chapter 12 for an explanation of J-strokes). In a tandem, bow paddlers tend to like slightly longer paddle shafts, by an inch or so, for a better reach. Stern paddlers often go with a slightly shorter paddle. If you switch between bow and stern, or occasionally stand up (canoes aren't *that* tippy) for a better look ahead, you'll like a bit longer paddle.

◆ **How do you paddle?** Paddlers who perfect a high or rapid paddle-stroke cadence tend to like a shorter paddle. That's true for both bow and stern paddlers. Couple a high paddle cadence with switching sides every six strokes, and the shorter paddle is an even better choice. A slower cadence and J-stroke course corrections work better with a slightly longer paddle.

◆ **Do you use a bent-shaft paddle?** Bent-shaft paddle advocates generally choose a paddle a couple of inches shorter than the standard paddle-length formula. Outrigger kayak sailors often pack a bent-shaft paddle well under 48 inches long overall. That works because of how low they sit in the hull, how narrow the hull is, and the restricted area between the kayak hull and the outrigger.

◆ **How long are your arms compared to the rest of your body?** If you have proportionately long arms, you may find a longer paddle shaft more comfortable. If your arms are on the short side, a shorter paddle may be more comfortable. Here's a quick little measurement: Grasp your paddle with one hand properly over the top grip, and the other where you normally place it just above the throat. Now lift the paddle over your head like a weight lifter. Bend your elbows, with your upper arms horizontal and your lower arms vertical. Your hands should be lined up vertically with your elbows. An inch one way or the other is well within the comfort zone. If your hands are spread far beyond your elbows, then you're not going to be able to use your muscles comfortably nor will you impart much power to the stroke.

What's a Paddle Made Of?

Like so much in paddling, your paddle's material should be determined by the kind of paddling you do. A heavy paddle with a thick plastic blade will wear you out in a half-day of high-cadence paddling. However, if you venture into shallow, rocky waters, and anticipate lending your stick to a brother-in-law with more ego than paddling skill, that same paddle may be a good choice. It all depends.

A paddle carved from a single piece of solid wood will either be the least expensive stick on the rack or a big-price-tag authentic replica of a traditional Native paddle. In either case, it will have a relatively narrow but thick blade, because that's the shape needed to cope with the stresses of paddling.

Paddles combining an aluminum shaft with a plastic blade and a plastic upper grip range from clubs better suited for prying clams out of the muck to some satisfactory paddles. They tend to be on the heavier side, with shafts too unyielding and blades too floppy for efficient use. They are more likely to have round shafts, and the bare aluminum will be cold to the touch (and to the bones, if you're sensitive that way). A minor but noticeable improvement is a coated shaft, but this, too, is a compromise. Coatings pad out the shaft diameter a bit and could make a shaft too large for your hands. That said, the better aluminum shafts with plastic blades can work for a loaner or for your own emergency spare. Test the paddle by throwing it in some shallow water. If it sinks, it will also sink when you inadvertently drop it in the drink.

If you're passionate about recreational level paddling, fiberglass may be your material of choice. It's light, stiff in the blade, durable, and reasonably affordable. Paddle makers have discovered how to build ovalized fiberglass shafts, and can also mount the blades at right angles to the long axis of the oval.

Laminated wood is lovely to the touch and a delight to the eye, but you'll pay for the work and technology that is poured into each of them. By laminating wood, a wider, thinner, and more efficient paddle blade can be fabricated, with edges reinforced to protect them from bangs and dings. A multispecies laminated shaft can be tuned for the best paddling characteristics: stiffer for white water or with a little snap and give to aid the cruising or flatwater stroke. Expect to see ovalized shafts, as well as a variety of nonwood reinforcing material.

A paddle made with a hard-setting resin reinforced with carbon fibers or graphite strands is featherweight and fantastically strong. Expect to fork over a lot of money for such a paddle, but if you want to leave miles in your wake each day, the price is well worth it. If you paddle for 8 hours at 50 strokes a minute, you'll lift your paddle 24,000 times. Reduce the total weight of your paddle by a mere 2 ounces, and you'll reduce the amount of weight you'll lift in a day by 3,000 pounds. That's a ton and a half you won't have to move.

A reasonably good casual-recreation canoe paddle weighs around 24 to 28 ounces, with some a half pound more than that. A lightweight composite marathon paddle can weigh under 8 ounces. If you can reduce the weight at the blade end of your paddle your paddle will feel far lighter than if you had reduced the weight in the shaft or upper grip.

Cost?

A top-quality competition canoe paddle can cost $300, compared to under $100 for a good-quality general-use paddle, and down to around $30 for the paddle you'll hand to youngish kids thumping around in shallow, rock-strewn water. Listen for the sound of the whack as that paddle's blade bounces off a rock, and evaluate just how important the high cost of a low-weight paddle is for its intended use.

A Final Review

So now that you know all about the features available for canoe paddles, here are general guidelines for selecting a paddle for your personal paddling style:

- **General recreation.** Look for a paddle with a generous pear-shaped grip or a soft tee grip with a comfortably curved upper edge. Try a paddle with a fiberglass shaft and a stout fiberglass blade with a reinforced tip and relatively thick and strong edges (so that it can take some abuse). As an alternative, try a paddle with an aluminum shaft and plastic blade. A laminated wood paddle will work as well for you as a fiberglass paddle, at similar or higher costs, but you'll have to revarnish it periodically.

- **Canoe tripping.** You'll be pushing a loaded canoe for hours and miles on end, so you want a lightweight and durable paddle. Try a pear-shaped grip with a smaller beavertail or tulip-shaped blade. You'll be most comfortable with a shaft that flexes a bit, to ease the shock of thousands of paddle strokes at a stretch. Laminated wood will be comfortable, as will a graphite or other lightweight composite paddle. A good fiberglass shaft/blade paddle will also be good company. If you'll be cruising on flatwater almost exclusively, try a 12- to 14-degree bent-shaft paddle, with a straight-shaft paddle in reserve. If you absolutely have to pry off the bottom or push off from shores, then make sure you have a reinforced paddle tip and edges—or better yet, learn to use your booted feet when pushing off from the shore.

 Rocks and Shoals

An ill-fitting paddle, too long or too short, will leave you with a pain between the shoulder blades in just an hour or two. Switch to a well-balanced paddle of the proper length and the discomfort will go away.

- **Marathon canoeing.** This demands ultra-light composite (graphite, carbon fiber, and the like) or laminated wood paddles, and a high percentage will be bent-shaft. Stow an equal-quality straight-shaft paddle within easy reach for more technical river descents. Most paddlers prefer a pear-shaped or offset pear-shaped grip and ovalized shafts.

◆ **White-water canoeing.** Control is all important, and a T-grip works best to establish the blade angle. A broad rectangular or tulip blade will grab best in aerated water, for best turning and acceleration. Currents can easily grab the square corners of the broad blade and unexpectedly twist the paddle in your hand. That's another good reason for the better leverage offered by a T-shaped upper grip. White-water canoers lean toward fiberglass or laminated wood, with very little shaft flexibility. Reinforced edges and tips are a must.

That's not to say that under the impetus of impending disaster you can't make do with whatever paddle you have at hand.

The Least You Need to Know

◆ Find the best paddle shaft length for you by sitting in your own canoe in the water with a paddle—the shaft should be from about your chin to the surface of the water.

◆ The shape of your paddle blade hinges on what kind of paddling you enjoy. Wider, short blades are better for shallow water and rivers while narrow and long blades are better for deep water and long trips.

◆ You should fine-tune your paddle shaft length by your paddling style: whether you paddle in the front or back of a tandem canoe, if you paddle in a canoe by yourself, and even whether you paddle with a slow cadence or a quick stroke.

◆ Get a grip on it: A T-shaped top grip offers you better control for paddling in rivers, while a pear-shaped grip offers more comfort for long-distance paddling on calm water.

Chapter 7

What Shapes a Kayak Paddle?

In This Chapter

- Learning your way around your kayak paddle
- Choosing the blade shape best suited to your paddling style
- The pros and cons of feathered blades and asymmetrical paddles
- What kayak paddles are made of

You can be the most proficient kayak paddler ever, with six-pack abs and arms the size of tree trunks, balancing easily in a toothpick-thin screamer of a kayak, and you won't be able to move an inch without the right tool. You need a paddle to transform all that potential power into motive force.

The best part is that if you're built more like the rest of us, you can pick up one of today's responsive paddles and, with remarkably little effort, send your kayak zooming across a river current or between islands in the wine-dark sea. Clever designers have shaped paddles that fiercely grip the water, that weigh only ounces, and that are so brilliantly twisted and hollowed that they almost correct the flaws in our strokes as we glide through the water. Paddle technology has become so good that most of us faced with a choice of a great kayak and an adequate paddle or a super paddle with a sluggish kayak are far better off going with the best possible paddle.

Parts of a Kayak Paddle

No matter the environment in which you paddle, the basic shape of the paddle remains the same. It is a stick, properly called a shaft, with a blade attached to each end. The area where the shaft merges into the blade is called the throat. A few kayak paddle blades are absolutely the same on each side of each blade. In that case, it doesn't really matter which side is the front and which the back. Most paddles, however, do have a distinctive front and back. On those paddles the blades are cupped or spooned, shaped to some degree much like the bowl of a spoon. The spooned blade is inserted just like a scoop into a tub of ice cream. The spooned shape stabilizes the blade in the water when force is applied to it, eliminating the tendency of some blades to wiggle in the water. This means that you can relax your death grip on the shaft and enjoying your paddling.

The very end of the paddle is called the tip. The grip is where the paddler grasps the paddle; there are two of them, and they are normally just a few inches in from the throats. Many paddles, primarily touring paddles, come with a multipiece shaft that can be taken apart. The shaft pieces are fastened together at the joint.

Shown is a typical kayak paddle, the same paddle that could be used for river paddling to kayak touring.

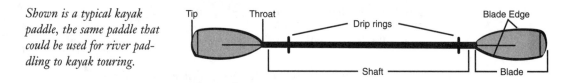

The Shape of the Blade

The shape of a kayak paddle blade defines the size, and the size defines the kind of paddling you love to do. I'll get into specific white-water and flatwater paddles later in this chapter; for now, let's look more closely at the blade features you should know about when shopping for a paddle.

Big vs. Small Blades

The decision to use bigger or smaller paddle blades largely depends on the fitness and paddling proficiency of the paddler. A super-fit racer with a beautiful paddle stroke technique can twirl a larger blade effortlessly—or apparently so. Most of us are far more comfortable with a smaller blade, no matter what kind of paddling we do. By choosing a small paddle blade we can increase our paddling cadence—the number of strokes per minute—and increase our pulse rate for cardio-vascular exercise. If we tried the same exercise with a larger paddle blade, we'd fatigue our muscles into exhaustion long before we exercised our hearts and lungs.

> **In the Wake**
>
> If you want a cardiovascular workout, go for very small paddle blades and a very high paddling cadence. If you want to build muscle mass, go for a larger paddle blade that will provide resistance training.

Asymmetrical vs. Symmetrical Blades

Draw a line right down your paddle shaft and straight across the blade of your paddle. The top half of the blade, above the line, may be a mirror image of the lower half. If so, this is a symmetrical blade.

The top half if the blade may be way bigger, may be longer and possibly wider than the bottom half. If so, this is an asymmetrical blade.

In the air, the asymmetrical blade looks lop-sided. In the water, however, it is a different story and that's why the asymmetrical blade is easier to paddle with and is much more efficient.

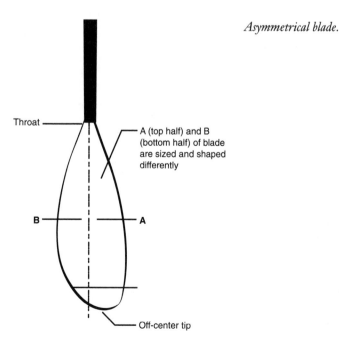

Asymmetrical blade.

Throat

A (top half) and B (bottom half) of blade are sized and shaped differently

B   A

Off-center tip

Symmetrical blade.

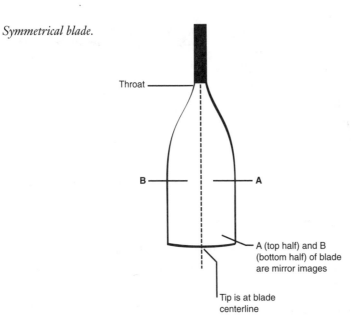

To understand why asymmetrical blades are so effective, imagine that you are floating just below the surface of a tropical lagoon, looking at the bottom of two kayaks. (You could just as well imagine yourself in a swimming pool, but why not go for a tropical paradise?) One paddler dips his or her asymmetrical blade in the water right in front of you, while the other paddler inserts his or her symmetrical blade right next to that. Look at the first, asymmetrical, blade (pictured on the right in the accompanying illustration). It pierced the water at an angle with the upper half of the blade reaching up to the air. You can see that the effective surface of the upper half of the blade has been reduced and now matches the surface area of the lower half of the blade. Equal effective areas above and below the centerline of the blade mean that there will be no twisting force exerted up the shaft.

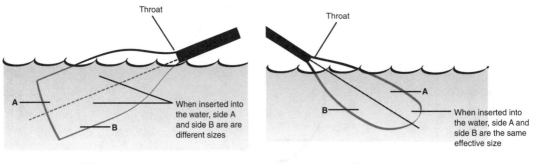

Symmetrical paddle.   *Asymmetrical paddle.*

Now look at the symmetrical blade (pictured on the left). It's at the same, correct, angle. The surface area of the top half of the blade has been effectively reduced, by the angle and the depth of the insertion. Unequal effective surface areas above and below the centerline of the blade result in a twisting motion that wastes some of your paddling energy and results in a less-effective paddle stroke.

Choosing the Right Blade for the Right Environment

The kind of paddle you choose depends on whether you'll be touring on flatwater or playing on whitewater. The touring paddler strives to get his or her kayak moving and attempts to use as little energy as possible with each stroke to keep his or her boat moving at an efficient speed. The river kayaker at play in whitewater demands instant changes in acceleration and blisteringly quick maneuverability. This mandates quick and enormous expenditures of paddling energy.

Blades for Flatwater Paddling

The touring kayaker really doesn't want to use a lot of his or her limited paddling power with each paddle stroke, so he or she will select a paddle blade that doesn't demand a lot of upper-body and arm strength—a small blade. Think of first gear in a car or the lowest gear on a bicycle. It's very easy to turn the crank one full rotation, but in doing so, you don't move ahead very much. However, and this is a big caveat, this kind of low-energy, low-result paddling yields up the absolutely fastest recovery time. He or she will recover most of the energy he or she expends in each paddle stroke during the time he or she she makes the stroke. It's not magic, just the combination of physics and blood chemistry.

Rocks and Shoals

Bigger, when it comes to blades, is not necessarily better. A large paddle blade will fatigue your muscles more quickly and give them little if any time for recuperation. Any speed you first gain will soon be lost and you'll soon slump into an exhausted and painful plod.

The touring kayaker also tends to paddle in deep water. That makes a long paddle blade an efficient choice. The paddler doesn't have to worry about banging a paddle on the bottom. Over centuries of paddling a number of touring paddle blade shapes have evolved. The Aleut blade from the far western islands of Alaska is very long and narrow. The quill is widest just beyond the throat and tapers to the tip. The asymmetrical touring blade is wider in proportion to its length, with the top half of the blade longer and wider than the bottom half. The square-end touring blade is relatively wide and relatively short, with a flat or square tip and is symmetrical. Any of these can work well for you, depending on what feels good in your hands.

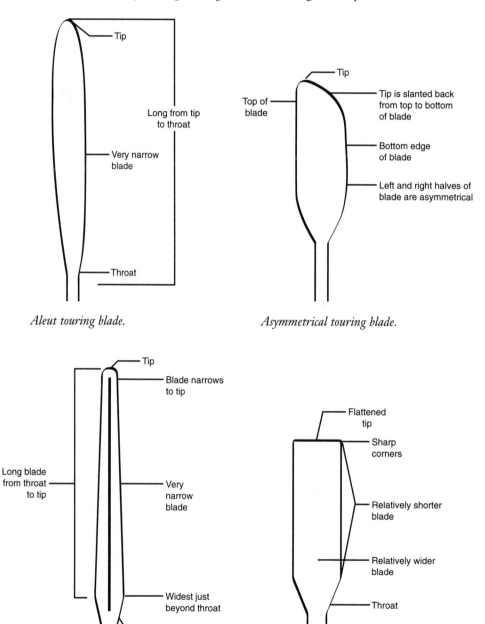

Aleut touring blade.

Asymmetrical touring blade.

Quill touring blade.

Square-end touring blade.

Blades for White-Water Paddling

River kayaks need a shorter paddle blade to avoid whopping a rock or digging a tip into a gravel bar. If you demand a greater surface area and long is out of the question, width is the only answer. To give a good bite into the mishmash of underwater currents, the white-water or river paddler should have a wide paddle blade.

The Old Paddler Says

Old-time voyageurs, the paddling engines of the fur trade, believed that some lakes were inhabited by evil spirits that slowed the progress of their big canoes. A modern look at those lakes supports their analysis, at least in part—the voyageurs were significantly slowed. The evil spirit was water dynamics. The wake boiling off their big canoes not only kicked up surface waves but also plunged vertically and dragged along the shallow lake bottoms. The friction of these rolling coils of water slowed the big boats.

There is no one best shape. The short, broad asymmetrical white-water blade feels very stable in the water for most paddlers. The elliptical blade, shaped almost like an egg, is the traditional shape for white-water paddling and is an easy shape with which to learn. The universal square-end blade puts a lot of surface area at the end of the blade, where the paddler can put the most leverage and force during a stroke.

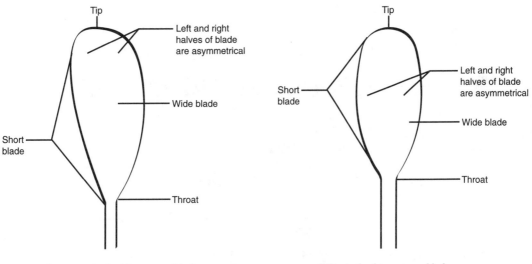

Asymmetrical white-water blade.   *Elliptical white-water blade.*

Universal square-end blade.

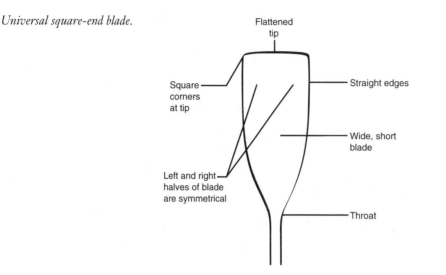

Flattened
tip

Square
corners
at tip

Straight edges

Wide, short
blade

Left and right
halves of blade
are symmetrical

Throat

Making the Shaft Work for You

Paddle shafts come in two flavors: round and oval. Oval shafts have two big pluses working in their favor: First, your fingers tend to wrap more comfortably around an oval shaft. Second, you can use the shape of the shaft to tell you the direction of the paddle blades. Nonetheless, some paddlers prefer a round shaft. Try 'em both, and go with the shape that works best for you.

Unfortunately, paddle makers around the world all have their own ideas as to the proper diameter for a paddle shaft—whether oval or round. Try paddles from a number of manufacturers until you find one that fits well in your hand. Too large a shaft will tire your hands. Too small a shaft will cramp your hands and forearms.

> ### In the Wake
>
> Some paddlers who suffer from neck and between-the-shoulder-blades pain find relief when they switch to a different paddle with a different shaft diameter. Is there a connection between shaft diameter and neck pain? Maybe. It could also be caused by the relative weight of the shaft compared to the blades, by a slightly longer or shorter paddle, or even by the heat-conducting characteristics of the shaft material. It's something to think about.

Some shafts, primarily white-water or competitive racing paddles, are a single piece from throat to throat. These are strong, lightweight, and with a consistent flex from one end to the other. That's good.

Some shafts, primarily touring paddles, come apart in the middle and are called *take-apart paddles.* These shafts are strong, but you have a potential wear and flex spot where the two halves slide together. The joint will also have a slightly different flex and will add a small amount of weight to the paddle. In most cases, the shaft halves will be held in alignment with spring-loaded buttons through precisely positioned holes. Other paddles may have set screws or twist-lock fastening mechanisms.

Some paddles even break apart into four pieces, making them easy to pack into a suitcase for easy transportation or stowage.

Paddlin' Talk

A **take-apart paddle** is a paddle that can be disconnected into two or more shorter sections. Merely moving a paddle from your garage to the put-in can be a major hassle, and stowing it as a spare can be a challenge. A take-apart paddle can really simplify your transportation and stowage chores.

Take-apart paddles have a number of advantages. Storage is one. Most touring kayaks don't have room on the rear deck for a spare 7-foot-long paddle. But there's plenty of room for a pair of 3½-foot paddle halves that can be joined quickly together.

A take-apart shaft also offers the paddler the choice of paddling a feathered or an unfeathered paddle (see the next section for an explanation of these paddle features). Just push down on the locking buttons and rotate the two shaft halves to re-align the blades. Most kayak paddle shafts are straight. Some are now fabricated with bends in the paddle shaft. This is an ergonomic development, attempting to keep the paddle blade in the most effective position and angle in the water while reducing the flex or angle in the paddler's own joints. It is a great idea. However, it is probably easier to learn the paddle strokes with a traditional straight-shaft paddle. Wait until you know the strokes and have a season or so of paddling in your wake before you start exploring the advantages of the bent-shaft paddles.

You won't have to commit to one style of shaft or the other. A few paddle makers are offering take-apart paddles with interchangeable straight or bent sections. You'll pay a hefty premium for this flexibility, perhaps more than you would for two different paddles, but these solutions can be found in the market.

Most recreational paddlers will be best served by a straight, oval shaft—one piece for river paddling and a two-piece take-apart for touring. River paddlers like the strength and simplicity of the one-piece paddle, while touring kayakers like the ability to take their longer paddles apart for easier stowage.

In an **unfeathered** kayak paddle, both blades are parallel, or in the same plane.

In a **feathered** kayak paddle, the blades are set at an angle to each other.

Feathered or Not

Take a look at any kayak paddle. If the two blades are exactly parallel, if you can lay the paddle down on the ground and both blades rest flat on the surface, then the paddle is *unfeathered*.

If the blades are not set in the same plane, the paddle is feathered. The blades may be at 90 degrees to each other or may be at less of an angle, sometimes as little as 45 degrees.

Feathered paddle.

Unfeathered paddle.

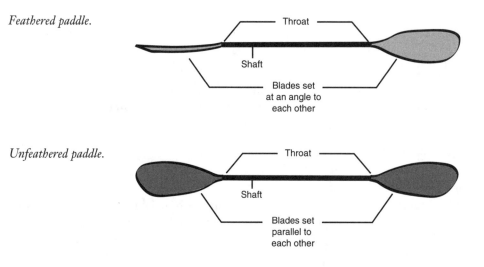

It used to be the case that all paddles were unfeathered. But in the early decades of the twentieth century, Olympic flatwater kayak coaches took on the project of stream-lining kayak paddles. The blade in the water worked fine, but pushing a broad blade through the air appeared to be a waste of effort and time. Why not, they reasoned, tilt the blades at right angles to each other and have the paddler rotate the paddle 90 degrees with each stroke. This would let the upper blade knife through the air edge first and reduce drag a bit.

In the Wake

Little improvements make a huge difference in kayak sprint racing. In the Seoul Olympics, American super-paddler Greg Barton won his second gold medal over the reigning world champion by just five one-thousandths of a second.

The offset paddle blades appeared in the Olympics, teams using them won the gold, and feathered paddles took the paddling world by storm.

So should you consider investing in a feathered paddle? If you're paddling into a head wind, or in a dead calm, you might gain a little with a feathered paddle. If you're paddling in a tailwind, you'll lose the minuscule boost the wind could give to an upper unfeathered blade. If you're paddling with a beam wind, a feathered paddle will present more surface area to the wind and you run a very slight risk of having your paddle lifted and twisted from your hand. Practically speaking, if the wind is strong enough to affect your paddle as it twirls through the air, then you would be far better off sitting on the beach with a mug of tea and a good book.

The majority of one-piece paddles made today are feathered and are designed so that the paddler's right hand controls the twisting and rotation of the paddle shaft. Because of that, most paddlers learn to control a feathered, right-hand-control paddle. Nevertheless, feathered paddles do come in two flavors: right-hand-control paddles and left-hand-control paddles. To determine what "hand" a paddle is, stand your paddle vertically in front of you with the *power face* of the blade on the ground facing your feet. Look up at the top blade. If it is facing to your right, you have a right-hand-control paddle. If to the left, you have a left-hand-control paddle. If it faces you, the paddle is unfeathered and you don't have to concern yourself with what hand controls it.

Paddlin' Talk

The **power face** is the face or surface of a kayak paddle blade that presses against the water during a stroke.

Rocks and Shoals

A take-apart paddle is a great choice for a spare on any trip. Most take-aparts can be adjusted for right-hand-control, left-hand-control, or unfeathered.

If you have a right-hand-control feathered paddle, gently grip the paddle with your right hand. Let the fingers of your other hand form a ring around the paddle shaft near the left blade. Your right wrist will rotate with each stroke to place each blade vertically in the water. A left-hand-control paddle works the same way, but with the opposite hand. Your left hand rotates the paddle shaft within the circle of your right fingers and palm.

Most white-water kayak paddles are made with a one-piece shaft, with the blades fixed in position. With a one-piece paddle, you can't alter or adjust the angle of the blades. What you buy is what you paddle, control-wise.

Most touring kayak paddles (but not all) are made with a take-apart shaft. The pieces join snugly with a sleeve, and with a spring-loaded button, a setscrew, or some other locking fastener holding the two parts. This gives you the option of paddling unfeathered, choosing your control hand if paddling feathered, and, in some cases, setting the angle of the paddle blade offset. Sometimes the offsets will be predetermined, and you'll be limited to a choice of feathered or unfeathered.

What's the Right Length?

Lincoln once said of the proper length of a dog's legs that they should reach the ground. Similarly, your paddle should reach the water.

You won't go too far wrong in white-water paddling if you pick up a paddle stretching 200 centimeters from tip to tip. That's the basic paddle size, and it works for 95 percent of the paddlers 95 percent of the time. If you're really tall with long arms or if most of your paddling will be on long stretches of flat water, you might be more comfortable with a slightly longer paddle, 202 cm or 203 cm. If you're on the short side, with shorter arms, or you're deep into the spins and moves of rodeo paddling, you might pare that down to 196 cm to 198 cm.

> **Rocks and Shoals**
>
> Watch yourself as you paddle. If you bob from side to side with each paddle stroke, you're probably leaning over to insert the blade in the water, and the paddle is too short for your paddling style and your boat.

> **In the Wake**
>
> Pay attention to what your mother used to say and sit up straight. If you slouch back as if you're in a chaise lounge, you'll lower your hands and you'll have a more challenging time reaching the water with a paddle that should fit you.

The touring kayak you paddle defines the length of the paddle you'll use. If you paddle a typical 23- to 24-inch-wide single touring kayak (and you're between 5 foot 4 inches and 6 foot 3 inches, give or take), then your starting paddle should be about 220 centimeters from tip to tip. If you are in a 17-inches to 22-inch-wide kayak, or you're 5 foot 3 inches or less, you may be more comfortable with a 210 cm to 220 cm paddle.

If you like to paddle in a hardshell double kayak, with a 29- to 32-inch beam, you'll want a slightly longer paddle somewhere around 230 cm. If you paddle a big frame-and-fabric kayak, with up to a 36-inch beam, then you should choose a 240-cm-or-longer paddle.

Some touring kayak paddlers hold their paddles fairly low, between their navel and solar plexus, and use a slower paddling cadence. If this describes you, consider a paddle 2 cm to 3 cm longer. If you prefer to paddle with a higher cadence and like your paddle approaching shoulder height, you'll be more comfortable with a slightly shorter paddle.

A Quick Guide to Fitting You and Your Paddle

So you're faced with a barrel full of unmarked paddles and friends on the beach frantic to get going for the day. Pick out a likely looking stick and grasp it 4 or 5 inches above the throats. Now hold it over your head, with your upper arms horizontal. Your hands should line up with your elbows. You can be off a finger's width or so either way, but that will give you a usable paddle length for your arms and a solo kayak. You'd be wise to try that paddle in the boat you'll be paddling. You don't want to have to lean sideways just to get the throat near the water's surface. And don't grab a paddle way longer than you need, because the extra weight will surely hammer you into the ground as the day progresses.

What's a Paddle Made Of?

When peoples of the high northern latitudes first took to the kayak, they paddled with a stick that had flattened areas out near the ends. From today's perspective, those first proto-paddles appear to be pretty primitive. They weren't. The earliest builders were just as concerned with shape, weight, balance, and durability as today's paddle manufacturers. Those early paddle makers developed an awesome cutting-edge design based on the materials available to them.

Paddle makers today have a menu of materials available to them. With these raw ingredients, they can cook up an amazing variety of shapes that are light in the hand and strong enough to face every intended use as well as quite a few unintended ones. You can pick up a featherlight sculpted work of paddling art that feels almost alive in your hands as you drive your kayak forward. Or you can go for a massive stick that could dig clams or shovel gravel, without nicking a blade. The choice is yours, once you work out where on the paddling spectrum you wish to sit.

Aluminum and plastic can team up for a tolerably good paddle. "Can" is the operative word, because you can also find poorly designed floppy blades stuck on a heavy shaft—a combination better suited for holding up a clothes line. Look for a paddle in the 2- to 2¼-pound range with an oval shaft and stiff but light

> **The Old Paddler Says**
>
> Paddle design is more important than paddle material. That said, each material it is better suited for certain kinds of environments. Select the design criteria you want, and then find the paddle meeting your needs and budget. Choosing a material and then looking for a paddle made of that, with the design criteria, can make for a long and usually fruitless search.

molded plastic blades. Bare aluminum is cold to the touch (and to your joints and tendons). You'll appreciate a coated shaft. Test the paddle's ability to float by chucking it into shallow water. It should float: If it doesn't during the test, it certainly won't when you accidentally drop it off the deck of your kayak. An aluminum/plastic kayak paddle you'd want to keep will cost under $125, and usable ones can be two thirds of that.

Fiberglass is the workhorse of kayak paddles. It forms a strong, comfortable shaft that doesn't suck the heat out of your hands. It can easily form complex shapes. It is reasonably lightweight, compared to its strength. It can be made quite light, or can be laid up with the strength and heft to bash through boulders as well as cobble beaches. Resin and fiberglass cloth, the main components, are inexpensive, and the long history of the lay-ups mean that manufacturing costs can be held to a reasonable level. The overall result is an affordable paddle with the light weight, strength, and flexibility options best suited to your paddling environment. On the downside, fiberglass is not the lightest, strongest kid on the block. If you want lighter, however, or stronger, you'll have to plunk down a good bit more cash at the register. A good fiberglass paddle will set you back $150 to $200.

Basic fiberglass proved that composite lay-ups work well for paddles. Light is better. Strong is better. The combination of light and strong is achieved with fancier resins and reinforcing materials such as Kevlar, graphite, and carbon fibers. Paddles made of such composites are so light that you can barely feel them in your hands. You will feel the cost of that lightness and strength in your wallet, however, which will also be lighter. If you're working your way through shallow, rocky waters or down a turbulent creek, you'll wince every time that $300-plus paddle whacks a rock or log. If you're racing at the level where hundredths of a second are meaningful, or cruising over vast distances, the weight and strength of the more esoteric lay-ups might be well worth the cost; otherwise, you might consider a compromise: a paddle that combines featherlight and steel-strong composite blades with a slightly heavier but less expensive fiberglass shaft. This reduces the weight out on the ends of the paddle, where you'll most feel it after a day on the way, with a slight paring of cost on the center section. Expect to pay $300 to $400 for a top-of-the-line composite paddle.

The Old Paddler Says

A paddle weighing between 35 and 40 ounces is a good compromise. The weight should be in the shaft, with the blades as light as possible, taking into consideration the use. River paddle blades need to be stout, and that means more weight. Touring blades are less likely to bang off rocks or the bottom, and can survive with thinner edges and a less-reinforced tip.

Wood is alive, and paddling with a good wooden paddle is like sharing the water with a great paddling companion. It is light and warm, and it flexes just the right amount under the power of your stroke. With all those pluses on one side of the equation, you'll have to add in a large price tag, more maintenance, and less durability on the other. Laminated wood can be bent into the most demanding and graceful shapes for the ultimate grab on the water. Shafts may be hollowed to pare away weight without reducing strength. A thin coat of resin can protect the wood without adding weight. Besides, wood is just flat-out pretty. A good wooden kayak paddle may run $200 or so, while a great paddle can top $600.

Some paddlers, especially those with the very narrow Greenland-style kayaks or with frame-and-fabric replicas of classic Native designs, have carved narrow-bladed copies of ancient paddles. These paddles were devised in a time predating laminations, and it was difficult or impossible for builders to find flaw-free wood wide enough for today's paddles. Are these paddles fun to use? Sure. Are they technically efficient? You'll work harder to cover the same distance at the same speed, but your own satisfaction of exploring kayaking's roots may make that added energy cost worth it.

The Least You Need to Know

- The kind of paddling you like to do determines the best paddle blade shape for you—short and wide for rivers, long and narrow for touring on lakes or oceans.

- The shape of the oval paddle shafts tells you the position of your paddle blades.

- Paddling style as well as the water you paddle determine your proper paddle length, but for most paddlers river kayak paddles should be about 200 cm long and touring paddles about 220 cm long.

- The most expensive paddle isn't necessarily the best. Discover what kinds of water you wish to paddle and look at the materials best suited for those conditions to find the paddle you really want.

Part 3

Gearing Up

You've just found the perfect canoe or kayak, in your favorite color, and you've added in the best paddles you could find. Hold on! It takes a lot of livin'—like the old saying goes—to make a house a home. And it takes a fair number of carefully chosen accessories to turn your new hull into the boat you really want to paddle.

In this part, we'll open the door to the accessories you really should include in your canoe or kayak, whether you're paddling rivers, ponds, or the saltwater. We'll also enter the world of high fashion for the clothes you'll find most comfortable when paddling in the summer heat or when the temperatures fall. There's no reason to store your canoe or kayak in the off-season, because as long as the water is running, you can experience great and comfortable paddling.

We'll also introduce you to the absolutely most important part of paddling—your life jacket. From proper sizing to proper care, your PFD is the one thing you must have.

Chapter 8

Gearing Up Your Boat

In This Chapter

- ◆ The basic gear for your canoe
- ◆ Stocking your kayak for river play
- ◆ Tools for a touring kayak
- ◆ Getting your boat to the water

It's happened! There, on the showroom floor, is the most beautiful canoe or kayak ever designed and built. You did it right. You studied all the brochures and boat reviews, went to the demonstration days and on-water boat shows, you paddled your way through a class from a school using boats similar to your dream, and you even rented this exact model for a long weekend trip just to be sure. And now you slapped your money down for this beauty, along with a perfectly fitting personal flotation device and a spiffy high-tech paddle.

So you're ready to launch, right? Nope. Between now and your first launch, you'll have to consider a passel of add-ons as you turn that perfect hull into a comfortable and efficient home on the water. You could well end up doubling the base price of your boat when all the extras are stowed aboard.

Before you start loading up the counter in front of the cash register, take some time to distinguish between what you really need and what you think you want.

Matching the Gear to Your Boat

As you're well aware by now, the kind of water you prefer to paddle determines the kind of boat you're buying. In turn, the kind of boat you buy determines which accessories you'll stow in, around, and on your boat. You won't need everything for your first time out on the water. And you might not have to pack everything along every time you launch. As you keep paddling you'll add to the basic list, and you'll possibly choose to leave some of the items hanging up in the garage.

> **In the Wake**
>
> When you're budgeting for your dream canoe or kayak, remember that the basic price of the hull is only a part of your total needs. Paddles, life jackets, carrying racks, and other items might cost anywhere from as half as much to as much as you pay for the boat.

The items described in the following sections have been tested by generations of paddlers and found to be useful in most paddling situations. Buy slowly, anticipate your needs, and draw upon the experience of your paddling companions to assemble the gear that best meshes with where and when you paddle.

Tricking Out Your Canoe

The basic canoe hull on the showroom floor is more than just a blank canvas, but less than a completed painting.

First of all, you want to keep it afloat and keep as much water as possible out of it. That requires flotation bags. To keep the flotation bags from simply floating away, you must attach a number of tie-downs inside the hull. Some paddlers like D-rings, and some like small inverted U-shaped brackets that will hold a cord. The shop where you buy your canoe will show you which type(s) work best with your particular hull. Some canoe float bags are long tubes laced in place along the bilges, some are blunt triangles placed in the bow and stern, and some are large square bags secured in the middle of the canoe. They all work.

Virtually all nonracing canoes should have painters—10-foot-long-or-so lines attached to the bow and stern. They help secure your canoe to a car rack, can be used to tie your canoe to a dock or to a shore-side object when beached, and can be used for a short tow line. Consider running a taut shock cord through a pair of holes in both the bow and stern deck plates and tucking your coiled painters under these shock cords.

Passionate wilderness trippers sometimes have an eyebolt carefully inserted through the forward stem, which they use for towing a canoe upstream or carefully lowering it downstream around a rapid.

If you'll be doing a lot of river paddling, you'll end up with your knees on the bottom of your canoe. That lowers your center of gravity (improving your balance) and gives you a more powerful stroke. It also hurts your knees. Either glue knee pads to the hull in the appropriate places, or buy less-comfortable but still-effective gardener or tile-setter knee pads, which you strap on your legs. In addition to the cushioning they provide, they all keep you from sliding around on a wet hull.

To improve your river paddling, install thigh braces or straps in your canoe. The simplest involve gluing a large D-ring on the center of the floor of the canoe, just in front of your seat or thwart, and gluing D-rings on the inner sides of the hull, immediately in front of where the seats fasten to the hull. Run a wide piece of webbing back and forth through the rings (looping around each outside ring and passing through the center ring), and fasten the ends together with a large buckle. Slide your knees under the straps. Brace your thighs against the straps when putting the muscle to your paddle and they will help keep you in the most efficient paddling position.

If you really get into white-water paddling, you can upgrade to adjustable metal straps for more efficiency.

If you're a dedicated white-water freak, you can install a rigid foam "saddle" in the middle of your canoe along the center line. You sit astride this saddle, with your thighs hooked under straps. You become part of the boat, and it responds instantly as you shift your weight. On the other hand, it really limits the use of your canoe for other activities. You normally see these in very highly rockered playboats and extreme white-water canoes.

Rocks and Shoals

Never tow a canoe, particularly a loaded canoe, behind a powered boat. Towing it at more than the efficient hull speed will suck the aft end down while forcing the bow to plane atop the water. As a result, the canoe will crack or bend between the middle and the rear seat.

The Old Paddler Says

You need three sets of knee pads for most recreational or tripper style boats with bench seats. One pair goes in front of both the front and rear seats. Place the third set behind the bow seat. That way, if you're paddling solo, you can sit in the bow seat but facing the stern. This keeps the canoe floating relatively level.

Some paddlers mount fasteners all around the outside rail of the gunwales, and attach a full-length *splash cover* to their canoe. These have openings for the two paddlers, and ward off an amazing amount of spray, splash, and rain.

You'll also want to protect the bottom of your canoe. Glue a strip of abrasion-resistant material as a *bang plate* along the bow and stern and along the full length of the keel to protect the canoe's hull, when launching or landing, from the bumps and nicks of running through shallows and the thump of occasionally touching a rock.

 Paddlin' Talk _____

A **splash cover** is a fabric cover over an open canoe or kayak with openings for the paddler or paddlers, designed to shed water. It is similar to a spray deck or spray skirt over the cockpit of a decked canoe or kayak.

A **bang plate** is a surface applied to the bow and stern of a canoe or kayak and along the keel line(s), to protect the outer skin from abrasion and wear. Also called a skid plate.

When two people carry a canoe, each person holds an end of the right-side-up canoe, normally just in front of the seats. If you must carry a canoe by yourself, however, you'll need a yoke at the center thwart. One style of yoke is a broad thwart, with a half-moon cut out of one side to wrap around the back of your neck while the canoe is balanced on your shoulders. An alternative is a pair of cushioned pads fastened to the center thwart (parallel to the keel) that rest on your shoulders. Two people can also carry a canoe that is inverted, normally each resting the edge of their respective seats—bow and stern—on their shoulders. This is a more comfortable way to carry a canoe for more than a few yards.

If you just toss things—energy bars, water bottles, binoculars, cameras—into a canoe when you launch, you might as well plan on them getting wet and sliding out of reach whenever you want them. Acquire a thwart bag, a small bag that you can lash to a thwart in front of you and keep everything in one accessible place. Place a small first-aid kit, a few repair items (lead off with good duct tape), and emergency supplies such as a Space Blanket, poncho, or huge yard-waste bag, and spare food in a second water-proof bag and lash it out of the way in your canoe.

Accessorizing Your River Kayak

A river kayak is a minimalist boat, stripped to the bare essentials, in the search for maneuverability and fun.

Foam Walls

The first accessories most river paddlers purchase are foam pillars or walls extending from the cockpit (or nearly so, in the bow) to the ends. Walls add a bit of flotation to the kayak, but, more important, they support the deck of a closed boat to keep it from squishing down around a paddler if the kayak becomes stuck against a rock or other obstruction by the pressure of the river current. It's very uncommon to have a kayak collapse, but the foam walls will help keep you from being stuck in the boat should such an accident happen. The walls should be firmly attached so that they don't shift.

Test the placement of your walls in a swimming pool. If you're bailing out of your kayak in a hurry during a *wet exit*, you want to make sure you have enough room in and around your cockpit to keep your legs and feet from hanging up on the walls.

Any space you don't occupy inside your kayak should be filled by inflated flotation bags. Because of the center wall, you'll need two narrow bags—instead of one bigger bag—for each end. Some two-person kayaks have room for more flotation bags between the two cockpits.

Handholds

All kayaks should have some sort of grab loops at the bow and stern. They provide a much-needed handhold in bouncy water for someone assisting you or for someone you're rescuing. Additional uses include serving as tie-down points when securing your kayak atop a car, or a place to grasp when two people are carrying a kayak. Grab loops may be constructed of webbing, rope, or molded plastic; no matter what they're made of, they must be capable of withstanding a lot of yanking and pulling. Some may be threaded through a hole bored through the bow (the hole encased in waterproof backing), or attached in two different places through

Paddlin' Talk

Getting out of a capsized or swamped boat is called a **wet exit**.

The Old Paddler Says

The more you fill your river kayak with inflatable air bags, the less the water you'll have to drain out when you miscalculate the outer boundaries of your knowledge. On the other hand, if you're not occasionally swimming, you're not probing the weaknesses in your paddling skills.

In the Wake

River kayaks are designed to be sleek and slippery. It's very difficult to hold on to the outside of a kayak in moving water—whether a boat is towing you to shore or you're pulling a boat as you swim to shore. That's why grab loops are so essential.

the deck to a stout backing plate. The loop should be large enough for a good hand-hold, but must be designed so that they can't twist tight and trap a hand by accident.

Many decked boaters install a large D-ring or a loop of cable ahead of and behind the cockpit, for use if they ever need to rescue someone. By and large, these tools are for advanced kayakers running big water or steep creeks.

Foot Braces

When you paddle forward, you don't pull your paddle blade through the water. You actually pull yourself up to a stationary paddle. To get the most out of this process, you need to brace your feet against something—and that something is called a foot brace.

For your first kayak, go for completely adjustable braces that can be fine-tuned to your precise fit. Some paddlers prefer a foam bulkhead that they can rest their feet against, but although these might be more comfortable, it's harder to adjust the fit. Furthermore, bulkhead foot rests aren't as convenient if two different-sized paddlers share the use of a kayak.

Hip and Thigh Pads

Any shifting or slipping around in your kayak seat is a waste of paddling energy. Install hip pads on the side of your seat to reduce side-to-side and twisting motions. You can add thin foam padding to the seat itself, to match the angle of the seat to your physique as well as to reduce slipperiness. Don't add enough foam to significantly raise your center of balance.

The Old Paddler Says

If you simply wedge a small waterproof stowage bag next to your float bags, tie a cord to one end and extend it back to the cockpit area. A small bag can and will migrate to the far end of your boat, and it is easier to retrieve it with an attached cord than to deflate your float bags and dive in after the wandering bag.

You'll also want to install thigh pads on the underside of the coaming at the front quarters of your cockpit. If your kayak doesn't have an adjustable seat back, install one.

All this padding enables you to lock your feet, legs, hips, and back firmly into the kayak, so that you wear your boat, rather than just sit in it. When you snugly wear your kayak, you can simply twitch your weight with a shrug to correct your balance or change your direction.

Waterproof Bag

Acquire a small waterproof bag to stow your lunch, first-aid kit, duct tape, and the odds and ends you positively need in your kayak. Lash it out of the way or tuck it atop a float bag.

Spray Deck

Far from least, you need a spray deck or spray skirt to keep water from pouring in through your cockpit. Most skirts are neoprene with an elastic cord or rubber edge that snaps around the cockpit coaming to hold them in place. Spray skirts made of coated nylon are more durable, less expensive, and more prone to letting water through.

A well-fitting spray skirt is tight in front of the paddler, so that water doesn't pool up. It should be snug around your waist, but not so tight as to be confining. If you really push down on the center, right ahead of the tunnel (the tube around your waist), the skirt should not pop off the coaming. It should be sticky enough so that when you hook the edge around the back of the cockpit coaming and pull it forward, it doesn't aggravatingly slip free. More important, it should not be so sticky or so tight as to be difficult to pop free when you want to release it. Every spray skirt should have a grab loop at the front, to help you release it. Tie a practice golf ball (one of those light plastic balls full of holes) to the loop to help locate it when you're first learning the Eskimo Roll.

Rocks and Shoals

Avoid really tight spray skirts. You want your skirt to come free when it is time to get out of your kayak!

Accessorizing Your Touring Kayak

Touring kayaks are the most customizable of all boats. Take any hundred kayaks a year old, all the same model produced by the same manufacturer out of the same mold with their hull numbers in order, and they'll all be just a bit different today.

Your kayak started as a vast, echoing chamber, pierced only by the keyhole-shape of the cockpit and the dangling seat. Everything else depends on you.

In the Wake

Hatches are a mixed blessing. They make stowing gear easier. They also offer new opportunities for a leak.

The Old Paddler Says

Tie a stout cord to the first bag you slide up under your deck. As you shove other bags in, this first bag will gradually get pushed to the very bow (or stern). When it comes time to unload, pull on the cord and the first bag will push all the other bags out into easy reach.

In the Wake

A bulkhead can be as comfortable as foot braces, if your distance from the seat back to the bulkhead fits you. It's okay to add a bit of closed cell foam to the face of a bulkhead if you want to adjust the distance a few inches.

Bulkheads and Hatches

Start by deciding if you want bulkheads with cargo areas accessed by hatches. They make it easier to load and unload your kayak, and they provide flotation if your cockpit is flooded. All hatches leak, though, so you still have to wrap everything in waterproof bags. If you choose to keep the inside of your kayak bare of bulkheads, you can dispense with those pesky but convenient hatches and reduce the price of your basic boat a bit. The downside is that if you opt to go without hatches, you'll have to stand on your head to cram dry bags up under the decks.

Rudders and Skegs

Do you want a rudder or a skeg? A skeg is a fixed direction rudder, that can be raised or lowered more deeply in the water and helps control your directional stability in cross winds. If you want a rudder, you'll need rudder pedals under your feet. If you want a skeg, you won't need rudder pedals (no secret, there) but you will need foot braces to rest your feet upon.

Spray Skirt

You'll need a basic spray skirt for your kayak. As with river kayaks, most skirts are neoprene with an elastic cord or rubber edge that snaps around the cockpit coaming to hold them in place. Some touring paddlers prefer a coated nylon spray skirt with a loose tunnel (where you sit) held up by suspenders. They are less confining and possibly less constricting. They do let in more spray and spume. A third choice, for balmy weather and calm water, is a half spray skirt, which just covers the front of the cockpit and has a hoop that keeps the skirt arched upward to shed water.

Grab Loops

Touring kayakers need the same bow and stern grab loops as their river paddling cousins. They're great for carrying a boat, for rescue work, or for tying a kayak when you land and don't want your boat to float away.

Some paddlers like to rig light grab lines from the bow to at least just aft of the cockpit along both sides of the deck, and some run them bow to stern. They're handy for a rescue, yours or someone else's. Others prefer to keep a clean—meaning uncluttered—deck. That's because any obstruction on the deck, from a thin shock cord to a paddle, will deflect the water—most likely right into your face.

Mount four pad eyes (small eyebolts) in a rectangle about 2 feet wide and a foot and a half deep on your deck right in front of your cockpit. Thread a stout elastic cord through the eyes, around the perimeter and also across the diagonals before tying the ends snugly together. You can tie your waterproof map case to the eyes or the cord, hook a removable compass to the cords, or use the elastic cord as a third hand to temporarily hold anything from a water bottle to your hat.

In Chapter 15 you'll learn how to use a temporary outrigger to stabilize your touring kayak, either to reboard from the water or to balance it for any purpose from fishing to skin-diving. That system is called a paddle float, and it can be mounted just behind your cockpit. When it is not in use all that shows is a few pad eyes and cleats (a small fitting that a rope may be fastened to).

If you have a take-apart spare paddle, then add some elastic shock cord across the stern deck to hold the blades, and some short lengths of shock cord behind your cockpit to hold down the spare paddle shafts.

A paddle park, a clip fastened to your deck that snaps around your paddle shaft and keeps the paddle from sliding away when you've put it down for a moment, is a handy attachment to your deck gear. It is very frustrating to drop a paddle and watch it disappear as the wind blows you and your kayak away. To be extra safe, also get a paddle leash. One end of a cord hooks to your paddle shaft, the other is secured to your wrist. It keeps you from being separated from your paddle.

A cleat centered on the deck immediately behind your cockpit works to tow another boat if so needed.

In the Wake

Every group should carry at least one 25-foot-or-longer tow line in case of emergencies. Two kayaks and two tow lines make easier work of assisting a paddler in need.

If you have a high fore deck—the area right in front of the cockpit—you well may have room for a long, thin "glove compartment" storage bag mounted on the inside above your legs. It's a good spot for a water bottle, binoculars, munchies, or sunblock. Anything you leave unattached and on the top of your deck will wash off.

Sea Anchor

Touring kayakers with a lot of miles under their keels like to park their boat in the water with a sea anchor or drogue. These can be streamed off the bow of your boat, to keep the bow into the wind. They are also a great fishing tool: Simply mount a cleat beside your kayak and stream the sea anchor off to the side. Your kayak will turn sideways to any wind and stop in the water. You'll stay right over your fishing ground.

Bagging Your Flotation Needs

Flotation devices, usually inflatable bags, will keep your boat afloat if you've had an upsetting experience. Not only will they provide buoyancy and stability, but they'll also limit the amount of water inside your boat that you'll have to remove. Less interior water means more stability. Cone-shaped bags filling the ends of your boat—canoe or kayak—are the minimum. Open canoes may add long tubes along the bilges or a large bag under the center thwart. Some cruising kayaks have watertight bulkheads fore and aft of the cockpit, to create air chambers in the ends. Still other cruising kayaks seat paddlers in a "sock" fastened around the cockpit coaming and sealing off the interior of the boat.

CAUTION

Rocks and Shoals

Insert inflatable air bags into your sit-on-top kayak if you're heading offshore. You could always lose a hatch cover, unplug a drain hole, or even open a seam, and the bag will help save you and your boat.

Some inflatable flotation bags can be opened and resealed, doubling as dry stowage bags. Bulkheads and hatches in cruising kayaks create sealed compartments that, like the dry stowage bags, provide an air chamber for flotation and a dry stowage area to protect your gear and equipment.

Whatever style you need—and employees at a good boat shop will advise you—make certain that there are plenty of lash points (places to tie ropes) to secure the bags.

Keeping the Dry Stuff Dry

A dry bag, not surprisingly, is a waterproof bag with some sort of sealable opening that keeps things dry. "Things" include clothes, camping gear, food, cameras—anything you want to take with you and that you must keep dry. Bag is a loose term. For those goodies that don't put up well with banging or crushing, you can choose from a variety of sizes of watertight boxes—the smallest boxes will be just big enough to hold a point-and-shoot 35mm camera; the biggest can hold a week's worth of food for a party of four.

Fortunately, paddlers have a neat way of doubling up their storage and flotation needs. Dual-purpose bags combine a large and sealable opening, enabling you to cram your dry-only goodies inside. Roll the opening shut, clamp it into place with a mechanical fastener (there are a number of different types, each the favorite of a different bag manufacturer), and then use the inflating tube to blow up the bag. Your goodies are safe from the wet, you've installed plenty of flotation, and the sheer size of the bag will displace a huge amount of water if you should capsize.

For delicate items—a camera, cell phone, or whatever—look for an air-padded small flotation bag. You place the delicate item in an interior bag, seal it, and then inflate a set of tubes pillowing the interior bag and shielding the contents from bumps and thumps.

> **Rocks and Shoals**
>
> Don't fill a combination flotation and dry storage bag completely with cast-iron cookware. At some point the weight of the iron will convert your flotation bag to an anchor.

Bailing Your Boat

Water will get inside your boat. That's a given. It will splash into an open canoe, and it will drip around a spray deck on a decked canoe or kayak. It will find the odd crack and seam. It will come in with your boots and damp clothes.

How should you send it back into the outside world?

If you're paddling an open canoe, a bailing scoop (a small pot or basin to scoop up water and toss it over the side) will remove a lot of water in a hurry. The odd drops can be sucked up with a thirsty sponge. If you take on a lot of water, you can beach your canoe and invert it to drain the water. Fast competition-cruiser canoes often have a small bailing hatch in the bottom of the boat. Just open the hatch when at speed, and the interior water will be sucked out. It's like opening a window in a moving car and having something sucked out.

A thirsty sponge is about the most effective way of taking a little water out of a river kayak. Pop your spray deck, and reach down into the bilge, leaning or tipping as necessary, to mop up the water. If there is a lot of water in your kayak, head for the beach. Tilt your kayak on edge to let as much water as possible pour

> **The Old Paddler Says**
>
> You can buy a bailing scoop, if you want. Or you can cut the bottom out of a gallon bleach jug and have a bailer that works with the best of 'em. Just don't forget or lose the screw-on cap.

out of the cockpit, and then invert the boat for the last few pints. You may have to rock your kayak, end to end, to get most of the water out.

You have a variety of choices for removing water from a touring kayak, starting with the large, thirsty sponge. A perfectly adequate solution is a simple push-pull pump, usually plastic, with a flotation collar to keep it afloat when you accidentally drop it over the side. Unfortunately, it also requires that you open your cockpit to reach the water inside. You also take both hands off your paddle, losing the ability to brace and aid your balance. A few minutes of vigorous pumping will clear a lot of water out of your hull.

The Old Paddler Says

In a tandem canoe or kayak, have one paddler pump and the other stabilize the boat. As one tires, switch roles.

A through-deck pump, usually just behind your cockpit with the handle within easy reach, will also shift a lot of water back outside. You don't have to pop your spray skirt to work a through-deck pump, but it does take one hand to raise and lower the pump handle, which means you lose the use of your paddle.

A foot-mounted pump, mounted next to your foot brace, moves plenty of water and leaves you with your spray skirt sealed around the coaming and your hands on the paddle. You can pump out no matter what the weather conditions.

Hard-core touring kayakers use electric bilge pumps. Battery life doesn't seem to be a concern, especially if you have a solar panel recharger.

Sit-on-top kayaks can take on water through anything from a loose hatch to an unplugged drain hole to a cracked hull seam. Because you can't see the bilge, it's harder to realize that you're taking on water. A simple tube push-pull pump and a sponge, reaching through a hatch, works as well as anything in keeping these hulls dry.

Rigging Your Personal Safety Gear

If you launch your canoe or kayak onto navigable waters (and on some others, as specified by state, provincial, or local laws) you're required to have a noise-making device aboard. Meet both the spirit and the letter of the law by hanging a very loud whistle on your personal flotation device—your life jacket. A good whistle, such as a Fox 40 or a Storm, will blast through the roar of a river, the crash of surf, or the howl of wind. Those same conditions will absorb the fragile sound of your voice and will soon render your throat hoarse and raw.

If you're going to be on the water after sunset or before sunrise (times set by law and not by how dark you think it is), then you are required to have at a minimum an electric torch (flashlight) or lighted lantern showing a white light, which you must be able to display in sufficient time to prevent a collision. If you're paddling between sunset and sunrise on many coastal and inland waters, you're required to carry approved flares (at least three) or an electric distress light that automatically flashes the international distress signal (..._ _ _ ...). Under Inland Navigation Rules of the United States, you may carry a high-intensity white light capable of flashing at regular intervals from 50 to 70 times a minute to be used as a distress signal.

In case you need to grab someone's attention during the day, stick a small signaling mirror in your pocket. A good combo mirror is silver on one side and red on the other. Although you're not required to carry them, orange smoke signals or an orange distress flag are also ideal for daytime use. The flag, if you choose to carry one, must be at least 3 × 3 feet, with a black square and ball on an orange background. Wave the flag from a paddle to signal that you're in trouble.

> **In the Wake**
>
> A whistle is equally valuable in locating a paddling partner who has temporarily misplaced the way back to camp. The blast of the whistle will carry an amazing distance, and you can hone in on each other by signaling back-and-forth.

 Rocks and Shoals _____

> Paddle at dusk and you face a major hazard: You are in a low and dark boat, which is difficult to see. Don't be shy about turning your powerful flashlight on any approaching powerboat, to alert the operator to your presence.

Yet another add-on that you'll need in a number of states and other jurisdictions is a registration number. Know the law in the area you live.

Getting to the Water

It is a common enough problem: You and your boat are here, and the put-in and the water you want to paddle are over there. How are you going to get there?

A multisport roof-rack system is the ultimate practical system, but it's not difficult to lay out hundreds of dollars for a top-of-the-line roof rack and its various components. They're stout, secure, and you can even lock them to your car and lock your boats to the rack. You can add attachments for skis, bicycles, or an overhead luggage rack. For paddlesports, you can equip the crossbars with gunwale blocks to carry an upside-down canoe, with cradles to carry a right-side-up touring kayak, or with center posts to stack a small fleet of white-water kayaks on edge.

If you're willing to put up with a little inconvenience and more time, you can get by with a simpler system. You make do with a pair of crossbars and a few blocks of closed cell foam whittled into shape or some pipe insulation. That, and some ropes or straps, are all you need to secure your boat to your rack and car. You can mount crossbars on their own feet (on your rain gutters or flat on your roof) or on the rooftop rails found on many cars.

Check out the strength and durability of car-top rails. Many are decorative at best, and can't stand up to the wind forces generated atop a car speeding down the interstate.

For a canoe, put a little padding—pipe insulation works well—on a crossbar and hoist your upside-down canoe atop the bars. For a touring kayak, hollow a small groove across the bottom of two foam blocks and a vee shape corresponding to the kayak's cross section in the top. Balance the foam blocks on the crossbars, and stack your kayak in the vee cuts. Most river kayaks can ride right side up on the crossbars.

You need at least three lines—and preferably four—on every boat you have atop your car. One line should go over the boat at each crossbar, snugged tight, and one should go from the bow to the front bumper or the frame underneath. A fourth line from the stern to the rear bumper helps keep the boat or racks from sliding forward during an abrupt stop.

Rocks and Shoals

Every once in a while, disassemble your rack, checking for loose bolts or worn components. Lightly oil the metal-to-metal parts, including bolts, and reassemble everything. You've just checked that all the critical parts are aligned and fastened tight—good for you.

The Old Paddler Says

Hauling your canoe or kayak atop your car can be one of the most dangerous (to the boat) acts you can do. More paddlers, than care to admit it, have forgotten to tie a bow or stern painter down and have driven over the flapping line. They discovered their error only when they heard the loud "crack" when they folded the end of their boat over!

If you only rarely have to move a canoe or kayak, look to the small foam blocks that fit over the gunwales of a canoe or the shaped foam blocks that cradle the bottom of your kayak, all of which rest right against the top of your car. Long tie-down straps run over the top of your boat and through your windows or doors. Elegant? Nope. But they work.

A variety of frame and crossbar members are available for pickup trucks—some that fold into the bed and some that remain fixed in place. Short lengths of artificial raingutter can be bolted to the sides of a pickup canopy, allowing a conventional multisports rack to be mounted on the canopy.

A handy gadget is a small boat trailer or cart. They're just a pair of wheels mounted on a frame, enabling you to roll your boat from your vehicle to the water. They are super if you want to roll your boat onto a ferryboat. A few will even hitch on to a bicycle for short trips to the water. Need to cross a wide, sandy beach? A wide-tired cart will float over loose sand.

For short carries, a pair of ropes or wide webbing makes a handy sling for four people. Thread one end of the webbing through a short length of plastic pipe, and then either sew or slice this end into a loop just large enough for a comfortable handhold. Measure out just enough webbing to loop under your boat and make a second pipe-and-loop handhold. The pipe handhold on either side should be just above the deck, to avoid barked knuckles. Rig the slings about a quarter of the way in from the bow and stern, enabling four people to share the weight of each boat.

The Least You Need to Know

- Flotation bags add buoyancy and stability to your canoe or kayak.

- Make your seat more comfortable with foam padding and straps.

- Make sure you have tools to remove water from your boat.

- A number of devices are available for moving your canoe or kayak to the water.

Chapter 9

Paddling's High Fashion

In This Chapter

- ◆ Clothing as a technical paddling tool
- ◆ Basic paddling garb from your closet
- ◆ Carrying a spare outfit
- ◆ Matching your outfit to the season

Paddling in the buff is not an option. Aesthetics aside, you really should be wearing your personal flotation device (also known as your life jacket) any time you're out on the water.

Think of your paddling clothing not as a fashion statement but as a tool. It should protect you from extremes of temperature. It should shield you from the sun's rays. It should act as a barrier between your body and the wind and water. It should help prevent chafing, blistering, and abrasions. That's a tall order in itself. Now factor in that it should do all those things while letting you stretch and twist to your limits without impeding you. It should be lightweight, extremely durable, and affordable. Oh, yeah, it should also have a pocket or two.

Fortunately, there are a number of clothing manufacturers who are also paddling enthusiasts and are building the garments the rest of the paddling world needs.

Choosing What to Wear

"What should I wear?"

To answer that question, you'll need to know where you are going. You'll dress differently if you're on your way to play in a white-water rapid than you would for a day's saltwater fishing or an expedition down a wilderness river. The scale of protection you'll require shifts from one part of the paddling spectrum to another, and although the goals of protection from the elements remain the same, the tools you need to shape that protection will vary.

Consider your first-ever paddling trip. You'll most likely go on a mid- to late-summer's day, because the warmth of the day and the water make a day afloat irresistibly attractive. We'll make it in a canoe, because you want to paddle with a friend. And for the heck of it, we'll make it on a gentle, meandering river. It could just as well have been a protected lake or a sheltered bay.

I'll describe specific kinds of clothing in a moment, but first I want to encourage you to layer your clothing. The weather doesn't always do what the forecast says it will, and that's when layering comes in handy. The concept is simple. Wear two light layers of clothing rather than one medium-heavy item, or three light layers rather than one heavy layer. Multiple light layers enable you to fine-tune your clothing comfort. You can add or subtract thermal protection in smaller increments, more akin to what you need at any specific moment.

The Old Paddler Says

It's nice to cram a thing or two in your pockets—a pocket knife, an energy bar, a match tin, or whatever. Keep in mind, though, that with each treasure you slip into a pocket, you're reducing the safety margin built into your life jacket. Put enough lead weights into your pocket and you'll sink!

In the Wake

Outdoor apparel manufacturers are now stitching their shirts, pants, and hats from good sunblock materials.

Start with a pair of long, synthetic material pants. You might hanker after jeans, but jeans are made of cotton and will sop up any stray water and stay wet for the rest of the trip. Pick a synthetic fabric that dries in a flash. Long pant legs shield you from the blistering bite of the sun. (Sitting in a canoe for several hours will give the sun easy access to tender skin.)

A long-sleeved shirt, also of a lightweight synthetic fabric, shades your vulnerable arms. A high collar— that you can button to the neck—keeps the sun away from your neck and tender throat.

Top everything off with a broad-brimmed hat. That keeps the back of your neck, your ears, and your scalp covered. It also shields your eyes from some of the sun's glare. Look for a felt crusher—a floppy-brimmed soft hat that will shade your face, ears, and neck—in your neighborhood outdoor shop. A baseball "gimme" cap shades your eyes, but leaves your ears and neck exposed. Remember those old movies about the French Foreign Legion marching across the sands of North Africa, and the silly caps they wore? They looked like a baseball cap with a skirt draped off the back over their ears and neck. You can find them in most angling shops, and they do offer a lot of protection.

Wear a pair of lace-up canvas tennis shoes. Lace-up, because you don't want to kick them off if you suddenly become a swimmer. Tennis shoes, because you don't care if you get the cloth tops wet, from splashes or from stepping in the water. If they get wet, they'll stay wet. You'll just have to live with it. Socks are optional.

> **Rocks and Shoals**
>
> Unfortunately, some folks who come to the beach were never taught to clean up after themselves. The most invitingly sandy beach is likely to be booby-trapped with glass from broken bottles and the sharp-edged remnants of pop-top cans. Shoes are a must.

If you have delicate hands, find an inexpensive pair of synthetic fingerless cycling gloves. They'll protect your hands from blistering or chafing if you're not used to the paddle, will comfort tender joints in your hands, and will keep some—but not all—of the sun off the back of your hands.

Add in a similar pair of pants, shirt, and underwear. Roll them up as tight as possible. If you have a big, sealable freezer bag that will hold your extra clothes, super. Second best is a heavy flexible plastic bag, normally called a fish or salmon bag and used by anglers. Put your clothes in the bottom, squeeze as much air out as possible, roll the top down for a tight seal held in place by a pair of big rubber bands, and then put this in a second bag. Third choice is an extra-sturdy garbage bag, with your clothes tightly wrapped in one bag and then placed in a second for added waterproofing. Admittedly, a good waterproof dry bag from a paddling shop offers better water-tightness and convenience, but for your first trip you'll have to make do.

Finally, keep a dry pair of shoes and socks in your car at the take-out for your drive home.

Many paddlers will keep a small, extra-absorbent pack towel in their personal *dry bag*. If you do get wet, from a learning experience or from a water fight, it's nice to dry off before changing into your reserve clothes.

> **Paddlin' Talk**
>
> A **dry bag** is a waterproof bag used to hold gear that should be kept dry in a canoe or kayak.

Finally, pack a fairly waterproof jacket that can double as a windbreaker. If you're damp, from splashes or perspiration, it takes a very little wind to chill you. When selecting a jacket to bring along, try to avoid one with a hood. If the hood is up and you quickly look to the side, all you're liable to see is the inside of the hood. If the hood is down, it can work just like a cistern collecting water—until you pull it up over your head. If you're naturally cautious or you like to plan ahead, a matching pair of lightweight rain pants will one day pay off.

The Old Paddler Says

Keep a complete change of clothes in the car for the drive home. You'll be so glad you did. If you don't need them after one trip, save them for the next.

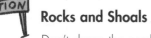

Rocks and Shoals

Don't drape the cord from a knife or whistle around your neck. In the unlikely event of an accident, you don't want to be swimming and have the lanyard snag on an obstruction.

That takes care of your clothing. A good pair of polarized sunglasses will protect your eyes from harmful rays, give you a better look at the water ahead and potential obstacles, and will help avoid headaches and painfully stiff necks caused by squinting. Good sunglasses aren't cheap, so secure them with a little cord that goes from earpiece to earpiece behind your head.

You'll find dozens of uses for a multiblade pocket knife, and, again, keep it on a cord to avoid losing it overboard. Stick a really loud whistle in your pocket, to grab someone's attention if it becomes necessary.

That's a basic, low-tech outfit for fair-weather canoeing.

Kayaking Chic

Unlike an open canoe, where you're exposed to the world, a decked kayak is its own little world. The kayak hull, deck, and the spray deck or skirt spanning the cockpit-to-paddler gap is a waterproof, weatherproof wall between the paddler and the environment. The wind may be blowing, it may be hailing, the sun may be beating fiercely down—but the kayak paddler from his or her toes to his or her solar plexus is sheltered by his or her boat.

Only the paddler's chest, arms, and head protrude from his or her floating world. However, the kayaker's paddle stroke puts him or her into more contact with the water. As the paddler inserts one blade into the water, the other blade, still dripping, is elevated well above his or her hands. Water trickles down the blade, drips past the throat, squeezes past the drip ring, and cascades down to the shaft to the paddler's hands. The next stroke brings water from the other side. Droplets fly into the air and shower the paddler. It gets damp out there.

The kayaker's first line of defense against all this water is a paddling jacket, with cuffs that snug down around his or her wrists and a collar around his or her neck that dams trickles of water. A durable paddling jacket will cost between $100 and $300. On a hot

day, or under a paddling jacket on cooler days, dedicated paddlers swear by paddling tops made of a four-way stretch material bonded to a thin layer of fleece and a rubber-ized, waterproof, and slightly breathable coating. The top seals out errant drops with a mock turtleneck and punch-through cuffs. Because a technical paddling top will set you back between $50 and $150, you might want to go without one until you're sure you'll be spending a lot of time paddling.

Sit-on-top kayaks are a lot of fun, but by their very nature, they are wet rides. You'll be sitting in a wet seat, getting splashed, and at times even see water bubbling up through the drain holes just below you. That's just part of paddling one of these versatile and fun boats, and when you realize that and dress for it, you'll enjoy them even more.

Rocks and Shoals _____

Dress for the tempera-ture of the water you might be in, rather than the temperature of the air.

Rocks and Shoals _____

Tape an extra-large plastic yard-waste bag inside your life jacket. You can pop neck and arm holes in it and use it for a poncho. It also works as a sleeping bag or a tent if you're caught out overnight, and can be used to clean up the mess others left at the take-out.

Coping With the Cold

A dipping thermometer is no reason to beach your canoe or kayak for the year. The days of summer are nice, but great paddling awaits you any time the water still moves freely. All you have to do is plan your wardrobe accordingly.

Historically, paddlers changed into 2.5 to 3 mm neoprene wetsuits once the temperatures started to ebb. A Farmer John/Farmer Jane wetsuit, looking much like a one-piece combi-nation of tights and a sleeveless vest, was rugged, kept you warm when combined with a paddling jacket, and was affordable—$50 to $70. It was also bulky, hard to keep clean, con-stricting, and uncomfortable. After a few wears, they became plagued with odors and developed

In the Wake

Although many paddlers simply hang their neoprene wetsuits up to air dry, this doesn't eliminate the odors and bacteria. Check with the manufacturer for specific instructions, but neoprene can be washed.

any number of chafing spots. But they kept you warm. Damp, but warm. They are still around, doing good work, but the paddler today has a number of options in the effort to stay warm.

Neoprene is still a good solution to the problem of cold water, and more so when price is taken into consideration. Cooling through evaporation can quickly chill a Farmer-wearing paddler, but that can be answered by a windproof paddling jacket. The Farmer John and Farmer Jane style of suits fit most paddlers, but neoprene pants and vests are also available separately. For added protection, a full neoprene jacket will cover your arms, shoulders, and neck.

Fuzzy Rubber

The new kid on the thermal protection block is familiarly called fuzzy rubber. They (there are a number of types on the market, under different trade names) are a fabric built around a stretchable base layer bonded to fleece on the inside for warmth and with a waterproof outer layer. They are more comfortable, easier to keep clean, and as thermally efficient as neoprene wetsuits. They are a lot thinner than bulky old wetsuits and significantly less constricting. Potential downsides are that they are a lot more expensive than neoprene wetsuits, so far less resistant to abrasion and wear, and they are form-fitting.

Drysuits

Drysuits do just what the name implies—keep you dry. They're made with a waterproof fabric, with tight cuffs at your wrists and ankles, and with a snug gasket around your neck. The downside is that you'll need some form of insulating liner to keep warm as well as dry. Lightweight fleece pants and top work well, as will a one-piece garment.

In the Wake
Fleece dries quickly and retains much of its thermal protection even when wet. It's more efficient than wool, long the paddler's favorite. Down loses most of its insulating qualities when wet. Cotton sops up water and funnels off your body heat.

Most canoeists do well with tightly woven synthetic-material pants that will shed splash and spray, worn with a waterproof yet breathable jacket designed to allow the full range of paddling motions. Start with a base layer of polypropylene (usually just called polypro) tights and top (your choice of long or short sleeves), adding a fleece pullover, a fleece vest for deeper chill, and a wind- and waterproof jacket. You'll appreciate a jacket with underarm zippers, to regulate the heat you'll build up paddling. Polypro and fleece will retain a lot of their insulating value even when damp.

Gloves

Paddling gloves (and mittens) are available in lightweight neoprene, in some of the stretchable insulating fabrics, and in coated nylons. In a pinch, rubber dishwashing gloves will do the trick. For just a little thermal protection, as well as good palm protection, try a pair of synthetic material fingerless cycling gloves.

Poagies are bag like things that fit snugly around a paddle shaft (for canoes and kayaks) with a gauntlet through which a bare hand can grasp the paddle shaft. Usually coated in nylon or neoprene, poagies protect your hands from chill and wet, while still allowing precise maneuvers.

Boots and Shoes

Recreational canoeists, wilderness trippers, and big-boat touring kayakers discovered long ago that mid- to upper-calf-height rubber boots are just fine for hopping in and out of shallow water. With fleece socks they're warm and comfy.

Manufacturers have developed a variety of lace-up water-friendly boots that protect but don't constrict your feet. When worn with waterproof breathable socks, they offer first-class thermal protection.

Sandals have long been the footwear of choice for water folks. They are quick-drying, surprisingly (to the uninitiated) supportive, and comfortable. Wear a pair of fleece socks for a bit more warmth, or a pair of waterproof breathable socks, perhaps over a light pair of sock liners for off-season comfort.

Rocks and Shoals

Rubber boots are great for wading, but miserable for swimming. Make sure you can slip them off if necessary while in the water or you'll find yourself wearing anchors.

Sports Bras

A lot of bras just don't work in paddling conditions. They're uncomfortable when wet, they chafe, and they restrict some paddling motions. Find an athletic-supply store that caters to women athletes and check out sports bras that combine support with comfortable materials and construction.

Dressing for the Warmth

The sun is out, the water's warm, and your boat is calling. It's time for shorts. Well, maybe. The sun can beat you up as bad as a blizzard, and you have to juggle a bunch of factors in deciding what to wear on the water.

Shorts

First of all, there's a lot more to a pair of paddling shorts than bare knees. Start with the basic material. If you're going to be playing in a wet environment, you need a garment that will dry almost instantaneously. A pair of cut-off cotton jeans won't. They'll suck up water and leave you feeling clammy and chafed all day. Go with a water-shedding smooth synthetic. You'll also be far more comfortable if the shorts have a mesh liner. Pocket-wise, you're better off with one that has a stout plastic zipper, and even more so with a flap over the zipper that seals with a button or hook-and-loop fabric. (Hook-and-loop—Velcro is the patron of this family, but there are others—works well, but can get clogged with sand and dirt.) Mesh pockets are great, because water will immediately drain from them. At the very least they should have several grommet drain holes.

The Old Paddler Says

When slathering yourself up with waterproof sunblock (look for it at most paddling and dive shops), don't forget the tender skin on the back of your knees if you're wearing shorts.

An adjustable waistband that stretches a bit for comfort and is secured with an adjustable plastic buckle will help keep your pants in place if you go over the side. Long pant legs, almost to the knee, won't bind or constrict you. They'll offer a bit of modesty and even more protection from sun, wind, bugs, and sharp brush.

Neoprene shorts are ideal for sit-on-tops, including surf skis. Some folks like full neoprene shorts, while others like neoprene butt and side panels and a Lycra or other stretchable front panel. With neat racer tech, we can ignore reality and bulges, and dream of how quick we might have been.

The Old Paddler Says

Sit-on-top kayaks, including surf skis, really expose your legs to the sun. At the same time, the frequent dowsings you'll experience can wash sunblock away. Slap on lots of sun block, wear a big-brimmed hat made of a sun-blocking material, wear a quick-drying long-sleeved shirt and long pants (both of sun-blocking material), and ration your time in the sun. That will reduce the odds of you getting burned, and will reduce the severity of the sunburn you eventually will get.

Stretchy materials bonded to fleece and a waterproof breathable exterior make great shorts and paddling tops. Put 'em on your gift list and maybe you'll be rewarded at the end of the year with a super present.

Long Pants, Tops, and Jackets

Long pants offer some major pluses. They'll protect your legs down to your feet from sun, bugs, brush, and the wind. Look for a lightweight synthetic; you can even find pants made with synthetic fabrics that block the burning rays of the sun. Avoid pants with cuffs—all they do is catch water and dirt.

On top, start with a high-collared long-sleeved shirt made out of a sunblocking material. Many will have vents under the arms and at the side seams. If you're too warm, roll your sleeves up. A lot of paddlers prefer a t-shirt under their PFD, but make it a synthetics one—synthetic fabrics are more comfortable than cotton and actually smell much better after a couple of days on the water.

If you're parking on the beach for a few days, flatwater or white water, add in a set of medium-weight Polarfleece sweatpants and a vest. It can get chilly down by the water during the evening. Fleece dries quickly and holds a lot of its insulating capabilities even when damp.

Keep a lightweight water- and wind-proof paddling jacket handy for rain showers or whatever, and think about a matching pair of rain pants. When shopping for jackets, keep in mind that fleece collars feel comfortable as long as they are dry, but many fleece collars will sop up rain and spray, and trickle it down your spine at the worst possible moments. That wet band pressing against your neck chills you quickly and thoroughly and can stiffen your paddling muscles.

> **In the Wake**
>
> If you're at the beginning of a long or steep portage trail, consider swapping your light in-boat shoes for all the support that good hiking boots can give. You'll be packing a lot of unbalanced weight, so protect your ankles.

Wilderness trippers will need to take a stout approach to paddling clothing. The pants, especially, have to stand up to the clawing and chewing of brush when you're searching out portage trails or building a camp on a jutting rock. Light weight takes a back seat to durability.

We mentioned bras a bit ago. Summer, with its accompanying heat and perspiration, demands more than just support. You're going to be twisting, reaching, and stretching, and a damp bra is going to provide a lot more chafing than support. Abandon cottons and sheers, and try on a few synthetic athletic sports bras.

Footwear

Sandals designed for water wear will protect your feet from all the nasty little sharp things poking up out of the beach as well as hot sand. A good pair supports your

Rocks and Shoals

Sandals protect the soles of your feet. They offer little if any protection against things that bite, from bugs to snakes.

arches and offers quite a bit of walking and hiking support to your feet and ankles. They don't protect the top of your toes from sunburn, though. If you're jumping in and out of the water, sandals will dry quickly. You can swim with them, and if they are a good fit, you'll still have them on at the end of the swim. Bottom line: Sandals work in a water environment. Put sunblock on your toes and be careful if you spill your coffee.

Water shoes, reef shoes, and a host of similar names describe a slip-on sort of moccasin with a solid sole and a stretchable synthetic fabric top. The good news is that they are cheap, and they offer protection for the bottoms of your feet on the beach and in the water. Don't expect great arch or ankle support. And if you swim, most will part company from you. If you understand their limitations, they'll do a good job for you. Just don't expect high-tech performance.

If you want the best all-around protection, support, and versatility, then look at lace-up water boots. They combine plenty of sole protection, a lace-up top that supports your foot and ankle, lots of drainage, and they will dry quickly and evenly. You'll pay for the advantages, and you'll have to decide if they are worth it for your kind of paddling and your paddling intensity.

Again, in the right environment—in and out of a canoe, in and out of a touring kayak with plenty of foot room—the old cheap and dependable rubber boot could well be the best footwear for your paddling. Look at where and when you want to paddle and determine whether they'll work for you.

Your Vital Topper

"If you want to warm your feet, put on a hat."

That might have been the best outdoors advice ever given. Your head works just like a radiator connected to the furnace of your body. It accounts for about 70 percent of your body's total heat loss. Not only does your head have a lot of blood circulating through it, but it's also exposed to the chilling effects of the wind. To reduce the amount of heat you're pumping out into the atmosphere, put on a hat.

If it's warm out, your head is exposed to the rays of the sun, and those rays heat your blood to the point that the rest of your body is sweating just to cool off your brain and body core. The solution is simple: Get your head out of the sun by putting on a hat.

Can a hat keep you both warm and cool? Sure. You can blow on your fingers to warm them and blow on your coffee to cool it. Your hat works the same way, seeking to insulate the blood flow through your head and scalp to keep you warm, or seeking to insulate your blood from the thermal radiation of the sun to keep you cool.

A hat will also protect your ears, neck, forehead, and scalp from sunburn. The bill or brim shades your eyes, giving you better vision as well as reducing the likelihood of a sun-induced headache. You'll paddle better, too, wearing a hat. Squint all day in the glare and you'll develop a painfully sore neck from the tension and a miserable sore spot right between your shoulder blades. Eliminate the glare and you'll avoid the squint and pain.

The hat you should choose depends on the kind of paddling you enjoy.

You won't venture there your first few times afloat, but most paddlers sporting in white water or playing in surf wear a helmet. With rocks, a hard bottom, and turbulent water, head protection makes a lot of sense. When the temperatures ebb like a tide, though, these paddlers will add a fleece skullcap under their helmets.

In warm and sunny weather, a big-brimmed light canvas hat with grommet holes for ventilation will keep the heat of the sun off your head and will protect you from sunburn. Select a hat with a chin strap or cord. Don't like cords or straps? You'll change your mind the first time an evil wind grabs your hat and sends it flapping away.

Rocks and Shoals

A hat offers your eyes some protection, but not as much as you need. Invest in a pair of good sunglasses, with side coverage.

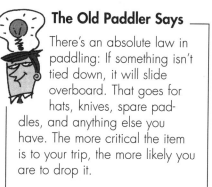

The Old Paddler Says

There's an absolute law in paddling: If something isn't tied down, it will slide overboard. That goes for hats, knives, spare paddles, and anything else you have. The more critical the item is to your trip, the more likely you are to drop it.

An offshore fisherman's cap, a baseball-like cap with a long bill and a skirt hanging down over your ears and neck gives you the same protection as a big-brimmed hat. Most come with a chin strap, as well as an adjustable headband for fit.

A baseball cap is the bare minimum. Your ears and neck will be exposed. If you go for this kind of cap, select one that's light-colored to reflect the heat, but that has a dark lining on the underside of the brim, to reduce glare.

Once the weather turns nasty, it's hard to beat the old-fashioned and eminently practicable sou'wester. You've probably seen them in a thousand old B movies featuring grizzled fishermen on the stormy sea. Traditionally, they are a bright-yellow oilskin with a short front brim and a long brim off the back to shed rain over your collar. And they have a broad ribbon of a chinstrap.

The Least You Need to Know

- You can find most of your paddling wear already in your closet.

- Layer your clothes for all-temperature comfort.

- Clothing made of synthetic materials such as polypro or fleece will keep you warm even if damp, and you *will* get damp when paddling a canoe or kayak.

- Keep warm: Wear a hat. Keep cool: Wear a hat.

Your PFD: Don't Leave Home Without It!

In This Chapter

- ◆ Why personal flotation devices (PFDs) are a must
- ◆ Choosing among PFD types
- ◆ Fitting your own PFD
- ◆ Caring for your PFD

When it comes to your *personal flotation device*, sometimes abbreviated as PFD, the accent is always on the *personal*. It's yours, and, as such, you should wear it whenever you're on the water. At the same time, it should be as comfortable and unobtrusive as any vital item of personal safety can ever be. Anytime it is wrapped around you, it should not bind or constrain your movements in any way.

The only times you should really know that you're wearing a PFD is when you've explored the far boundaries of your stability and have known *deeply* the difference between swimmer and paddler. Even in the water, it's the support you want and not the constricted (or, worse, too-loose) feeling of an ill-fitting PFD.

Paddlin' Talk

PFD is boater—canoeist or kayaker—shorthand for **personal flotation device.** That's the familiar life jacket or vest you should wear at all times while in your boat, for those unexpected moments when you come out of your boat.

Rocks and Shoals

Most drownings occur when there is a PFD stowed in the boat. Few people are fast enough to pick up and don a PFD when they are toppling out of their boat, the time when they most need it.

Fortunately for you, there's a huge array of personal flotation devices that can give you the support you need without clamping you into a restricting sleeve.

When to Wear It?

Common sense dictates that you should wear a PFD whenever you venture out onto the water in a canoe or kayak. Some states, some provinces, and a scattering of local agencies go beyond this and demand that you wear one anytime you're aboard your canoe or kayak. Some agencies address the safety question with a more flexible attitude, and only rule that children under a certain age must wear PFDs while underway. No matter what the laws say, since perhaps only 1 out of 1,000 boaters has the skills to slip into and zip up a PFD sometime between when they first lose stability in a boat and when they hit the water (and trust me, at some point you *are* going to take a spill), you should always wear your PFD.

The U.S. Coast Guard Types

There are four "classes" of wearable PFDs: the big and bulky high-flotation Offshore Life Jacket (Type I), the familiar "horsecollar" Near-Shore Buoyant Vest (Type II), the Special Use or Hybrid Inflatable (Type V), and the comfortable Flotation Aid vest usually referred to as a Type III. Throwables—the square cushion or the life ring— are Type IVs.

The Type I, with 22 pounds of buoyancy (11 pounds for a child), is constraining, heavy, and hot. It will turn an unconscious wearer face-up under most conditions. The Type II, the familiar orange "horsecollar" that wraps around your neck and has front ties, provides 15.5 pounds of buoyancy in adult sizes, 11 pounds of buoyancy for a medium-sized child, and 7 pounds for a small child. The horsecollar is not the most comfortable for a day of paddling, but will turn a nonswimmer or an unconscious person face-up in most conditions—although not as effectively or in as many conditions as the Type I. Type V PFDs are dubbed "special purpose," and are only effective under specified conditions. It is the least bulky of all PFDs, with a small amount of built-in buoyancy and an inflatable chamber that brings it up to the Type I, II, or III standards listed on its label.

For canoeists and kayakers, the Type III life vest is the way to go. Even better is the Type III vest designed specifically for canoeists and kayakers. It meets all federal standards but has narrower shoulder straps and large arm holes to allow a full range of paddling motion. This is the kind of PFD you should buy and wear whenever you are out on the water in your canoe or kayak.

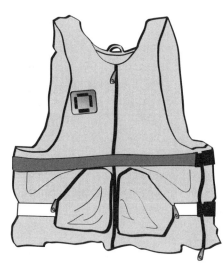

Today's Canoe and Kayak Type III Personal Flotation Device is a life vest tailored for your paddling movements, whether on the river, freshwater lake, or saltwater. It features large armholes, adjustable shoulder and side straps, an adjustable waistband, quick-draining pockets, and a rugged zipper.

In addition to the vest-style Type III, there's a coat-style Type III PFD, which offers the same buoyancy. It is, however, bulky and quite warm to wear in even moderate paddling situations. Some type III PFDs have what are called "impact class" ratings; these are designed to withstand the impact of hitting the water at high speed while water skiing.

Adult Type III PFDs come in a variety of sizes, ranging from small to extra large, but those sizes can be a little deceiving. The sizes have nothing to do with the wearer's weight—they indicate only chest size, and all have the same amount—15.5 pounds minimum—of flotation. All adult sizes contain this same flotation. Adding to the confusion, a few PFDs may be rated as 90 lb. or more, which is just a manufacturer's way of saying "adult."

Youth PFDs have less flotation, corresponding to a child's different body mass and flotation. A PFD labeled "medium child" has at least

In the Wake

Some Type III PFDs are constructed with shaped foam panels, while others are made with a series of vertical foam-filled tubes looking much like giant corduroy. The shaped panel PFDs tend to be a bit more comfortable for most paddlers, while the vertical tube PFDs tend to be a little less expensive.

11 pounds of buoyancy, while those labeled "small child" size have 7 pounds of buoyancy. Since an average adult needs about 7 pounds of buoyancy to support his or her head above water when he or she is awake and conscious, you can see that PFDs offer more than enough buoyancy when sized appropriately.

What You Have to Have!

U.S. Coast Guard, as well as state and provincial, regulations call for all canoes and kayaks on navigable water and not engaged in specified competition to carry at least one Type I, II, III, or V PFD for each person on board. Figure that to mean virtually any stream, lake, bay, or ocean in North America, although there are a few limited exceptions. Federal law—and this doesn't include possible state and local laws, which may be more restrictive—requires that Type V PFDs must be worn, and must have use restrictions on them that must be observed. Federal law does not require PFDs on racing shells, rowing sculls, and racing kayaks under limited conditions. If you're not familiar with each comma and dot in the law, assume that you aren't affected by the exemption.

The old square floating seat cushion and the throw ring don't cut it for canoes and kayaks. You can't wear them, and you don't have a way to carry them.

What You Want in a PFD

You should start with large armholes and narrow shoulder straps, allowing you the greatest range of arm and paddling motion. Adjustable shoulder straps allow precise fitting from shoulder to waist. Compression straps under each armhole snug the PFD to your torso. A waist belt cinches the PFD snugly.

The Old Paddler Says

The back foam panels in your PFD protect your back from injury if you hit rocks or other obstructions when you're upside down in your canoe or kayak, or swimming in turbulent water. It also provides additional insulation for your vital body core.

Most Canoe and Kayak PFDs (check on the label for this designation) are waist length. A few are hip length, with a skirt or flap of flotation extending below the waist. Waist length are definitely preferable in decked boats—canoes or kayaks—because they don't bump against your spray deck. Same goes for most sit-on-top or wash-deck kayaks. Paddlers who tend to slump in their seats (remember Mom telling you to sit up straight?) find that their PFDs catch on the back of their coamings, usually with the feeling that their boat is too deep for comfortable paddling. Actually, it's merely a case of poor posture.

In a canoe or some inflatables, the PFD skirt stands clear of the thwarts or seats, and you can go with whatever style you think looks cool.

Pockets are optional and sometimes even come in handy. You want some sort of closure at the top of the pocket, either a hook-and-loop cloth or a zipper. Beware of metal zippers that corrode, or hook-and-loop closures that clog with sand. Best is a zipper top, covered with a hook-and-loop flap. Mesh drains well, and, at a minimum, choose a pocket with grommet drain holes. A loop and snap inside the pocket is great for car keys. Hang your whistle cord from a ring on the PFD, or on the pocket zipper.

Lots of reflective tape or patches make you more visible in less-than-ideal conditions. Some reflective material may be sewn on the PFD itself, but you can usually add more over shoulder straps. Some PFDs have what is called a four-way lash pad high on the back. The lash pad has four openings, into which such things as small lights may be clipped. If you paddle at dusk, a small clip-on flashlight hung there is a bright and easily-visible beacon.

Fitting Your PFD

The best way to know if your PFD fits is to try it on! Don all your normal paddling clothes, slip into your PFD, and clamber into your boat with paddle in hand. Adjust (and call on help if you need it) your shoulder straps so that the PFD's waist and yours line up. Snug down the compression straps under each arm and then the waist belt until your PFD feels somewhat tight but not binding. Stretch through every paddling maneuver you can think of. Does the PFD bind any of your motions? If it does, then adjust the straps or try a different size. Once you can move around without having the PFD impede

Rocks and Shoals _____

Think of your PFD as a bank account filled with buoyancy you may need. Every item you cram into your pockets is a withdrawal from that account.

The Old Paddler Says _____

When your PFD is adjusted to fit you properly, put your name on it. It is one of the few things your kindergarten teacher was wrong about—it is not for sharing.

Rocks and Shoals _____

What if your shape just doesn't match up with a PFD, no matter how you adjust shoulder and side compression straps? You can find PFDs with straps (sometimes as a PFD option) that lead from the back edge through your legs and snap to the front. The straps aren't as comfortable as strapless models, but will offer you support.

your motions, have a friend stand behind you and lift up on both shoulder straps. If the shoulder straps of the PFD lift up around your ears and your nose gets buried in the zipper, it's not a good fit. Try another size, or readjust the straps.

After you've completed this test for yourself, repeat it for your children. When you do, think about the PFD shoulder straps sticking above the surface with a circle of hair floating between them. That's gross, ugly, and will induce nightmares. It's not nearly as horrible as seeing the same image drifting away from your boat.

Caring for Your PFD

Your PFD isn't meant to be altered in any way. If you can't get the one you own to fit comfortably by adjusting the straps, buy another one that does. You alter it at the risk of your life.

Rocks and Shoals

A PFD is not a seat cushion. The crushed foam in a munched PFD is like a flat spare tire on a car. It just won't work when you really need it.

It is not a kneeling pad, a fender for your boat, or even a substitute car-top rack. And it is not a beach chair. When you crush the foam in your PFD, you are sacrificing its buoyancy.

Drip-dry your PFD thoroughly before stowing it away. Always stow it in a dark, well-ventilated space. Never dry it over a radiator, heater, a fire, or any other direct heat source.

Don't leave your PFD in your boat for long periods when you're not paddling. Mold can attack and weaken the fabric if put away damp. Vermin can chew on it. Metal parts may rust. If you don't take care of it, it will not take care of you.

It's easy to tell when it's time to retire your old PFD. Put it on and jump into the water. If it doesn't keep your chin out of the water, then it's time to retire that faithful friend. Inspect it for rips, tears, or holes, and make certain that seams, fabric straps, and hardware are in good shape. If it smells of mildew or has a weathered or faded appearance, beach it. Hey, your personal flotation device (and the emphasis is on personal) has to work perfectly in that instant you need it. Your PFD is the one thing you can cling to when the rest of your paddling day has turned topsy-turvy.

The Least You Need to Know

- The law says you have to *carry* a personal flotation device; common sense says you have to *wear* it.

- The most comfortable PFD for paddling will be stamped "Canoe and Kayak."

- When a PFD states it has 15.5 lb. of flotation, take into consideration that it only takes about 7 pounds of flotation to keep an average adult's chin above the water.

- Check your PFD for signs of wear, stains, mildew, or fraying seams. Retire it when it starts showing signs of age.

Part 4

At the Water's Edge

A canoe or a kayak in your backyard may be a thing of beauty, but it's not living up to your expectations while resting on the grass.

In this part, we'll start at the beach by getting into your canoe or kayak. There are techniques you can use when pushing off into a lake with small waves or into the current of a river that will make your first trip way more pleasurable.

You'll also learn how and when to use the paddle strokes that propel your canoe or kayak, and how to use your paddle as a temporary brace when your boat runs into somewhat tippy conditions.

Oh, you'll also experience falling out of your boat. You'll be surprised at just how hard it is to tip over. You'll also be surprised over how much confidence you gain once you've gotten the top of your head wet.

Chapter 11

Getting Underway

In This Chapter

- How to carry your canoe or kayak
- Scrambling aboard your canoe
- Launching your kayak
- Learning the wet exit
- Bow to the waves, current, or wind

You've read the book, you've tried on the clothes, and you even have a paddle right at hand. You're not a paddler yet, no matter how carefully you've visualized each stroke. You still have to get in your boat and onto the water.

Carrying Your Boat to the Water

There are four distinct carries you can use to get your boat from your car to the water's edge. That's if you even want to carry it. You may just want to put it on a little cart and roll it down to the water. In any case, you should be aware of the carrying techniques:

♦ **One-person technique.** *For a canoe*, grip both gunwales just ahead of the center thwart. Lift the boat to your thighs, letting the stern rest on the ground. Lift the canoe over your head, rotating it upside down, and let that center thwart rest over your shoulders. You'll be a lot more comfortable if the thwart is curved or padded to fit your neck and shoulders. Use your hands to raise the stern, and start walking for the water. *For a kayak*, roll the boat up on one edge, the cockpit facing you, and slip the cockpit over one shoulder with your hand gripping the inside of the coaming.

Rocks and Shoals

Paddlers have a host of very funny stories about portagers carrying their canoes over a trail and meeting a canoe team coming the other way … with a great whack. They also share stories of canoeists ramming a tree while wearing a canoe as a hat. If you can't see, you're a hazard on the trail.

♦ **Two-person technique, version #1.** *For a canoe*, you and your partner should stand beside the canoe, just in front of your respective seats. Grip both gunwales, and, with an agreed-upon signal, swing the canoe upside down over your heads. Rest the gunwales on your shoulders. The taller paddler (and portager) should be in the front, because this enables you both to see a bit better.

♦ **Two-person technique, version #2.** Or, *for a canoe or kayak*, have the two paddlers stand at each end of the canoe or kayak, one on each side. With a *canoe*, grip the gunwale near the deck, and lift. With some canoes you may grab the deck to lift. *For kayaks*, grab the loop at the bow and stern. One person, for either boat, will use the left hand and the other, the right hand. Switch sides when your hands get tired.

♦ **Four-person technique.** Four people make carrying a canoe or kayak a light load. *For an open canoe or kayak*, place two people just in front of each seat. They can grasp the gunwale or, depending on the boat, lift at the seat or at the deck. An easier variation is to use two straps with broad, comfortable handholds fastened at the ends. The straps go under the hull, with the people lifting the straps rather than the gunwales. This is the lightest way of carrying a touring kayak, and works well for most canoes. It is awkward with very short kayaks.

Boarding Your Canoe

In the good old days of canvas-covered wood canoes, rubbing the fragile hull against any kind of beach was spectacularly against the rules. With today's plastics and composites, you can touch the earth as you launch and land. It still makes sense to keep that touch as light as possible. The following sections describe two easy ways to make the transition from shore to water.

From the Beach

Climbing into a canoe is a simple, two-step process. However, like dancing, you can get your feet tangled and end up in a heap. On the dance floor you'll be dry. Tumbling out of a canoe leaves you wet, sputtering, and confounded, with your paddle drifting away and your pockets full of sand. Make it easy on yourself.

If two of you are set to board a tandem open canoe, you have a couple of options. If there is any current or wind (forget about launching through any waves bigger than a ripple for the time being), then put your canoe in the water parallel to the shoreline with the bow pointing into the wind or current. The canoe should be barely afloat.

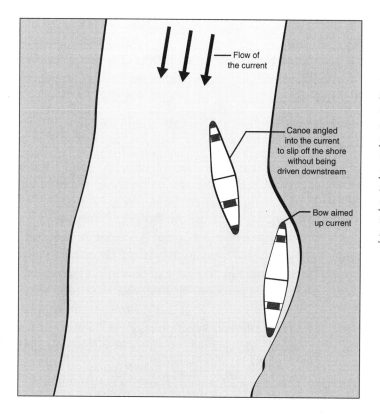

Flow of the current

Canoe angled into the current to slip off the shore without being driven downstream

Bow aimed up current

Launching while heading into the current allows a canoe or kayak to easily angle offshore without being pushed downstream. Launching heading downstream lets the current push your canoe or kayak back against the bank, bounces you through the bankside shallows, and doesn't give you a chance to pause in mid-current and look for your best route downstream.

The bow paddler stands next to the boat (on the shore side), reaching over the canoe to grasp the gunwales on each side just ahead of the bow seat. This stabilizes the canoe. As soon as the bow paddler is braced, the stern paddler reaches across the canoe and grasps each gunwale, and places the foot that will end up on the far side of the canoe directly on the center line of the canoe, about 12 inches or so in front of the seat. Keeping the body relatively low (that old center-of-gravity thing), and balancing the weight equally on two arms, the stern paddler brings his or her foot quickly and smoothly into the canoe. No jerking! Still holding the gunwales, the stern paddler smoothly sits down.

The Old Paddler Says

The paddler (and the canoe) will be more stable immediately after boarding a canoe if he or she edges forward off the seat and supports his weight on his knees, with his or her feet back under the seat. He or she should be resting against the front edge of the seat, and his or her knees should be spread out to as close to the bilges as possible. This lowers the center of gravity, which makes the canoe more stable, as well as giving the paddler better leverage while shifting his or her weight to balance the canoe.

The stern paddler then braces his or her paddle either off the shore or off the shallow bottom, stabilizing the canoe. The bow paddler goes through the same sequence as the stern paddler does the balancing.

When both are ready, the bow paddler shoves off the shore side (switching paddle sides if necessary) and both push ahead to move the canoe into deeper water.

If there is no wind or current action, you can slide the canoe at right angles to the shore with the bow pointing outward and the stern resting on the shoreline. The stern paddler straddles the end of the canoe, locking the gunwales between his or her legs, and grasps the gunwales with his or her hands while the bow paddler steps aboard with hands on the gunwales for balance. The bow paddler, staying low in the canoe for balance, steps directly down the middle of the canoe and over the front seat. The bow paddler sits, and braces with his or her paddle—either off the bottom or with a bracing stroke. When the bow paddler is ready, the stern paddler moves to one side of the canoe, brings his or her canoe-side foot into the canoe, right at the center line in front of the stern seat, and pushes off the shore with the other foot. As the canoe glides into deeper water, the stern paddler brings his or her other foot aboard and sinks to his or her seat.

Rocks and Shoals

If just your stern is on the beach and the bow in the water, your canoe is balanced on the narrow knife edge of the keel end. This is potentially very tippy, and a paddler attempting to balance the canoe on shore should be braced for quite a bit of effort and twisting.

The solo paddler boarding his or her canoe goes through the same steps as the first paddler in a tandem canoe. If the water depths make it possible, begin with the canoe floating in very shallow water parallel to the shoreline. If you paddle a solo canoe with a center seat, grasp the gunwales just in front of the center seat. Carefully step to the center of the canoe with one foot, and shove off from shore with the other as you bring that foot aboard. Sit down, pick up your paddle, and go. If the canoe hangs up on the bottom, use your paddle to shove off on the shore side, scooting yourself into deep water.

In the Wake

Just lightly slosh the sole of your shoe at the surface of the water before you place your first foot in the canoe. As you bring your second foot aboard, also rinse off the sole. A few drops of water can easily be sponged out of your canoe, but if you bring aboard a small piece of gravel, it is bound to end up under your knee. Mud is just as bad because it spreads when it is wet and is a beast to clean up at the end of the day.

Launching a solo canoe straight out from the shoreline works well, as long as you remember that you're balancing on a very narrow part of the canoe's keel. It will be far tippier.

There's one important change if you're paddling a standard recreation canoe by yourself—turn it around. You'll sit on what had been the front seat, but you'll sit on the back edge of the seat—facing what you had thought of as the stern—and will paddle in that direction. One seat, if you look at it, is placed a fair distance from the end of the canoe. That leaves room for the bow paddler's legs. If you're paddling by yourself and use that seat, you bring your weight up near the center of the canoe. This permits the canoe to float flat on the water, for far more efficient paddling and control.

Boarding from a Dock

Climbing aboard your canoe from a dock can be simplicity itself or can be nerve-janglingly difficult. If it is a very low dock, even with or lower than the gunwales of your canoe, you have it made. Board the canoe just as if it were in shallow water parallel to the shoreline. You can stand on the dock next to the canoe or you can kneel on the dock, whatever feels better to you. It works for one paddler or two.

If the canoe is several feet below the surface of the dock, your best bet is to move the canoe over to the shore. If that's impossible, tie your bow and stern *painter lines* to the dock, to prevent the canoe from abruptly sliding well away from the face of the dock. Sit on the edge of the dock, with your feet over and preferably in the canoe. Roll over, keeping your feet in the canoe, until your stomach is on the edge of the dock and you are supporting much of your weight with your hands. Carefully lower yourself into the canoe, placing your feet on the center line, and gradually transfer your weight from your hands to your feet. Keeping a hand on the dock to maintain your balance, lower yourself until you're low in the canoe and can grasp both gunwales. Sit or kneel at your seat. If you're paddling alone, ask a friend on the dock to cast your lines off. If you're the first person of a tandem team, you should be in the stern and balancing the canoe as your bow paddler joins you aboard.

Paddlin' Talk _____

Painter lines are short lines or ropes attached to the bow and stern of a canoe or kayak.

Who Boards First?

There are at least two schools of thought, and practice, regarding which paddler should board a tandem canoe first. From a mechanical perspective, the bow paddler gets the nod. That's because the bow seat is set well closer to the center of the canoe than the stern. A person settling into the bow seat will only slightly sink the bow end and raise the stern. A paddler sitting in the stern will significantly sink the stern and raise the bow. This will make the canoe a bit more unstable, with its waterline and underwater profile so dramatically changed.

CAUTION

Rocks and Shoals _____

It is easy enough to upset a canoe while launching: Simply put both hands on the same gunwale and rest your weight on them, or put your foot way to the side of the canoe when moving ahead. Don't worry, though. As long as you keep your weight over the middle of the canoe and low, you're very stable.

From a visibility and paddling standpoint, the stern paddler gets the nod. The stern paddler can easily keep a close watch as the bow paddler boards, and with this knowledge, can move to compensate the shifting weight of the bow paddler. Also, it is far easier to control a canoe with a solo paddle in the stern, which is important as the canoe begins to move and the bow paddler may not have his or her paddle immediately ready.

Try both ways. Then practice the one that works best for you, and develop the ability to use the other approach for when conditions dictate.

Coming Ashore from Your Canoe

Landing from a canoe is definitely on the easy side, with today's tough and resilient hull materials. If you have a sloping beach, just come ashore with a bit of care—aim for the soft spots and avoid big rocks—just until the bow touches the ground.

The bow paddler hops out, grabs the deck or the gunwale, and gives the canoe a firm pull, up onto the beach. The stern paddler can then step ashore over the side, or if the beach is more sloped and the stern is still in deep water, can walk down the middle of the canoe bracing on the gunwales. The bow paddler steadies the canoe while the stern paddler disembarks.

If you're landing on a very steep beach or on rocks with deep water alongside, paddle up parallel to the shoreline. Head your bow into the wind or current, if there is any. Some tandem teams, facing wind or current, like having the bow paddler step out first and control the canoe while the stern paddler comes ashore. This does put the bow up in the air, as the bow paddler exits, which increases the canoe's tendency to twirl about back into the current. It's also easier for a stern paddler to control a canoe than it is for a person alone in the bow. Other teams choose to have the stern paddler exit first with the bow paddler bracing the canoe. This prevents the bow from swinging out. The stern paddler then stabilizes the canoe as the bow paddler scrambles ashore.

Rocks and Shoals

When landing, either tie your painter lines to something well-attached to the shore or bring your canoe well above the water. You really don't want your canoe drifting away when you're catching a nap on the beach.

Boarding Your Kayak

Sliding yourself into the snug cockpit of a kayak looks challenging, more challenging than it actually is. You use a temporary outrigger support so that you can slip right into your kayak seat.

The outrigger support is something you have right at hand. Just use your paddle.

Two things first:

- If you have adjustable foot braces in your kayak, including rudder pedals, make sure that they are adjusted for you before you launch. Yes, with some models you can adjust the footpegs when you're on the water. But sticking your head into the cockpit and fumbling around in a rocking kayak is way harder than you believe, until you try it.

- Slip into your spray deck. Again, you can do this on the water but it's far easier to do this standing ashore before you put on your personal flotation device.

Boarding from a Beach

Place your kayak, whether river kayak or touring kayak, in a couple of inches of water, as close as possible to and parallel to the shoreline. Crouch or squat next to your cockpit. Put your paddle behind you, with one blade flat on the ground and the other blade just past your deck. Wrap your boat-side hand fingers around the back of your cockpit coaming, with the paddle shaft under your palm. Place your other hand on the paddle shaft, close to or just behind your hip. You should be able to raise and lower your body with your arms. Lift your weight onto your hands, so that you are supporting most of your weight at the cockpit, and using the other hand as much for balance and stability as anything. Start to shift your body toward the cockpit, bringing your boat-side leg up and into the cockpit. As soon as the first leg is in the cockpit, raise your other leg and place it in the cockpit. As you place your legs in the cockpit, your body will naturally be over the cockpit, and your legs will be extended under the deck. Lower yourself down into the seat, and bring your paddle in front of you.

Boarding your kayak from a beach or a dock is the same: building a supporting bridge with your paddle to help balance as you move your weight into the boat. The shore-side blade is flat, the paddler's hand wraps around the paddle shaft and the rear of the coaming, and the paddler supports his or her weight with both hands as he or she squats beside the kayak cockpit.

(Suzanne Stuhaug)

Paddlin' Talk

Huli is a Hawaiian term meaning to turn over or to turn upside down. Polynesians have been paddling canoes for at least a couple of thousand years and their language reflects their knowledge of paddlesports.

This sounds way more complicated than it is in practice. But be warned: Boarding your kayak for the first couple of times exposes you to the greatest likelihood of getting wet. You can practice entering and exiting with your kayak while resting on your backyard lawn. There is an unfortunate law of physics and public humiliation that if you do *huli* your kayak while boarding, there will be a large crowd on that same beach.

Snap your spray deck around the coaming, slightly lean your kayak away from the shore (to lift the keel line and to bring the bottom of the hull parallel to the slope of the water bottom), and, with your hands, scoot yourself over into deeper water.

The Old Paddler Says

The first time you shift your weight to the rear of your cockpit, your kayak—especially if yours is a fiberglass boat—will moan and groan a bit. You'll panic, with visions of your kayak being crushed. Don't panic. Sometimes this noise is caused by the fiberglass hull moving against a foam wall, sometimes by the flexing of the fiberglass, and sometimes because boats just make those kinds of sounds. Swallow your heart back out of your throat and go about your boarding.

If beach conditions permit, you can bring your kayak down to the water's edge, with the bow up to the front of the cockpit on the water. Board your kayak just the same way, and when you're in the cockpit with the spray deck snapped into place, use your hands and a couple of good hip thrusts to propel yourself into the water.

Keeping your kayak parallel to the shoreline (or a low dock) is the best way for two paddlers to board a double kayak. Once in a while you'll see a big double launched bow first, with the bow paddler coming aboard as the front cockpit is at the shoreline, and the stern paddler boarding as the front two thirds of the kayak (or more) is afloat. If you're launching into waves, this really is your best option; otherwise, you'll be battered broadside by each curl coming onto the beach. It is very, very difficult to turn into the waves from a parallel-to-the-shore launch, when you have no momentum and the water is too shallow to lower your rudder.

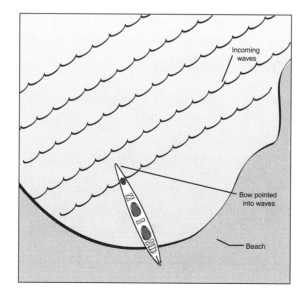

In calm water, you can board more conveniently if your kayak is parallel to the beach. If there are waves, even small ones, you'll find it far easier and much drier to launch with your bow pointing right into the waves. It is challenging to get a boat moving ahead and, at the same time, to turn into the waves when you're being thumped on the side by those waves. The waves also have a sneaky habit of splashing aboard and in your face.

The bow-on launch, for doubles or single kayaks, comes with a problem that grows worse with longer kayaks. If the beach is steep, you could end up with your bow afloat, your midsection up in the air, and your stern teetering on a knife edge. Apart from stressing your kayak unduly, you could end up flipping your kayak and falling out.

A steep beach launch.

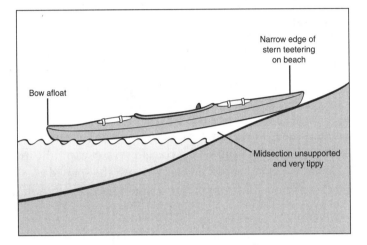

Boarding Your Sit-on-Top Kayak

The very first time you board a sit-on-top kayak, you'll understand why these boats are so deservedly popular. The easiest way is to put the sit-on-top in the water, step over it right ahead of the seat, and sit down. As an alternative, stand sprattle-legged and pull the kayak between your legs until you come to the seat. Then sit down. The sides of the kayak will lift your legs and drop your heels right into their divots.

Coming Ashore from Your Kayak

Exiting your kayak is even easier than boarding. Swing into shallow water parallel to the shoreline, and extend your paddle straight out to the side just as you did when boarding, with one hand holding the paddle shaft to the back edge of the cockpit and the other out on the shaft. Lift yourself up and back from the cockpit. Swing one foot and then the other to the ground, and you're home free.

Taking a Spill on Purpose

Most paddlers, at one time or another in the pursuit of their favorite hobby, will find themselves upside down in the water. That ain't a bad thing. It should, for the development of your paddling skills, come sooner rather than later. Bear with us for a moment.

The paddler who has never dumped over is particularly apprehensive about the possibility of a swim. You're relatively confined in most kayaks or canoes and a little corner of your mind worries that you will become entangled in your boat if you're upside down. The very idea of being inverted, unable to breathe, and with water up your nose, will prey upon you every time you're out on the water.

Your paddling will become excessively defensive as—consciously or not—you do everything in your power to prevent an upset. Excessive, because you will sacrifice efficiency and power in a rigid effort to preserve your dignity and a dry face. Excessive, because, without that fear, you'll be able to concentrate on learning the strokes and the balance to keep yourself upright.

What's the remedy? Fall over and dispel those concerns. Don't paddle alone far from shore on a snowy day to try this. Your best spot is in a heated swimming poll, followed closely by an enclosed swimming area in a tepid lake. The water should be relatively shallow, more than waist- but less than chest-deep. That's so you won't bump the bottom and yet will feel comfortable standing. You should be wearing your life jacket, both to see just how effective it is and to prove that it won't snag on your boat

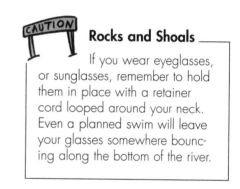

Rocks and Shoals

If you wear eyeglasses, or sunglasses, remember to hold them in place with a retainer cord looped around your neck. Even a planned swim will leave your glasses somewhere bouncing along the bottom of the river.

Be with a good instructor. Spouses, significant others, and parents usually bring too much baggage to the classroom to qualify. You and they will create all sorts of mandatory goals, rather than relishing the learning process. You can wear goggles and nose plugs if they add to your comfort. Other than that, all you'll need are swimming togs. And your boat, of course.

Once you're comfortable in your boat, lean to the side and see how far you can lean. When you lean over far enough, and you'll be surprised how far that is, you'll flop into the water.

If you try this in a canoe, by now you've fallen out. Come up alongside your canoe, check for your partner if you paddle tandem, and swim toward shore towing your boat.

If you've been paddling a kayak, take a moment to reflect on where you are. Curl your body forward so that your face is near the front of your cockpit, grab the loop at the front of your spray deck, and tug it free from the coaming. It may have already popped off. Relax the pressure of your feet on the foot braces and you'll likely float free. If not, put a hand on each side of the cockpit and push yourself out (and back a little) with the same movement you use to slide off a pair of pants.

Your PFD will pop you right back to the surface.

Many of the best paddling instructors in North America firmly believe that the very first things you should learn is how to exit an overturned boat, followed immediately by how to rescue yourself and resume paddling. It gives you a huge boost of confidence.

Recovering from an Upset

The Eskimo roll is the quickest and most elegant way to recover from an upset. With a brace from your paddle and a flick of your hips, you'll be back upright with nary a drop of water in your kayak. If you come out of your kayak, you'll want a paddle float outrigger for a safe and secure reboarding. Sponsons, inflatable tubes belted to the hull of your kayak, also work like mini-outriggers to assist you in reboarding a swamped boat. A second kayak can stabilize your kayak as you pump out water and clamber back in your cockpit. You need to know how to do these before the need to do such arises. Practice, while it doesn't always make perfect, does make possible. We're saying kayak, but these techniques work just as well for canoes. So what are you waiting for? Read on.

The roll begins (the second half, really, the first half being you going from upright to upside down) with positioning your paddle straight out from the side of your kayak. The blade should be just below the surface and parallel to it. Allow your body to float up on the paddle side of your boat. Your PFD will help, lots. Hold your paddle with both hands, at your normal grips. Obviously, your paddle shaft will be above—closer to the surface—your wrists. Don't lift your head. You have plenty of air and plenty of time. Using your paddle as a brace (you're in a bracing position) use your hips and knees to rotate your boat underneath you. Your head should be the last part of your body out of the water. Let it follow, not lead, the movement up. Lifting your heavy head is the surest way to foil your roll.

You can practice the rolling maneuver in a pool or in a lake near a dock. Position your kayak parallel to the edge of the pool (or dock), rotate your torso to face the edge, and grasp the edge with both hands. Use your lower body and your hips to rotate the upper deck toward the pool edge, while supporting yourself with your hands. It's easy to lean your boat way over on its side, far beyond vertical, with your spray deck deep in the water. It is equally easy, as you hold the edge of the pool, to use a flick of your hips or a shift of your weight to rotate the hull back underneath you.

To Eskimo roll a canoe, you need knee braces or straps. Without them, you'll simply fall out. It is also harder to Eskimo roll a canoe than a kayak, because the canoe is bigger, beamier, and will fill with water. With a little practice, though, you can learn.

A word of caution: We don't know many people who learned to roll on their own, and we know a lot of people who quickly learned to roll with the help of an instructor.

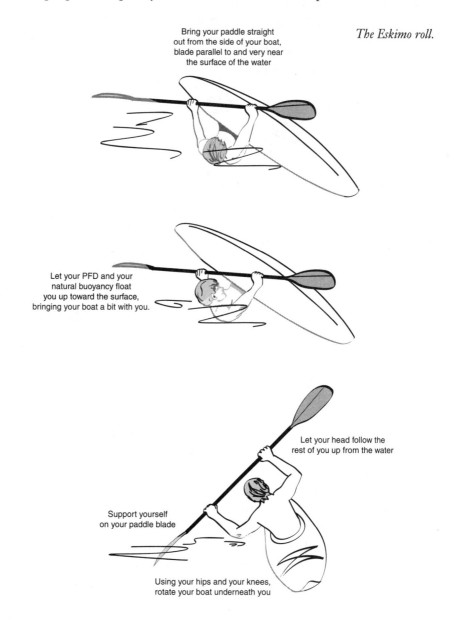

Bring your paddle straight out from the side of your boat, blade parallel to and very near the surface of the water

The Eskimo roll.

Let your PFD and your natural buoyancy float you up toward the surface, bringing your boat a bit with you.

Let your head follow the rest of you up from the water

Support yourself on your paddle blade

Using your hips and your knees, rotate your boat underneath you

Paddlin' Talk

A **paddle float** is an inflatable bag attached to one kayak paddle blade while the other end of the paddle is secured at the kayak deck at right angles to the hull. It functions as an outrigger to aid re-entry and water removal after an upset or swamping.

Building a Paddle Float Outrigger

For whatever reason, assume you are in the water next to your kayak and you want to climb back aboard. First of all, a wet kayak is slippery. The waves are bouncing you around. A kayak wasn't designed to carry your weight on the deck without weight inside to stabilize everything. Now what do you do?

Because you were prepared, you can quickly rig a *paddle float*—a temporary outrigger—to help you back aboard.

Lash your paddle across the rear deck of your kayak just aft of the cockpit and place an inflatable float over the outstretched paddle blade. This works just like an outrigger, enabling you to squirm aboard from where you are in the water at A, pump your boat dry, and resume your passage.

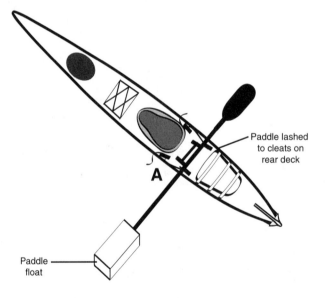

Paddle lashed to cleats on rear deck

A

Paddle float

At its simplest (and it is simple), you lash a paddle to your rear deck with the shaft sticking straight out to the side. Secure a small inflatable bag to the outboard paddle blade, and the paddle float will support you as you squirm back into your cockpit. Position yourself alongside your cockpit, facing the stern and with the paddle shaft in your hands. Using the shaft as a brace, slide up and over the shaft onto the rear deck, facing down. Shift your feet into the cockpit and rotate your body as you slide in. Keep your weight on the paddle float side, or else you might find yourself toppling over the other way. It sounds simple, but requires practice and preparation.

The Old Paddler Says

You're better off leaving your favorite paddle on its leash and building the paddle float with your spare paddle, which should be secured on your rear deck. That way, you have your motive power at hand, and you're ready for a brace at any moment once aboard. You can turn yourself about, to keep water from splashing into your cockpit. You may then disassemble your spare and paddle float at your leisure.

First, mount the cleats and pad eyes (fittings you'll use to tie the paddle firmly into position) for the paddle float on your rear deck. Your boat shop can do this, and they will know where and how to mount the hardware. You also can do this under the tutelage of a skilled paddling club co-member, one who might also teach you the technique of reboarding.

Second, stow your deflated paddle float where you can reach it from the water. It will fit nicely behind your seat, tied in place.

Third, on dry land, make certain all the parts fit together, the lashing is long enough, and that you know how to inflate the float. Try a couple of practice runs and you'll be ready for business.

We've done this with a canoe, lashing a paddle to the center thwart. A long paddle, or better yet a double-bladed kayak paddle, makes it easier.

Sponsons Balance Your Act

If you're planning to do something that might unbalance your boat—casting a fishing line, focusing a picture, or just settling back for a bit of a breather and a well-deserved lunch—consider strapping on a set of sponsons. Sponsons are longish, narrow tubes that strap to each side of your kayak. With the air squeezed out, they add a little resistance to your forward progress. When inflated they look like puffy bumpers on each side of your cockpit, and they dramatically stabilize and support your kayak. They also make it fairly easy to clamber back into the cockpit (that's relatively speaking—climbing onto a wet kayak in open water is plain hard work, but without a paddle float or sponsons it becomes extremely challenging). If deployed before needed, they well may prevent your having to exercise self-rescue skills.

An interesting variation of the sponson is a big square inflatable (usually with a gas cartridge) pillow. If you do huli (capsize), inflate your pillow and use it for a brace to roll back up.

Rescue with a Little Help from Your Friends

If you suddenly find yourself upside down without a paddle, and the water is not too bumpy, lean forward and stick your hand as far as possible above the water's surface. In a perfect world, one of your paddlemates will glide swiftly into position and nudge his or her bow right into your hand. You can use that bow to brace yourself as you roll up.

CAUTION Rocks and Shoals

Climbing into a boat in open water is hard, whether or not someone is balancing it for you. If the rescuing paddler stretches his or her paddle over both boats just behind the coaming, grasping a coaming and paddle shaft with each hand, it helps to create a stable platform. Now, for a foot up, hang a $2^1/2$-foot-long-or-so loop of rope over the paddle shaft and use that for a first step to slide aboard. Keep your weight as low as possible when coming up out of the water, making each move as smooth as possible.

If you're out of your boat, a second kayak can pull alongside yours. The second paddler can grasp your coaming to stabilize your boat as you squirm back aboard.

If conditions are bouncy, a two-boat rescue system might be too difficult. Your best option may well be for you to climb on a rear deck for a piggyback ride to shore or shelter and have another member of the party tow your boat there.

In the Wake

We've seen descriptions of "Capistrano Flips," where a canoe is held out of the water by two wet paddlers and flipped over. We've seen boat-over-boat and any number of other plans that work well in a protected pool. It's not been our fortune to paddle with anyone who can do these on a river.

If you overturn in the river, get upstream of your boat. A water-filled boat can weigh 1,000 pounds or more, and you don't want to get pinched between it and a rock. If you're paddling tandem, look for your partner. It might be difficult to spot a head in the waves and water, but you must locate anyone else in the water.

With your partner spotted and safe, grab the upstream grab loop or painter on your boat and begin to swim with it toward shore. You'll have to angle into the current to successfully ferry toward the near shore.

The Least You Need to Know

◆ Learn four easy ways to carry your canoe or kayak.

◆ Boarding your canoe or kayak from the side is easy.

◆ Keep your bow to the waves, wind, or current.

◆ Practice tipping over, to be more comfortable when you're paddling.

Chapter **12**

Making Your Canoe Go

In This Chapter

◆ The parts of every stroke

◆ Propelling your canoe forward (and backward)

◆ Using J-strokes to go straight

◆ Sweeping through a turn

◆ Prys and draws for quick turns

You've found the perfect canoe, discovered a paddle that fits you to a T, donned your personal flotation device, and scrambled aboard. Now it's time to learn how to go somewhere. Time to learn how to put the paddle in the water, to head in the direction you want to go, and to turn where and when you want.

Fortunately, that's easy. Every paddle stroke that moves or turns your canoe is made up of small and easily grasped steps. If you can learn to smile, you can learn to paddle!

The Four Canoe Stroke Movements

Every canoe paddle stroke, from extreme whitewater to placid pond play, is made with four distinct and interrelated movements. The start of the stroke, as the paddle blade enters the water, is the catch. You apply power. You remove the blade from the water at the exit. You bring your paddle back to the starting position with the recovery.

When you plant your paddle blade in the water during the catch, you thrust it almost like a spear, with the force aimed right down the shaft. Water shouldn't spray off the face of the paddle blade, and there shouldn't be a sharp splash as you insert it. The blade face should be at right angles to your canoe's keel and as vertical as you can comfortably hold it. The blade should be completely in the water before you start to apply power.

The power in the power phase of the stroke doesn't come from your arms. Your upper hand on the top grip sets and maintains the angle of the paddle blade. Your lower hand, the one nearest the blade, guides the paddle. The power comes from the major muscles of your torso. You wind up those torso muscles as you place the blade in the water, and then you unwind them to bring your canoe up to the paddle.

Your paddle shaft should be long enough so that when you are in the middle of a forward stroke, the upper grip is about mouth or nose high, and the paddle throat, where the blade and shaft meet, is at the water's surface.

(Suzanne Stuhaug)

Extract the paddle from the water at the exit point. Just pull the paddle right up along the line of the shaft. Don't swing the paddle in a huge arc from your shoulder, as if you were attempting to scoop a shovelful of water up at the end of the stroke. Rather than adding power to your stroke, you're merely pulling down against the paddle as you force the canoe downward. That misuse of energy slows you down and tires you out!

Recover by returning your paddle from the exit to the catch. Some paddlers extract their paddle from the water, and then rotate it edge-first to reduce air resistance as they swing it forward. Instead of lifting the paddle out of the water to return to the catch, some paddlers rotate the paddle while it's still in the water, so that the blade edge points along the direction of travel (at right angles to the blade during the power phase), and slice the paddle forward to the catch. This might slightly increase your stability because the blade is in the water and capable of instant bracing (which we'll discuss later in this chapter).

Take careful note of your top hand on the top grip, controlling the angle of the blade. That's the key to many of the paddle strokes you'll be learning in this chapter. Draw an imaginary line straight down your forearm. Draw another line across your four knuckles atop your paddle grip. If the line across your knuckles is more or less per-pendicular (at right angles) to the line down your forearm, your paddle blade is at right angles to the power being exerted during your paddle stroke. Your thumb is neutral, not angled.

During some strokes, as you'll see, the outside edge of your blade—the edge away from the side of your canoe—should be rotated so that it is slightly in front of the other edge during the power portion of the stroke. You set this angle by rotating your upper grip hand so that your thumb points toward you. You don't have to look at the blade to see the angle, just feel your thumb pointing at you.

In other strokes the outside edge should be rotated so that it is somewhat behind the other edge during the power portion of the paddle stroke. You establish this angle by rotating your upper grip hand so that your thumb points away from you, more or less toward the bow.

In all three cases your thumb is the indicator of how much you're angling your paddle blade and in which direction you're angling it.

By changing the angle of the blade during the stroke, you can pull your canoe side-ways, you can turn your canoe, you can prevent your canoe from turning, and you can support your weight on the paddle blade as you regain your balance. And it is all due to the direction you point your thumb.

Your upper grip hand controls the angle of your paddle blade. A neutral thumb, when the line of your knuckles is more or less perpendicular to your forearm, keeps your paddle blade at right angles to the power of your stroke.

(Suzanne Stuhaug)

If you rotate your thumb forward, away from your body, the edge of the blade away from the canoe is rotated ahead of the edge, closer to the canoe.

(Suzanne Stuhaug)

By rotating your thumb inward, toward your body, you rotate your paddle blade so that the outer edge of the paddle blade is behind the inner edge.

(Suzanne Stuhaug)

Don't lean way forward from the waist when initiating your paddle stroke. All this does is make your canoe bob up and down, and every down-bob sinks the bow into denser water—in effect slamming on the brakes.

Keep erect in your canoe. The urge to lean to your paddle side is seductive. Concentrate on rotating your body and keeping your upper arm about shoulder to chin height and across your body so that your upper hand is over the water. If you lean to the side, you'll tilt your canoe to that side. That changes the whole underwater profile of your canoe and the resistance of the water on the left and right sides of the hull. Your canoe turns, in a spiral, away from the side to which you are leaning.

Moving Your Boat Forward

Rotation is the key to comfortable paddling. You'll see paddlers pushing mightily with their top hand and pulling furiously with their lower hand, but you won't see them paddling that way for long, because their relatively small arm muscles quickly fatigue. Bring the big muscles of your torso and thighs into play and you'll put miles in your wake and still feel refreshed.

Rotate your paddle-side shoulder forward, with your lower (paddle-side) arm straight, at the beginning of a forward stroke. You'll untwist your torso, which pulls your straight arm back, to apply power during the stroke.

(Suzanne Stuhaug)

End the forward stroke just past your hip, with your shoulders at right angles to the canoe's keel line, and your upper hand across your body and over the water on the paddle side.

(Suzanne Stuhaug)

Here's how to paddle properly:

1. Keep your back erect, leaning very slightly forward—no more than about 5 degrees—as you plant your paddle at the catch. Your arms should be fairly straight, and you shouldn't bend your elbows during the stroke.

2. Bring your paddle-blade-side shoulder forward by rotating your body as you bring the blade forward to the catch, where you insert the paddle blade. You're winding up your power.

3. Thrust your paddle blade into the water. You'll feel the blade grab the water and stick in place. Your upper hand thumb should be in the neutral position, with the paddle blade at right angles to the keel line of the canoe.

> **In the Wake**
>
> Keep the paddle shaft as close as possible to the side of your canoe. The farther out from the side of the canoe your paddle (and paddling force) is, the greater the tendency of the canoe is to turn away from the paddle side.

4. Unwind by rotating your body toward your paddle. Your paddle-side shoulder will come back, until a line drawn across your shoulders will be about at right angles to the centerline of the canoe (the imaginary line drawn directly from the point of the bow to the point of the stern). Rotating beyond that point doesn't add anything to your stroke. Your upper hand keeps the paddle blade at right angles to your canoe's centerline. Your upper hand should be just out over the water on the paddle side of the canoe, keeping the paddle vertical. Your lower hand should be above the gunwale.

5. The rotation of your body pulls your straight lower arm on your paddle shaft. Because of the position of the blade, the water is providing a lot of resistance—and you can feel this in your hips and legs. Pull your canoe up to your stationary paddle. If you are able to concentrate on your paddle, where the blade enters the water, you might see a few small lines of turbulence curl out from the power face of the blade. There is a bit of paddle motion. If you were actually pulling the paddle blade through the water, there would be a wake boiling off the blade, stretching ahead of the blade toward the bow of the canoe. That wake ain't there.

6. When your lower hand is back near your hip, and your upper hand has been rotated out over the paddle-side gunwale (the paddle will be tilted approximately 15 degrees forward), you've transmitted all the effective power you can to the blade.

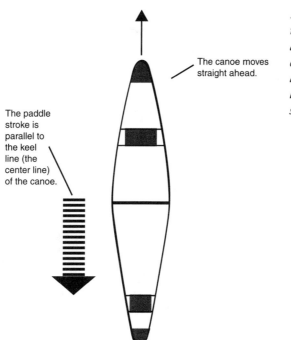

The canoe moves straight ahead.

The paddle stroke is parallel to the keel line (the center line) of the canoe.

During the forward stroke the paddle blade is at right angles to the keel line of the canoe, and the power is applied parallel to the keel line. The canoe moves straight ahead.

7. If you're the bow paddler in a tandem canoe, it's time to recover and prepare for the next stroke. If you're the stern paddler or if you're paddling solo, segue into a J-stroke to keep your canoe heading in a straight line. (You'll learn about corrective strokes such as the J-stroke in just a little bit.)

Heading Backward

There are two good reasons to do a back stroke: to slow down or to back up. And there's one way to do a back stroke: reverse the sequence of actions of a forward stroke.

Start by rotating your upper body toward your paddle side. Insert the paddle blade in the water at or just behind your hip, with your upper hand out over the water, at about chin height, to keep the paddle vertical in the water when seen from the front. Seen from the side, the upper grip may be inclined

CAUTION

Rocks and Shoals

A moving canoe has a lot of inertia. When you insert your paddle blade at the start of a back stroke, a lot of pressure will suddenly be applied to the paddle. This force can yank the paddle out of your hands if you're not prepared, or can wrench your back or shoulders if you're not expecting it. Be ready.

slightly forward, up to about 15 degrees. Your upper hand thumb should be in the neutral position, with the blade at right angles to your canoe's centerline. Your lower hand should be above the line of the gunwale. Unwind your power by rotating your body toward the bow of the canoe and bracing your straight, lower hand against the paddle shaft. Keep your upper hand over the water and the paddle shaft vertical.

Slow or stop your canoe by inserting your paddle blade in the water, right alongside yourself, blade at right angles to the keel line and your direction of travel. To back up, apply power to the paddle blade face toward the bow, with the power parallel to the keel line. Your canoe will move directly backward.

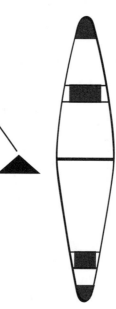

Slow or stop your canoe by inserting your paddle blade in the water right alongside yourself, blade at right angles to the keel line and your direction of travel.

Rotate until your paddle-side shoulder is slightly in front of your off-side shoulder. Your lower hand will probably be a tad bit in front of your upper hand. Pluck the paddle blade from the water.

If you're merely slowing down, you can simply insert the paddle blade in the water at right angles to the canoe's centerline and hold it there. The resistance of the broad face of the paddle will rapidly bleed off your speed.

The Old Paddler Says

During a back stroke, keep your paddle shaft close to the side of your canoe and keep the force applied parallel to the centerline of your canoe. If you start with the blade close to your canoe but let it slew out from the side, you segue into a back sweep, a turning and bracing stroke that turns the bow of the canoe (if done by a solo or stern paddler) toward the paddle side.

If you're backing up, remember to look behind yourself to see where you're going. It will probably be slightly easier to look back over your paddle-side shoulder at the beginning of each back stroke.

Correcting Your Course

You'd have a more efficient forward paddling stroke if you could jam your paddle straight down through the hull of your canoe at the centerline and pull your canoe right over your paddle. In this case, efficiency competes with physics, and efficiency loses. Instead, we paddle just outside of the gunwale, some distance from the centerline, and this lop-sided effort makes your canoe want to turn away from the paddle-side force.

J-Stroke

For most of us, paddling solo or in the stern of a tandem canoe, a J-stroke works just fine to keep our canoe on course. It comes, seamlessly, at the end of a forward stroke. At the exit point, slightly rotate the *power face* of the paddle outward or away from the canoe. The slight outward force kicks the stern of the canoe away from the paddle.

The forward stroke itself tends to turn the canoe bow away from the paddle side, while the J-stroke pushes the stern sideways and negates the turning.

If you were paddling on friction-free ice, the canoe would make a big swooping turn one way (the forward stroke) and then abruptly the other way (the J-stroke). You'd look like a snake trail or a series of linked "S" shapes wiggling forward. In the real world, with a canoe's natural inclination to resist turning, you'll carve a straight wake.

The name of the corrective stroke describes the apparent path of the paddle relative to the canoe. The blade really stays fixed in one place and the canoe moves around it, but it looks as if the paddle carves a capital "J" in the water.

> ### In the Wake
>
> You can learn to do a J-stroke in a few minutes, and can master the mechanics of the stroke in an hour or so of paddling. It will take you 50 miles of paddling before you start instinctively making little corrective strokes just before your canoe starts to curve off course.

> ### Paddlin' Talk
>
> The **power face** is the face of a canoe paddle pressed against the water during a stroke.

Begin the J-stroke more than midway through your forward stroke. As the shaft passes your thigh, rotate the upper grip, putting your thumb forward. This turns the power face outward, away from the canoe. Push the power face of the paddle outward, no more than a few inches. Some paddling instructors advocate levering the paddle shaft off the gunwale if you need a more powerful outward thrust.

The J-stroke corrects the tendency of your canoe to turn away from the paddle side. At the end of a forward stroke, rotate your upper hand so that your thumb is forward, which twists the angle of the paddle blade in the water. Lightly flick the paddle blade outward, which scoots your stern away from the paddle side and your bow slightly toward the paddle side. Done subtly, this keeps you on a straight course.

(Suzanne Stuhaug)

Beware of the rudder as a paddle technique for correcting your canoe's course. It works, to be sure, but it also bleeds off some of the speed and momentum you've worked so hard to achieve. The rudder involves rotating the upper grip so that your upper hand's thumb turns toward you and your little finger follows the extension of your arm. This rotates the power face of the paddle blade toward the canoe. If it is just held in place, the resistance on the back face of the blade functions as a rudder and the canoe bow turns toward the paddle side. If you push the back face of the blade outward, moving the stern away from the paddle, you're prying or levering the stern over a bit. Not only are you losing energy, but a pry works against a canoe's stability. You're losing balance, rather than increasing it. If you really have to yank the stern sideways to avoid a problem, you'll save time and energy by levering your J-stroke off the gunwale, rather than wasting time setting up and pushing a weaker combination of a rudder and a pry.

Paddling with a Switch

Marathon or competition cruiser paddlers have developed a high-efficiency technique to keep their canoe heading in a straight line. Their switch paddling style calls for a set number of paddle strokes on one side of the canoe, and then a switch to the other side—without missing a beat—for a set number of strokes. Their carefully choreographed technique moves a well-tracking canoe very swiftly, without the little slowdowns and extra motions of J-strokes. It works extremely well for practiced paddlers in the right kind of boat.

Off in a New Direction

Changing direction in a canoe is not difficult—in fact, it sometimes happens without your planning for it to happen. Changing directions when you want, as you want, and in the direction you want, is slightly trickier.

At the most basic, altering your course in a canoe involves an act as simple as paddling a little harder on one side. The canoe will gradually arc in the other direction. If you prefer, you can tilt the canoe slightly so that it balances on one of its bilges. This changes its underwater profile, and the canoe will spiral—more or less sharply, depending on the lean—away from the direction of the lean.

You have in your hands, however, the tools to swing a canoe to a new heading within a few feet. Your paddle, and the power to put to that paddle, can make a canoe pirouette and spin like a ballet dancer gone mad. The pry, the draw, the forward sweep, and the reverse sweep are the four overlapping building blocks of quick maneuverability, as well as the foundation for all river paddling.

Making Sweeping Changes

Just for a moment, imagine that your canoe paddle is a humongous spatula and you're about to spread icing on a cake. You've just figured out how to execute a sweep stroke, a combination of a bracing or stabilizing stroke with a sharp turn.

Forward Sweep

The forward sweep is a tool every canoeist needs, because it both turns your canoe and adds speed. Think of it almost as a forward stroke, but with the blade carving a great arc from bow to stern rather than staying close to the canoe hull. The first half of the stroke pushes the bow away from the paddle, while the second half pulls the stern toward the paddle. As a result, the canoe pivots around its midpoint as it maintains or gains speed. That's how the solo paddler does it. The bow paddler in a tandem does only the first half of the stroke, with the paddle going from ahead to straight out to the side of the paddler. The stern paddler catches the paddle as far out to the side as he or she can, straight out from him- or herself, and brings the blade back to the stern very close to the hull.

To start a sweep stroke, rotate your torso just as with a forward stroke, but insert the blade with the power face pointing away from the side of the canoe.

(Suzanne Stuhaug)

Sweep the paddle through an arc, extended to your full reach, from bow to stern with the paddle blade just under the surface. We kept the blade above the surface here, just to show its extended position out from the side of the canoe.

(Suzanne Stuhaug)

Start by keeping your upper grip hand low—no more than shoulder height—while fully extending your bottom grip arm forward to insert the paddle blade well forward. Rotate your lower-hand shoulder forward, just as you did for the forward stroke, to increase your reach. Your upper-grip thumb should be up, on the upper side of the paddle shaft, and the power face of the blade should be out and away from your canoe. Keep your upper-grip hand about breast-pocket high and comfortably bent so that it stays near your chest. Unwind your torso to swing your paddle in a wide arc. Your low upper hand and your straight lower arm will keep the blade in the water but will hold the shaft at a low angle. The paddle blade will be near the surface through-out the stroke. Continue the arc, rotating your shoulders to keep the line of your shoulders following the blade. The farther your paddle extends from the side of your canoe, the better, as this increases the turning force. At the midpoint of the stroke, with the paddle straight out from the side of the canoe, the power face of the paddle is aimed directly astern. From that point on, the power face turns more and more toward the canoe until the exit point at the stern, where the power face is pointing directly at the canoe.

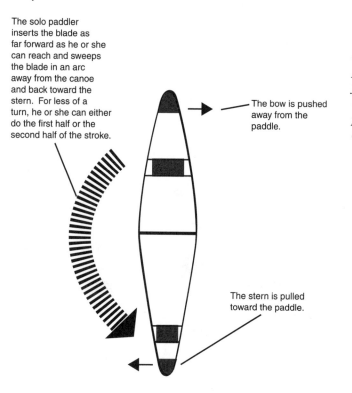

The solo paddler inserts the blade as far forward as he or she can reach and sweeps the blade in an arc away from the canoe and back toward the stern. For less of a turn, he or she can either do the first half or the second half of the stroke.

The bow is pushed away from the paddle.

The stern is pulled toward the paddle.

The forward sweep stroke quickly turns your canoe away from the paddle. The paddle should be extended as far out as possible completely through the stroke, with the paddle blade near the surface of the water.

The Old Paddler Says

Some bow and solo paddlers like to turn the top edge of their paddle just slightly toward the power face, by turning their upper grip thumb a slight bit toward their chest during the sweep stroke. This provides just a bit of lift, helping to lighten the bow and making the canoe turn a little easier. Think of the way you angle a spatula when smearing icing over a cake.

If the bow paddler in a tandem attempts the second half of the stroke, the motion from the midpoint to the exit next to the canoe merely and inefficiently attempts to pull the entire canoe sideways. If the stern paddler in a tandem attempts the first half of the sweep, it's wasted energy, as the stroke attempts to force the entire canoe side-ways, away from the blade.

The bow paddler's forward sweep stroke in a tandem canoe first pushes the bow away from the paddle, beginning the turn, and ends by moving the canoe ahead. The paddle blade, extended as it is from the paddler, also increases the canoe's stability of balance much like reaching out your hand to a tabletop to catch your balance.

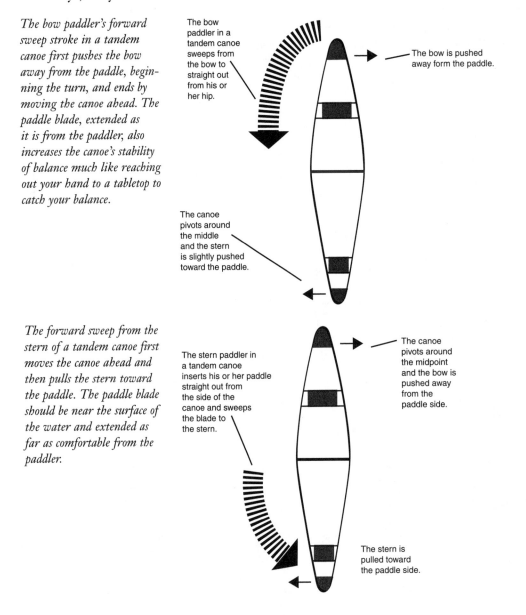

The bow paddler in a tandem canoe sweeps from the bow to straight out from his or her hip.

The bow is pushed away form the paddle.

The canoe pivots around the middle and the stern is slightly pushed toward the paddle.

The forward sweep from the stern of a tandem canoe first moves the canoe ahead and then pulls the stern toward the paddle. The paddle blade should be near the surface of the water and extended as far as comfortable from the paddler.

The stern paddler in a tandem canoe inserts his or her paddle straight out from the side of the canoe and sweeps the blade to the stern.

The canoe pivots around the midpoint and the bow is pushed away from the paddle side.

The stern is pulled toward the paddle side.

Reverse Sweep

The reverse sweep is a massively effective stroke for a sharp turn when you're not worried about losing momentum. It not only stops the boat, but can actually send it scooting backward while executing the turn.

The beginning of the reverse sweep is a mirror image of the end of the forward sweep, other than that the power face of the paddle blade now faces away from the canoe. As you rotate your torso through an arc until your paddle-side shoulder is aimed at the bow, your straight lower arm will push the paddle blade in the same arc.

(Suzanne Stuhaug)

Start by placing the paddle blade next to the boat and behind you, with the power face away from the canoe and your upper-grip hand close to your chest, with your thumb uppermost, aimed toward the sky. The imaginary line across the knuckles of your upper grip hand should be vertical. Your lower-grip arm should be extended straight, and your shoulders and torso should be rotated to the paddle side of the canoe. Unwind your torso, swinging the paddle in a broad arc from bow to stern. Exit just before you bang your paddle into the bow of your canoe.

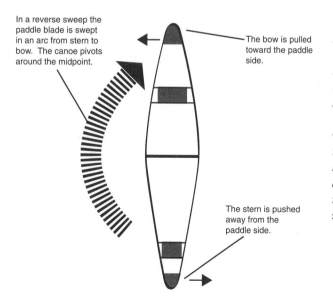

In a reverse sweep the paddle blade is swept in an arc from stern to bow. The canoe pivots around the midpoint.

The bow is pulled toward the paddle side.

The stern is pushed away from the paddle side.

Turn your upper-grip thumb a bit away from you, so that the top edge of the paddle blade is ahead of the lower edge as the paddle is swept in an arc from stern to bow. This angle during the stroke will push the blade upward toward the surface. You can lean your weight on the paddle making your canoe easier to turn and at the same time making the canoe more stable.

Again, you can turn the top edge of your paddle blade slightly forward, rotating your upper-grip thumb slightly away from you, while you execute the stroke. The paddle blade will have a tendency to rise toward the surface, and you can rest some of your weight (a surprising amount, with a little practice) through your lower arm onto the paddle shaft. This lightens the canoe, making it easier to turn.

That's how the solo paddler does the reverse sweep. The stern paddler in a tandem sweeps his or her blade from the back of the canoe to straight out from his or her side, while the bow paddler swings his or her blade from straight out to the side to the bow.

The reverse bow sweep first slows your canoe, much like a back stroke, and then strongly pulls the canoe's bow toward the paddle. It is a very effective stroke while maneuvering in tight quarters.

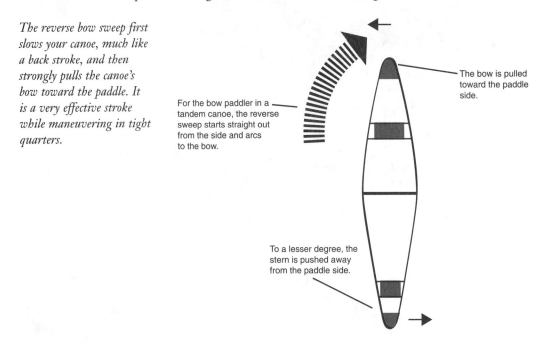

For the bow paddler in a tandem canoe, the reverse sweep starts straight out from the side and arcs to the bow.

The bow is pulled toward the paddle side.

To a lesser degree, the stern is pushed away from the paddle side.

Quick Turns

Most of the time, a gradual turn is best. Any sharp change in direction comes at the cost of boat speed. You've worked hard enough to get your canoe moving and to keep it moving, so why slow it down if you don't have to? You will, however, one day find yourself in a position where you have to turn *right now*. Draw strokes and pry strokes will do that for you. Draws and prys are also the foundation for much of today's canoe river and whitewater techniques.

Drawing Yourself Sideways

The draw stroke is a powerful, bracing stroke that moves your canoe sideways. If you're a solo paddler sitting in the middle, your entire boat will slide sideways when you apply this stroke. If you are a bow or stern paddler in a tandem, your end of the boat will move sideways, pivoting around the canoe's midpoint, and the canoe will swing to a new heading. If the bow paddler does a draw stroke in one direction and the stern paddler duplicates it but on the other side, the boat will spin about its midpoint. If the bow and stern paddlers both do draws on the same side, the canoe slips sideways.

In a draw stroke, you stick the paddle in the water, blade parallel to the keel line of your canoe and straight out from your hip, and pull your canoe sideways toward it.

(Suzanne Stubaug)

Creating that effect is easy if you take it one step at a time:

1. Rotate your torso until your shoulders face the direction that you wish to go.

2. Catch the paddle in the water straight out from your hip, at least a foot and a half away from the side of the canoe and as far as you can comfortably reach. The blade should be parallel to the centerline of your canoe. Your top hand should be arched, higher than your forehead and just in front of it, and out over the water past the gunwale. Both arms should be comfortably straight, and your paddle should be close to vertical in the water.

3. Now try to pull your hip toward the paddle, almost as if you were attempting to twist into a C and touch your hip to your shoulder. Apply more power by pushing down with your upper hand. Your lower hand, holding the shaft, is just the pivot point—you don't actively pull with your lower arm. The net result is that you just scoot yourself sideways up to the paddle.

You can move your canoe directly sideways with a draw stroke, a very effective maneuver in both moving water and on flatwater. You can add a bit of forward or back movement to your canoe by angling the path of your draw stroke slightly forward or back.

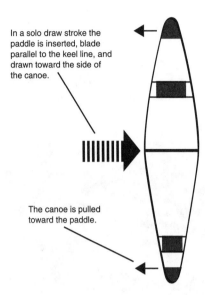

In a solo draw stroke the paddle is inserted, blade parallel to the keel line, and drawn toward the side of the canoe.

The canoe is pulled toward the paddle.

Because you've put the blade well out to the side and put a fair amount of power to the blade, you've really stabilized your boat. To illustrate this point, imagine that you're sitting on the ground with your knees tucked up to your chest. It wouldn't take much of a push to send you rolling over on your side. If you put your hand on the ground, though, with some of your weight on it, you'd be much more stable. As long as you're doing a draw stroke, your hand is out there supporting you.

People often think of a draw stroke as being straight out from the centerline of a canoe. It doesn't have to be, though. You can angle it toward the bow or the stern, combining the sideslip of the draw with a bit of back- or forward stroke.

The draw stroke in a tandem canoe does double duty. If the bow and stern paddlers do draw strokes on opposite sides of their canoe, the canoe spins in a very tight turn. If the two paddlers do their draw strokes on the same side, the canoe is moved sideways, just as if a solo paddler was doing a draw stroke.

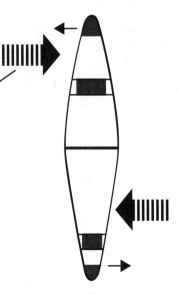

If both the bow and stern paddlers in a tandem do draw strokes, the canoe spins about its middle.

Reaching for a Cross Draw

Sometimes instead of turning toward your paddle side, you'll want to turn quickly away from it. If you're the bow paddler in a tandem canoe or solo, one of the most elegant and precise ways of swinging your bow to the off-paddle-side is with a cross draw. It is a draw stroke, but one with which you reach over your canoe and grab the water on the far side. It works for a bow paddler as well as a solo paddler.

Start your cross draw by inserting the paddle in the water on the opposite side of the canoe. You do this by bringing your upper-grip hand down and toward your chest at breast-pocket level. Your thumb should be pointing up. Swing your lower hand, holding the lower grip, across your canoe. You'll probably want to slide your lower hand up the shaft a few inches, depending how flexible you are. Insert the paddle into the water as far from the canoe side as you can, rotating your shoulders toward that side. The blade should be parallel to the centerline of your canoe. The shaft will point back toward your upper-hand shoulder, because that's how we're assembled. Don't be concerned that the blade is not vertical.

In a cross draw, the paddler reaches over the canoe and executes a draw stroke on the other side. It gives the same general effect as a pry, but offers a little more stability.

(Suzanne Stuhaug)

Unwind your torso so that you face forward, with your shoulders now at about a right angle to the centerline of your canoe. This pulls you toward the paddle blade. During the rotation, your upper-grip hand will push against the grip, bringing the paddle to near-vertical as the canoe approaches. Just before your canoe thumps into the paddle, lower your upper-grip hand (still holding the upper grip) and lift your lower shaft hand to pluck the paddle from the water.

Pry Power

You don't have to cross over to briskly move your canoe away from the paddle side. For sheer power, it's hard to beat the pry. Done in the bow or stern, it pivots your canoe around the center in an abrupt change of direction. Done amidships, it shoots your canoe sideways. The power comes at a price. Draw strokes stabilize your canoe as they move it. A pry stroke does not. You must balance your canoe as you pry.

In a pry stroke, the paddle is inserted in the water as close to the canoe as possible, with the blade parallel to the keel line and perhaps even a bit under the gunwale. The paddler pulls back on the top hand, literally prying the canoe sideways. This is a very powerful stroke, especially in a current, but requires balance, as it doesn't add stability to the maneuver.

(Suzanne Stuhaug)

Insert your paddle blade into the water near the front of your hip, with the blade parallel to the centerline of your canoe. Your upper-grip hand, with your thumb toward the stern, should be around nose to eye height. Rest your lower-grip hand on the gunwale, holding the shaft of the paddle against the gunwale. Rotate your torso toward your paddle. Your top arm should be comfortably straight. The rotation should bring your upper hand out over the water (past the gunwale) and catch the blade of the paddle underneath the edge of your canoe at an angle. Unwind your torso, bringing the line of your shoulders at right angles to the centerline of your canoe and facing you forward. As you do so, in the same motion, strongly pull your top hand toward the center of the canoe. This pivots your paddle around the gunwale, forcing the paddle blade out and pushing your canoe away from the paddle.

Rocks and Shoals

Don't lean away from your paddle during a pry. If you do lean away while executing the stroke, the paddle can exert an upward force against your chine (where the bottom and side of the canoe meet), which can send you toppling over into the water.

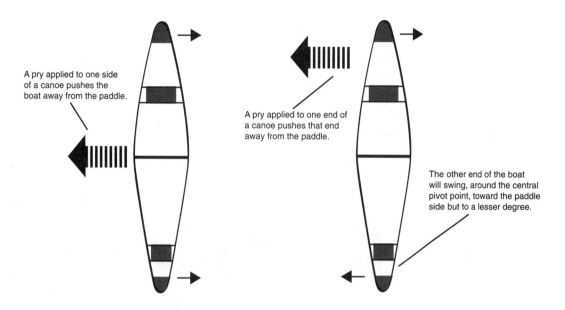

A pry applied to one side of a canoe pushes the boat away from the paddle.

A pry applied to one end of a canoe pushes that end away from the paddle.

The other end of the boat will swing, around the central pivot point, toward the paddle side but to a lesser degree.

A pry stroke by a solo paddler moves the canoe sideways. It can be done very quickly but, unlike the cross draw, it doesn't make the canoe more stable.

A pry stroke applied at either end of a tandem quickly and sharply turns the canoe away from the paddle. If both paddlers do pry strokes on opposite sides, the canoe can completely turn around within its own length.

Bracing Yourself

Braces don't move your canoe or change its speed or its direction. What they do, and do well, is to re-establish your balance once you've lost it. A high brace (merely because the paddle shaft is higher than your wrists) enables you to pull yourself back upright. A low brace (surprise, your paddle shaft is lower than your wrists) enables you to push yourself back upright. You choose which one to use by which way you are toppling over. If you're falling toward the paddle side, a low brace will stop you and push you up. If you're falling away from your paddle, a high brace will catch the water and let you pull yourself toward it, and upright.

Learning to lean your canoe is the key to happy paddling, and learning the bracing strokes is your key to confident leaning. When you can catch your balance at will you won't feel as if you're teetering over the edge of the water. Lean your canoe and you stabilize—balance, if you prefer—when crossing from one current to another. A lean helps you to maintain a course in wind, avoid getting a face-full or lap-full of water in waves, and is the foundation for many paddling maneuvers. Braces are the paddle maneuver you need when you've misjudged your lean and it is a case of paddle or swim. Learn to lean for happier paddling. Learn to brace to keep paddling.

High Brace

The high brace will support your lean while guiding you through a turn. It is a critical part of a quick turn into an eddy across the line between two currents flowing in opposite directions. (You'll learn about eddies and their currents in Chapters 14 and 15, when we go paddling on rivers and on flat water.) It's not as powerful or as controlled as a low brace.

A high brace enables you to stick your paddle in the water, with the shaft above your wrists, and to pull yourself back up if you have lost your balance and have toppled away from the paddle side.

(Suzanne Stuhaug)

Start by putting your paddle across the gunwales just in front of you, with your hands on the paddle grips. Bend your elbows and bring your hands and the paddle up to your chest. Extend the paddle to your *onside*, the same side as your paddle blade, and place the paddle blade on the water. Keep the elbow of your lower-grip arm forward and low to prevent joint or shoulder injury. By pulling with your lower arm, you'll pull yourself to the paddle and erect.

Paddlin' Talk

The same side of a canoe as a paddle stroke is called the **onside**.

Sculling High Brace

You can increase the effectiveness and length of a high brace, even taking into consideration its normally lower power, by sculling the blade. Start your high brace, but as you place the blade on the water, slightly lift one edge of the blade and move the blade a couple of feet or so in the direction of the raised blade. This will cause the blade to rise to the surface, much like you did as a kid when you put your hand out the window of a moving car and tilted it to let your hand rise in the airstream. At the end of the lateral motion, reverse the angle of the blade, so that the other edge is up, and bring the blade back. You can, with practice, keep this back-and-forth motion up for quite some time and, in doing so, totally support your brace (and canoe!).

Low Brace

Start the low brace with your hands low, with your upper-grip hand across your body and over the water outside the gunwale and your lower-grip arm extended straight from the shoulder. Your top-grip thumb should face the bow. Your top-grip hand should be lower than your bottom-grip hand. Rotate your torso and shoulders, facing your paddle. Flop your paddle blade flat on the water. (Some people like to slap their blades down with a bang and splash. It doesn't make them grab the water any faster, but it is kinda fun.)

Paddlin' Talk

Offside is the opposite side of a canoe or kayak from a paddle stroke.

In a low brace, lay your paddle blade flat on the water and push up to regain your balance if you've started to topple toward your paddle side. Note that the paddle shaft is below the paddler's wrists. The low brace can be combined with a stern reverse sweep when angled back toward the stern for a smooth and powerful turn.

(Suzanne Stuhaug)

Keeping your body rigid, lean like a bell out over your on-paddle side. The precise moment you begin to feel your weight on the paddle shaft, lift up on your on-side knee (the knee closest to your paddle) and push down with your other knee. This will bring your boat back to level. Pull up and in with your upper-grip hand, and push down (against the water) with your lower-grip hand. As you finish the brace, your upper-grip hand will be right in front of your belly button.

You don't want your big old head (we're not kidding, or teasing) unbalancing everything. Keep your head down throughout the whole bracing maneuver, and recover by bringing it low in front of you as the brace is completed.

Want to hold that brace longer? Try sculling, just like in the high brace.

A low brace is easy to do and it gives you a lot of confidence while paddling. It can be *too* comfortable to use, and you might be tempted to rely on it rather than using a high brace or balancing your canoe with a lean. Remember that a low brace is only one of many paddling techniques at your disposal.

The Old Paddler Says

Practice the strokes, prys, and braces in calm water, and, if you have a choice, in warm water. Paddlers make many jokes about swimming as a component of learning, and all the jokes have a large kernel of truth within them. You should explore the outer limits of your skills in controlled situations, so that you know just how far you can stretch the boundaries of possibility. Capsizing is not an act of failure, but an affirmation of your willingness to learn. Push, practice, and push some more.

Doing It in Tandem

Two paddlers functioning as a team are far more powerful than their individual parts. On the other hand, two paddlers each attempting to dominate a paddling situation lead, at best, to confusion and, more likely, to discord and an upset.

It's up to the bow paddler to set the paddling cadence. If the bow paddles raggedly or irregularly, the stern paddler will be frustrated and exhausted. The timing of the paddling strokes has to be such that the stern paddler can match the stroke or provide a supporting stroke following the bow paddler's lead. The bow paddler must remember that the canoe extends out behind his position, and he must make allowances for how wind, wave, obstacles and current affect the back half of the canoe.

The stern paddler has to follow the short term lead of the bow. Whatever course of action the bow initiates must be followed by matching strokes out of the stern. The bow paddler has a far better view of the water immediately in front of the canoe, and can react more quickly to what he or she sees. The stern paddler has a far better view of how the canoe aligns to the projected course and has a great range of strokes to align the canoe with the bow's movements. If the bow paddler prys, for example, to line up with a narrow opening, the stern paddler must draw to bring the canoe sideways. If the bow paddler sees an obstruction immediately ahead and begins to back-paddle, the stern paddler must not only aid in the back-paddle, but can draw, sweep, or pry to maintain the proper alignment to the wind, to the waves, or to the current.

Paddling a tandem canoe is much like waltzing, with the stern following the lead of the bow.

Practice the strokes slowly, if need be, and see how you can link one stroke to the next in a combination that moves your canoe to where you wish to be.

The Least You Need to Know

- ◆ Rotating your torso is the key to effective paddling.

- ◆ Going ahead involves a combination of strokes, forward as well as a J-stroke. Learn to use the strokes in combination to control your canoe.

- ◆ You can pry to pull your canoe around a tight corner, whether you are in the currents of a river or in calm water.

- ◆ A bracing stroke allows you to quickly regain your balance.

Chapter **13**

Making Your Kayak Go

In This Chapter

- ◆ The twists and turns of going ahead
- ◆ Putting on the brakes
- ◆ Changing your course
- ◆ Supporting yourself with a brace

It's funny that we speak of the sport of kayaking. The kayak simply floats there, with us in it, while it's the paddle that propels us across the water. We also tend to think of a number of different kinds of strokes. Yet paddlers out on the water meld the motions of several strokes together, seamlessly blending one into the next in a ballet of energy-conserving motion.

All of us learn the basics of each stroke as a series of steps leading us through the mechanics of each action. We paddle, however, as a flow of energy throughout our bodies, along the paddle, toward our destination. We also, as we think about it, discriminate between the kinds of strokes. In the kayak, we'll start with a bit of one stroke, segue into the power of another, and end with a little kick-turn from yet a third paddle maneuver. We mix and match our basic strokes, creating variations and in-between strokes as the situation and our perception of it dictate. We invent paddling as we paddle.

The Art and Truth of Paddling

Paddlers, as a community, have discovered certain truths. To avoid reinventing the wheel—or, in this case, the paddle—take these tips to heart:

♦ **Use the big muscles of your torso and upper body, to paddle efficiently.** Those big muscles are way more powerful than the smaller muscles of your arms, and will enable you to put more power into play over a longer period of time without fatiguing yourself.

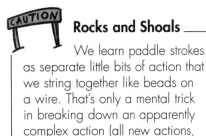

Rocks and Shoals _____

We learn paddle strokes as separate little bits of action that we string together like beads on a wire. That's only a mental trick in breaking down an apparently complex action (all new actions, in any activity, at first appear complex) into easily understand-able motions. In the real world, a paddle stroke is a seamless flow of action, itself part of a greater constant motion.

The Old Paddler Says _____

Some veteran paddlers talk of a hip flick, and others of a knee lift. They're speaking of the same technique: being able to roll or rock your kayak around its long axis by shifting your lower body. You can rotate your kayak from bal-ancing on one edge to balancing on the other only by changing the weight balance in your hips, and you can do this while keeping your upper body erect and rotat-ing for powerful strokes.

♦ **Keep your arms straight.** Your arms connect your torso to your paddle, and you apply power to your paddle by rotating your torso. If your arms are straight, you pull (with the rotation) right down the line of your bones and tendons, and the muscles of your arms remain pretty well relaxed. If you start a paddle-stroke rotation with your arms bent, you're going to have to burn up energy to keep your arm crooked. Hey, if your arm is bent as you start to rotate and you let your arm straighten, you're not putting any tension or power on the paddle. And you won't be going anywhere.

♦ **Use your lower body to balance your kayak.** Your upper body may be quite busy rotating power into your paddle with a great array of strokes and braces, but your lower body calmly goes about its business of leaning your kayak to the left or right—perhaps to set up a turn or to restore your balance. That's not to imply that you have a physical split personality. It's just that these two activities, so separate in function, take place at the same time.

♦ **Keep your arms in front of you.** That's where the stroke happens. Nantahala Outdoor Center instructors, a canny bunch of paddlers all, encourage beginners to imagine a box in front of them. It's as wide as your shoulders, as high as the crown of your head, and extends down to just above the deck of your kayak.

Anything you do with your paddle happens inside the box. It is a moveable box. If you want to work off the side of your kayak, you may rotate your upper body to face that side and the box moves with your body.

♦ **Last, the muscles of your face determine how well you paddle.** The paddler with a clenched jaw and a grip on the paddle so hard that his or her knuckles are a ridgeline of white mini-mountains is not paddling well. The paddler with a loopy big grin is paddling very well indeed.

Paddlin' Talk

The **throat** is the transition from the paddle shaft to the paddle blade.

Mechanically speaking, you can apply the greatest force to your paddle when your hands are about 4 inches up the shaft from the throat (where the shaft and paddle blade merge into each other), and if you held the paddle over your head with your upper arms horizontal, your elbows would be at right angles.

You can paddle at a higher cadence (the number of strokes per minute) if you bring your hands in a bit more, to where, if you held your paddle up to your shoulders in front of your body horizontally, the knuckles of your index fingers would be just outside of the bone at the top outer edge of your shoulder. You pay for this faster cadence by not being able to apply as much power to each individual stroke.

When you really need to dig down for power, shift into your low paddle gear. You can find it by putting your paddle over your head with your upper arms horizontal and your elbows bent at right angles. Your hands will be in the power position.

(Suzanne Stuhaug)

For a fast paddle cadence, bring your hands in to the high-gear position. Raise your paddle horizontally to shoulder height with your elbows fairly close to your sides, and bring your hands in, right in front of your shoulders. You'll put less power in each stroke, but will multiply your effort with the high number of individual strokes.

(Suzanne Stuhaug)

Forward with Your First Stroke

The kayak forward stroke is a subtle stroke. With a blade on each side, you don't need the corrective moves that keep a canoe heading straight. Every canoe paddle stroke, since it is a couple of feet out from the centerline of the canoe, tends to slew the canoe away from the power of the paddle. In a kayak, the twisting motion on one side is almost instantly countered by power on the other side.

Kayakers aren't concerned with the recovery phase of a forward stroke. Pulling the paddle blade through the power portion of a paddle stroke on one side of the kayak lifts and moves the blade on the other end of the paddle through its recovery phase. When the power portion of the stroke on one side is complete, the blade at the other end of the paddle is poised to plunge into the water to begin the power portion of the stroke on that side. On the surface, this means that a kayak is easier to control—at least while going ahead in a straight line—than a canoe. What it also means is that a kayak requires many more subtle nudges and corrections than a canoe.

Start by sitting erect in your kayak, perhaps leaning forward just a bit. Rotate your upper body away from the side you wish to initiate your first paddle stroke, and extend forward your arm (without a noticeable bend in your elbow) and shoulder on the paddle side. Your offside hand (on the opposite side of the kayak from where you want to place the paddle blade in the water) should be up around eye level and your arm on that side should be just slightly bent and perhaps just a bit forward of your shoulder. Stick your paddle blade in the water, almost to the throat, and feel it grab. Unwind your torso. You'll feel a pull through your lower arm, on the paddle side, and you'll be pushing on the top-hand (paddle blade out of the water) side.

The power part of your stroke dissipates as the shaft passes the front of your cockpit, and ends as the shaft passes your thigh. As you stop rotating your torso, lower your offside hand. Start to bend your onside arm. This will lift the blade from the water around your hips. Extend your offside hand—the hand at the opposite side of a canoe or kayak from a paddle stroke—at about shoulder level, and as the paddle blade comes fully forward you'll find yourself in the proper position to begin a stroke on the opposite side.

> **In the Wake**
>
> If you have tight hamstrings, you'll have trouble rotating. You'll slouch down in your cockpit and lose power. Before you get in your kayak, practice touching your toes to loosen up.

> **The Old Paddler Says**
>
> Force your kayak forward with your feet. As you drive a stroke on the left side, press against your right foot brace. As you drive on the right, press ahead with your left foot.

Wind up your body at the start of a paddle stroke for power and efficiency. The paddle-side arm is straight, the paddle-side shoulder forward, and the torso is rotated to face away from the paddle side.

(Suzanne Stuhaug)

The catch, where the paddle is inserted smoothly into the water, should be up around the paddler's foot.

(Suzanne Stuhaug)

The paddler's upper, nonpaddle-side hand should be out over the water on the paddle side, with the upper arm straight and the torso rotated toward the paddle side.

(Suzanne Stuhaug)

The lifting motion as the paddler extracts the paddle from the water at the end of one stroke positions the other blade for insertion at the start of the next stroke.

(Suzanne Stuhaug)

Keep the paddle blade at right angles to the keel line, and make the apparent motion of the paddle blade through the water parallel to the keel line (the broad arrow). The kayak will move ahead (in the direction of the small arrow).

Stopping with a Back Stroke

Kayaks generally don't come with brakes. If you want to stop, your options are to hit something (bad form) or to learn how to paddle backward. Paddling backward is the easier of the two.

Paddling backward is the foundation of the back-ferry, the technique of paddling in reserve into a current. This enables you to either cross a current without being washed down-current, or enables you to hold your position in a current while you peer down-current to see what awaits you. It's a technique you need in both river and flatwater paddling, and is as vital for tidal flows, waves, or wind as it is in the flow of a river.

If paddling bow-first into a flow strikes you as more efficient, that's because it is. But there are moments when you don't have the time or the room to swing about, and there are times you absolutely must look down-current, and it is more convenient to paddle backward than to crane your head to sneak a peek over your shoulder.

Backing up is like going forward, only the other way around.

Rotate your upper body to your onside, so that you face the side for the first paddle stroke. Bend your onside arm a bit so that you can place the paddle blade in the water at your hip. Your upper, offside arm should be bent at the elbow with that hand at about eye level. The top of your paddle will be canted (or leaning) slightly toward the bow. When seen from the back, your hands will appear to be almost directly one above the other (although from the side your upper hand will be closer to the bow). Now unwind, letting the rotation of your torso power the shaft with your bottom hand. You'll feel as if you're pushing the paddle forward. (You're actually pushing your kayak backward.)

> ### In the Wake
>
> Most paddlers seem to find it convenient always to look back over the same shoulder when back-paddling or back-ferrying. Others switch from one side to the other, with the paddle strokes. Whatever your cup of tea, remember to keep a sharp eye on what's behind you!

Continue the rotation until your onside shoulder is pointing toward the bow and your onside arm is fully extended. You're not going to turn so far as to have a line drawn between your shoulders be parallel to the centerline of your kayak, but push it around as far as you comfortably and smoothly can. At that full extension, lower your offside hand and raise your onside hand. This lifts one blade out of the water and places the other in the catch position to begin the next stroke. If you're paddling exactly the same on both sides, you'll back in a straight line. If you're not, you're going to turn, and this is a good self-check on how you're paddling.

Be careful when stopping. You're slowing a heavy boat with a lot of inertia.

Insert the paddle blade at right angles to the keel line and hold it vertical in the water to slow or stop.

Changing Your Course

Your first time on the water, you'll swear that paddling in a straight line is impossible. You'll wiggle along like a snake on ice. Within a surprisingly short time you'll have those big looping curls shaved down to a reasonably straight line. You can hurry the process along by looking at an object well ahead of you rather than at the bow of your kayak. As the distant object bobbles off your course, you'll instinctually begin to make smaller and smaller corrections—a tad bit more power on one stroke, a bit of a sweep to bring a bow around, or perhaps even a minor lean to initiate a slight turn. You'll discover how to recognize tiny drifts off your course and the mini-corrections that will bring you back on your heading.

That's well and good when you want to go straight. Somewhere, not too far ahead, you're going to want to turn. Here are the strokes and maneuvers you need to initiate those turns where you want them and as sharp as they have to be. Practice them on flatwater, and know that you'll use them on every flatwater and every river trip in your paddling future.

The Old Paddler Says

If you're paddling a touring kayak, don't turn your rudder to smooth out your course. Every time you move your rudder, you add friction and resistance, and that forces you to use way more energy to paddle a given distance or hold a given speed.

Sweeping Ahead with a Turn

The key to happy kayak paddling, whether on a river or on flatwater, is the forward sweep. It enables you to control how fast and how sharply you turn and, while doing so, drives you forward. That keeps your speed and energy balance in the black, since you're not needlessly tossing away the momentum you worked so hard to build. Also, most kayaks are much more stable when they are moving than when they are just bobbing about.

The stroke begins with your paddle midway to low across your chest, with your offside (the side away from the paddle stroke) hand about as high as your breast pocket or the top of your PFD zipper. Straighten your onside (the side nearest the paddle stroke) arm and rotate your upper body so that you're facing away from your stroke side. This puts your paddle blade as far forward as you can reach. Catch the water with the blade. With your onside arm straight, your torso rotated away from the paddle blade, and your offside hand low and near your chest, the power face of the blade in the water will aim out and away from your kayak. Unwind your upper body, bringing the paddle in a broad arc from bow to stern. Keep the blade as far away from your kayak as you can, to accentuate the turning power of the stroke.

Some hints:

- Watch the tip of the paddle blade throughout the arc. This will help you to rotate your upper body to face the paddle side.

- Keep your offside hand (since that side of the paddle is higher during a stroke, it is sometimes called the upper hand) low, about the same height as the top of your PFD zipper. That will keep your paddle shaft as horizontal as possible, emphasizing the outward arc of the paddle blade. Keep the paddle blade submerged throughout the stroke.

- Finish with power! Drive your offside, top hand across your chest at the end of the stroke. This powers the blade toward the stern of your kayak, accelerating the turning motion. Your onside hand is the pivot point around which the paddle shaft swings. Your offside shoulder should be almost pointing at the bow as the stroke is completed, and you should be looking at the blade. At the end of the stroke, the power face of the blade faces the kayak.

During the foreword sweep stroke the paddler rotates his torso as if starting a forward stroke, but inserts the paddle blade with the power face aimed away from the side of the kayak.

(Suzanne Stuhaug)

The blade is swung through a large curve from bow to stern, with the blade extended as far as possible from the kayak at the mid-point to increase the turning force. The blade should be just under the surface. Here the blade is above the surface, merely to show its position.

(Suzanne Stuhaug)

Practice your torso rotation by watching and facing your blade the whole way through the stroke. You can add a little extra kick at the end by driving your upper, non-paddle-side, hand forward as the stroke is completed.

(Suzanne Stuhaug)

The first half of the forward sweep pushes your bow away from the paddle blade, pivoting your kayak around its midpoint. The second half of the stroke pulls your stern toward the paddle, still pivoting around the kayak's middle.

In a double kayak, in moving water or on flatwater, only half the sweep is used by each paddler. The bow paddler uses the first half of a forward sweep to push the bow away, and the last half of a reverse sweep to pull the bow toward the paddle. The stern paddler uses the last half of the forward stroke to pull the stern toward the paddle, or the first half of a reverse sweep to push the stern away from the paddle.

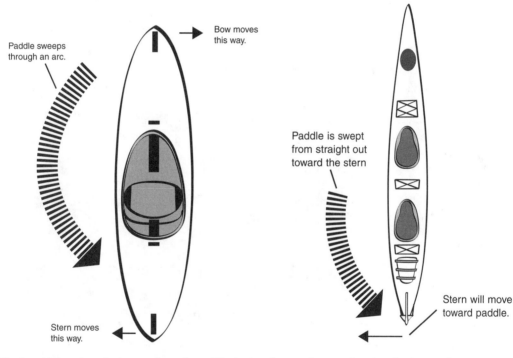

The kayak's bow is pushed away from the paddle during the first half of the solo paddler's forward sweep stroke, and the stern is pulled toward the paddle blade during the last half of the stroke. The combination turns the kayak quickly.

In a tandem kayak, the arc of a sweep stroke is limited from straight out from the kayak to the bow or stern.

Rocks and Shoals

If a bow paddler in a double kayak uses the back half of a forward sweep, he is attempting to pull the midpoint of the kayak toward his paddle rather than helping with a turn. The stern paddler, using the first half of a forward sweep, attempts to push the entire kayak away from her paddle blade, rather than initiating a turn. The same holds true, in opposite, for the reverse sweep.

Reverse Sweep for a Powerful Turn

The reverse stroke is the quickest way to crank yourself around in an immediate turn. It also burns away your forward momentum in one spectacular slew. Newcomers to the water like the reverse sweep because of its great leverage.

To do a reverse sweep, think of a forward sweep, but then do everything backward. Start with your upper body rotated toward the paddle-stroke side, your onside arm straight and fully extended, and your offside hand about breast-pocket height, just in front of your chest. The power face of the blade faces away from your kayak. Keeping your onside arm straight, rotate your upper body so that the paddle scribes a great arc from stern to bow. At the midpoint of the stroke, the paddle blade should be as far away from the side of your kayak as you can reach with your body comfortably erect. At the end of the stroke, with your onside shoulder aimed more or less at the bow and your onside arm still fully extended, the power face of the blade aims at your kayak.

To begin a reverse sweep, the paddler rotates his torso toward the paddle side, inserting the paddle next to the stern with the power face of the blade aimed away from the kayak hull.

(Suzanne Stuhaug)

The paddle blade should be just under the surface of the water (here, it is shown above, but just to illustrate that it is extended away from the hull), and should be vertical in the water as it is swept from stern to bow. The power in the stroke comes from rotating your upper body, not from your arms.

(Suzanne Stuhaug)

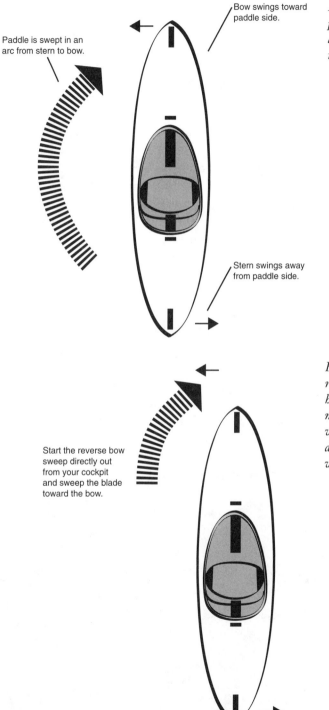

Bow swings toward paddle side.

Paddle is swept in an arc from stern to bow.

In a reverse sweep by a solo paddler, the kayak pivots around the midpoint of the kayak.

Stern swings away from paddle side.

Start the reverse bow sweep directly out from your cockpit and sweep the blade toward the bow.

For a less-abrupt turn, reduce the reverse sweep by half and stroke from the midpoint until the bow. This will pull the bow to the paddle side, but not as much as with a full reverse stroke.

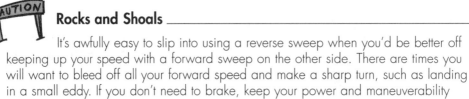

Rocks and Shoals

It's awfully easy to slip into using a reverse sweep when you'd be better off keeping up your speed with a forward sweep on the other side. There are times you will want to bleed off all your forward speed and make a sharp turn, such as landing in a small eddy. If you don't need to brake, keep your power and maneuverability going with the forward sweep.

A neat technique, especially if you're backing up out of the turbulent water in a hole or crossing the bouncy line between two counter-flowing currents, is to tilt the top end of the power face forward, to 45 degrees or thereabouts. When you implement the sweep, the angled blade will attempt to rise to the surface. You can rest a surprising amount of weight on your paddle shaft to keep the blade in the water, stabilizing your kayak and whipping around the turn.

Drawing Yourself Sideways

Want to kick your kayak sideways just a bit? Then draw yourself over there. Rotate your upper body so that you're facing the direction you want to slide your kayak. Both your hands should be out over the water, with your top, offside hand directly over your lower, onside hand. Insert the paddle blade. The power face of the paddle blade should be pointing at the side of your kayak, right about at your hip. Press out with your offside hand, which becomes the pivot point for your paddle shaft. Pull strongly with your lower, onside hand to pull your kayak toward the paddle blade.

The draw stroke is a simple and powerful maneuver that pulls your kayak sideways. It helps steady your kayak, and is a key factor in many turning maneuvers.

(Suzanne Stubaug)

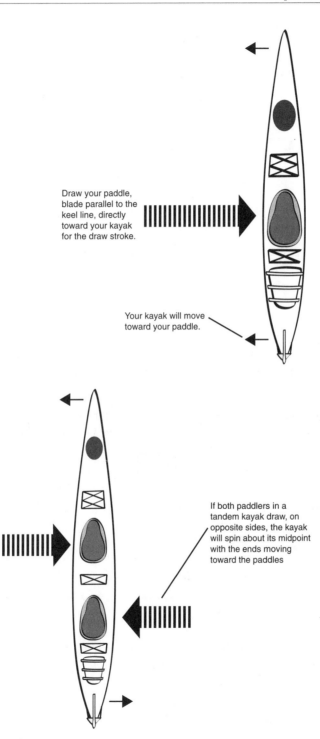

The draw stroke, done in the middle of your kayak, moves your entire boat sideways.

Draw your paddle, blade parallel to the keel line, directly toward your kayak for the draw stroke.

Your kayak will move toward your paddle.

If either paddler does a draw stroke, that end of the kayak will move toward the paddle. If both draw on the same side, the entire boat will slide sideways toward the paddles. If the paddlers draw on opposite sides, the kayak will pivot about its middle.

If both paddlers in a tandem kayak draw, on opposite sides, the kayak will spin about its midpoint with the ends moving toward the paddles

To make your draw stroke work easier, slide your boat toward the paddle blade. Using only your hips, lean your kayak just slightly away from the paddle. Keep your body vertical. This is called, if anyone ever asks, a J-lean—your body is the vertical part of the letter while your leaned or tilted boat is the curved part at the bottom. By leaning your kayak away from the paddle, you raise the side of your kayak and let the relatively flatter surfaces of the bottom of the hull slide toward your paddle blade with less resistance.

> **In the Wake**
>
> Can you pry with a kayak paddle? Sure. But it's easier, in far and away the most circumstances, to use the blade at the other end of your stick and draw yourself over. A draw is more stabilizing than a pry and takes less time to set up and do.

Dragging your kayak sideways through the water isn't easy work. The draw stroke works best for quick, minor corrections. In a double kayak, in flatwater or on a river, a draw stroke will quickly pull the paddler's end of the kayak sideways for a rapid turn.

Using Your Scull to Draw

To smoothly move your kayak directly sideways, and as a neat exercise to feel just how changing the angle of your paddle changes the way it feels and works, try a sculling draw.

Start by rotating your upper body and placing the paddle in the water, with the same hand positions that you'd use to start the regular draw stroke. The blade should be 6 inches to a foot from the side of your kayak—whatever is comfortable. Now, rotate the paddle shaft so that what will become the leading edge of the paddle blade is at a shallow angle—15 to 30 degrees, but you're going to continually adjust this—away from your kayak. With a graceful motion, move your paddle blade through the water parallel to the centerline of your kayak in the direction of the paddle-blade edge you've called the leading edge. The paddle, because of the angle and the play of the water past the moving blade, will try to pull away from the side of your kayak. Your arms are already straight, so instead of widening the gap between the paddle blade and the kayak, your kayak is towed sideways by the blade.

> **Rocks and Shoals**
>
> It's easy to tell if you've reversed the angle of the blade, so that the leading edge is toward you rather than away: The paddle will dart right at your kayak. If you're leaning out over the water, you may follow your nose right into the water.

A sculling brace looks much like a draw stroke or a high brace, other than that the paddle is sliced back and forth (a couple of feet or so) with the leading edge of the blade canted away from the kayak. This pulls the kayak along behind the advancing blade and adds to the boat's stability.

(Suzanne Stuhaug)

After your paddle has moved a couple of feet fore and aft (parallel to the centerline), bring the blade to a halt. Reverse the angle of the blade so that the other edge is now angled away from your kayak. Bring the paddle in the other direction, still parallel to the centerline of your kayak, and feel the blade pull against your arms. The paddle is dragging your kayak along behind it. You only have to move the paddle about 2 to 2¹/₂ feet fore and aft, but seamlessly link the back and forth motion and the reversal of the angle of the leading edge. Play with changing the angle of the blade and the vigor of the stroke.

Brace Yourself for Balanced Paddling

Balance is the key to fun in kayak paddling, and most of your balance comes from your lower body. If you allow your hips and legs to keep your kayak in balance, then your paddle can attend to its business of keeping you moving in the direction you want. That said, most paddlers have mislaid their balance on occasion and learned to appreciate a great brace. The alternative is a roll, and in frigid water or rocky shallows, the brace is a far better choice.

Generally speaking, you hang below a high brace and you pull yourself toward the brace to come upright (or hold yourself upright). You are above, from the perspective of your wrists and elbows, a low brace. You push yourself away from the brace to come upright or to support your position.

Hanging from a High Brace

Because of the double-bladed paddle and because of a lower position in their boat, kayakers tend to rely on their high brace.

Initiate the brace, while you're learning, with your paddle across your deck and hold-ing it with both hands. Bend your elbows and bring your hands up to your chest, less than shoulder high. Keep your elbows close in to your body. Extend the paddle blade out on the side where you're going to put the blade in the water. The shaft should be right over your elbows. Rotate your control hand to put the power face of the blade flat against the water. You'll feel the blade grab the water. As soon as you feel this grab, drop your head toward the blade and use those good balancing hips and legs to lift up on the onside and push down on the offside to regain your balance.

Think of the high brace, with the paddle shaft higher than your wrists, as a fence pole that you can use to lift yourself back vertical if you are falling away from it.

(Suzanne Stuhaug)

If you just want a little support and your kayak is moving, get into a high brace posi-tion, but instead of keeping your paddle blade flat on the water, tilt the leading edge of the blade slightly up. As long as you are moving, the blade will attempt to force its way to the surface and, in trying, will offer support. You can use a current instead of forward movement for the same net effect.

Rocks and Shoals

Protect your joints by keeping your hands at shoulder height or lower, and keeping your elbows tucked in to your body. You can have a lot of force on your paddle blade, and extending your arms can place damaging stress on your shoulders.

If you are relatively still in the water, you can scull the paddle blade back and forth, just like with the sculling draw, and you can support yourself for as long as you keep the scull going.

If you are in white water or surf, a practiced sculling motion will keep your bracing blade from plunging deep into the wet.

Easy Bracing with a Low Paddle

The low brace is a fairly effective stabilizing stroke, as well as a great tool for advanced white water play. It works much like a reverse sweep to hook yourself around in a turn. It also doesn't demand the strength of a high brace.

The low brace is like the arms on a comfortable rocking chair. Push down on the paddle shaft to lift yourself, just as you would on the arms of the chair.

(Suzanne Stuhaug)

Start with the paddle across your deck. With your wrists and elbows above the paddle shaft, lift it and extend the paddle blade over the water. The nonpower face of the paddle should be flat on the water. As soon as the blade is grabbing the water, drop your head to your onside, press down on the paddle shaft, and lift your onside knee to bring your kayak into balance. You can hold that brace for a long time, by sculling the blade as you did in the sculling draw.

A low brace may easily be switched into a reverse sweep by first moving the paddle from straight out to a bit behind your hips, and then propelling the blade forward in an arc. The blade may be rotated until it is vertical, or may have its upper edge angled ahead to provide a bit of support.

Balancing On A Rudder

Imagine that you're balanced on the front of a wave. If you're very brave it could be 6 feet high, if you're cautious 6 inches. Whatever the height, you're sliding down and across this wave in an exhilarating ride. There are little bumps in the water as well as some wind, and your bow wiggles back and forth a bit. You also feel the need for a little more stability. Fortunately, there is the stern rudder.

If you're moving forward, the stern rudder will turn your bow toward the paddle side. You can also balance on the paddle blade when you're surfing on a wave on flat-water or on a river.

(Suzanne Stuhaug)

Start by holding your paddle near the stern of your kayak, with your blade nearly vertical in the water. The paddle should be on the side toward the top of the wave. You can control the direction of the bow just by moving the paddle blade in or out a bit.

Now, rotate the top edge of the blade out away from the side of the kayak a bit. Experiment for a while, to find the angle that works for you. Now you can control the direction of the bow. Feel the water pushing against the inclined blade—it is offering you support and stability as well as control.

The stern rudder is also a handy technique when you are paddling up to a dock or beach in calm water. You can glide toward your landing place, and use a stern rudder to make the final little turns needed to put yourself in exactly the right slot.

The Least You Need to Know

- Body rotation moves your kayak ahead.
- Sweeps turn your kayak to a new direction.
- Draws and prys move your kayak sideways.
- You can support loss of balance with a brace.

Part 5

On the Water

You've spent a lot of time getting ready for it … so now is the time to pull all the skills you've acquired together and head out on the water.

You'll get a pretty good idea of how water works while flowing down a river, as well as a look at the major kinds of obstacles you're liable to encounter along the water. Even better, you'll see how to put your paddling skills to work in coping with those obstacles. These tips and techniques work for canoeists and kayakers alike.

Touring boaters, in their canoes and kayaks, explore lakes, bays, and the ocean itself. You'll see how you can paddle in wind and waves, can find quiet beaches for launching or landing, and even predict the flow of tides and currents. You'll even discover how to cope with an upsetting experience, and do it on your own. We'll also touch on the fundamentals of finding your way on the water.

Chapter **14**

Running the River

In This Chapter

- ◆ Understanding rivers and their difficulty ratings
- ◆ Ferrying your way across currents
- ◆ Turning into and out of eddies
- ◆ Navigating holes, waves, and pillows

Walk up on a sunny hillside some afternoon, balancing a glass of water as you quarter up the flower-dazzled slope. It might be steep enough to make you huff and puff on your way, or it might be so gentle an incline as to be unnoticeable. All that matters is that after a bit of hiking you've gained a few meters of elevation.

Now, with whatever ceremonies you desire, splash the water out over the ground. In that act, you'll find out all you need to know about rivers. They are water running downhill. That little pulse of water might throw itself over an edge and fall free as it sunders itself into foam, might pool up in a declivity, or it might snake along in a series of interconnected S-bends and oxbows. Those are some of the characteristics of rivers. Water flowing downhill.

What All Rivers Have in Common

We've paddled heart-freezing descents when the average *gradient* is 200 or more feet per mile, with turbulent water mounding up on the upstream sides of snaggle-toothed boulders. We've ridden the broad, pulsing breast of Canada's remote Mackenzie, which descends less than 500 feet over 1,000 miles. The loudest noise in the Everglades is the hum of mosquitoes, and you can't even see the tea-dark water nudging its way through the thick water weeds. No matter how different all these waterways are, they all have one thing in common: They are water flowing downhill.

Paddlin' Talk

A **gradient** is a measure of the vertical drop over a given distance. The greater the descent, the steeper and more turbulent the river. However, the river may have miles of near-flat interrupted by a high waterfall, so gradient isn't the sole factor you have to know.

Rocks and Shoals

Imagine that you're leading a group of 47 boats down a river, with skill levels ranging from a very first river trip to paddlers who can (and have) competed at the highest Olympic or World Championship levels. How on Earth are you going keep track of each boat, offer the needed support to those who require it, as well as offer the freedom and space to those who desire it?

Never Paddle Alone

There are rules by which we paddle, evolved by literally hundreds of generations of paddlers, everywhere that people face forward in their boats and propel themselves along the waterways with a paddle. The first, the most basic, is that we never paddle alone. For safety's sake, we travel in no less than groups of three. In the terrible event of accident (and no matter how careful we are, accidents can happen), a party of three boats means that one can stay with the damaged boat or injured paddler on the beach and one can carefully, very carefully, proceed in a search for whatever help is needed.

A party of five boats is probably better than three. It means that one boat can stay with the damaged boat, providing such aid as may be needed, and a party of three can press on in the search for aid.

Bigger is not always better when it comes to paddling parties. Somewhere around seven or nine boats seems to become unwieldy. The group occupies huge sections of river as they spread apart, and communication turns into sporadic bursts of sound. The challenges the first boat discovers and conquers are far out of sight of the middle of the group, much less the back, and carefully planned routes dissolve into mud. The duties of the trip leader become overwhelming as the size expands, too.

Paddlers have learned more than the minimum safe number of boats on the river over the years; they've also learned an effective way to organize the group, taking full advantage of experience and the willingness to learn.

There are two key people on every river paddling trip: the trip leader and the sweep boat.

The Trip Leader's Responsibilities

The trip leader …

♦ Knows the river segment to be paddled, either having paddled it in the recent past or by studying guidebooks, maps, and relying on the experiences of others who have descended that pitch. The trip leader identifies the put-in and take-out, the possible lunch or rest stops, and the alternate take-outs in the event of difficulties.

♦ Usually is the first boat down the river. He or she may delegate another boat to lead a particular segment. No member of the group should ever pass the lead boat.

♦ Determines who will be included on the trip, based on the strength of the overall party, the weather and water conditions, and the skills of each paddler or team.

♦ Explains the route to each paddler, outlining any particular challenges.

♦ Organizes safety backup for any stretch or rapid requiring it. This may range from landing above a rapid and scouting it from the bank to positioning people with *throw bags* (a rope stuffed into a soft bag, which prevents tangling and makes it easy to throw to a person in the water) below a stretch judged challenging for some party members.

♦ If conditions warrant, cancels a trip or cuts a trip short at an alternate take-out.

Paddlin' Talk

A **throw bag** is a fabric bag holding up to 60 feet of line, making it easier to throw one end to a person in the water.

In the Wake

Without fail, keep the boat behind you in sight. If you lose track of the boat behind, signal ahead that you are waiting. By waiting, you keep the party together and will be close enough to offer aid and assistance if necessary.

The Sweep Boat's Responsibilities

The sweep boat is generally occupied by a paddler as skilled as the trip leader, and is literally the last boat in the party, sweeping all else in front of him or her. Because the sweep boat is up-current of the other boats, the paddler can quickly speed to rescue a boat or boaters in trouble.

The sweep boat should carry a full complement of rescue gear and a first-aid kit, with the paddler knowing how to use all of it. Several other boats in the party, including the trip leader, should be similarly equipped.

A third important member of the trip isn't on the river. That's the friend or family holding a copy of the float plan, which outlines the route, the people paddling, the boats, cars left at each end, and the time the party is due home. Few paddlers ever need such a plan, but it is far better to have someone know where you are just in case of the unexpected.

How Difficult Are the Rapids?

Whatever we face we often consider to be the biggest, meanest, most beautiful, tallest … well, you get the picture. We are subjective creatures, all too willing to judge whatever is happening at this moment to be the Plimsoll mark against which all other events are measured. That, however, does us no good when we attempt to determine just how difficult a particular segment of river is. We need an objective, rather than a subjective, standard. Fortunately, such a standard exists.

How difficult will it be to paddle today's stretch of river? What challenges will I face? Although your best advice will come from a paddling buddy who has just run that section of river, you can get a pretty good idea of the skills you need from the International Scale of River Difficulty, as adopted for North American paddlers by the American Whitewater Affiliation. It is a six-step scale of white water difficulty. Within each step are a bunch of sub-classifications, all of which are shaded by the paddlers making the evaluation.

The International Scale of Difficulty

Here are the classifications:

◆ **Class I:** Easy. Expect fast-moving water with riffles and small waves. Few obstructions, all obvious and easily missed with little training. Risk to swimmers is slight; self-rescue is easy.

- **Class II:** Novice. Expect straightforward rapids with wide, clear channels that are evident without scouting. Occasional maneuvering may be required, but rocks and medium-size waves are easily missed by trained paddlers. Swimmers are seldom injured and group assistance, while helpful, is seldom needed. Rapids that are at the upper end of this difficulty range are designated "Class II+".

- **Class III:** Intermediate. Look for rapids with moderate, irregular waves that may be difficult to avoid and that can swamp an open canoe. Complex maneuvers in fast current and good boat control in tight passages or around ledges are often required; large waves or strainers may be present but are easily avoided. Strong eddies and powerful current effects can be found, particularly on large-volume rivers. Scouting is advisable for inexperienced parties. Injuries while swimming are rare; self-rescue is usually easy but group assistance may be required to avoid long swims. Rapids that are at the lower or upper end of this difficulty range are designated "Class III-" or "Class III+" respectively.

- **Class IV:** Advanced. Expect intense, powerful but predictable rapids requiring precise boat handling in turbulent water. Depending on the character of the river, it may feature large, unavoidable waves and holes or constricted passages demanding fast maneuvers under pressure. A fast, reliable eddy turn may be needed to initiate maneuvers, scout rapids, or rest. Rapids may require "must" moves above dangerous hazards. Scouting may be necessary the first time down. Risk of injury to swimmers is moderate to high, and water conditions may make self-rescue difficult. Group assistance for rescue is often essential but requires practiced skills. A strong Eskimo roll is highly recommended. Rapids that are at the lower or upper end of this difficulty range are designated "Class IV-" or "Class IV+" respectively.

- **Class V:** Expert. These are extremely long, obstructed, or very violent rapids that expose a paddler to added risk. Drops may contain large, unavoidable waves and holes or steep, congested chutes with complex, demanding routes. Rapids may continue for long distances between pools, demanding a high level of fitness. What eddies exist may be small, turbulent, or difficult to reach. At the high end of the scale, several of these factors may be combined. Scouting is recommended but may be difficult. Swims are dangerous, and rescue is often difficult even for experts. A very reliable Eskimo roll, proper equipment, extensive experience, and practiced rescue skills are essential. Because of the large range of difficulty that exists beyond class IV, class V is an open-ended, multiple-level scale designated by class V.0, V.1, V.2, and so on. Each of these levels is an order of magnitude more difficult than the last. Here's an example: Increasing difficulty from class V.0 to class V.1 is a similar order of magnitude as increasing from class IV to Class V.0.

♦ **Class VI:** Extreme and exploratory. These runs have almost never been attempted and often exemplify the extremes of difficulty, unpredictability, and danger. The consequences of errors are severe, and rescue may be impossible. These are for teams of experts only, at favorable water levels, after close personal inspection and taking all precautions. After a Class VI rapids has been run many times, its rating may be changed to an appropriate class V.x rating.

From this scale you'll glean an indication of what other paddlers think of a particular rapid or river segment. Although it's a good indication, you must remember that a river is a constantly changing and evolving physical environment.

The challenges of finding your way through a rapid fluctuate with changing water levels and flows, with downed trees, with the scouring of a flood or the damming of a landslide. Relative difficulties climb as temperatures plummet, when the river itself is more remote or inaccessible, or even with the frequency you encounter white water. A single, short Class-III rapid along an otherwise placid river may seem easy, while several essentially similar rapids packed close together may seem dauntingly challenging. It's easy to misunderstand the nuances of a region.

It boils down to paddling cautiously until you develop a feel for the local interpretations of the scale … whether that locale is the other side of your state or at the far end of another continent.

The Three-Step Gauge for Non-White-Water Rivers

If you've taken the classes and acquired the skills to paddle white water with pleasure (and, we suspect, with a bit of élan), the International Scale of River Difficulty is an invaluable tool in assessing the challenges you'll discover on the river.

Many of the rivers in North America, and certainly the huge majority of rivers explored by casual recreational canoeists and kayakers, are placid in nature. Their currents are soft, their shores inviting, and the scenery along their banks a far greater draw than the adrenalin of charging through their riffles. For these rivers, a separate, but no less important, scale has evolved:

♦ **Class A:** Currents of less than two knots. Motion of the current is barely noticeable.

- ◆ **Class B:** Currents of two to four knots. Paddlers may backpaddle against the current relatively easily.

- ◆ **Class C:** Currents of four knots or more. Paddlers may paddle against these currents with some difficulty and for short distances, but will find backpaddling difficult.

What You'll Meet on the River

The river is a dynamic environment. The water moves, and it moves around objects in the river channel. This sets up currents that sometimes collide, sometimes merge, and on occasion reinforce each other. That's just what happens when water runs downhill. As the water surges along from the hilltop to the ocean, it shapes its own channel and builds a variety of identifiable and predictable patterns. You need to look, immediately ahead and well downstream, always watching the water and the space immediately above it. The following sections help you identify what you'll encounter as you ride that water running downhill.

Going with the Flow

A current is simply water in motion. It prefers to travel in a straight line from where it began as rain or snow to where it rests in the ocean. It is deflected, bounced, slewed about, and changed by the various physical features found in the river channel. Get in the habit of looking at the current and figuring out why it moves about as it does. Why is the current stronger on one side of a river, and why does the stronger current suddenly shoot over to the other side? Is this an indication of a deep channel blocked by a large submerged rock?

Generally speaking, the river current will be fastest in the middle of the deepest part of a channel. That may not be in the middle of the river. At a bend, for instance, the river is deepest and swiftest on the outside edge of the river.

The current will increase in speed where the river is constricted, allowing more water to move past a given point, and will decrease in velocity when the river spreads out.

On a typical bend of a river the current will be swiftest along the outside of the bend, where the river will also be deepest. The outside bank will be steep, while the inside of the bend will have a gentle bank often with gravel or sand bars deposited close by the shore.

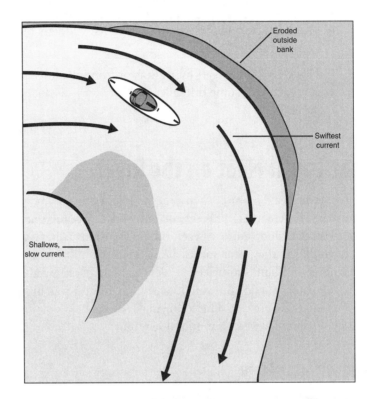

The water current flows to the outside of a bend, moving more swiftly and eroding the river bank on that side. It usually results in a steeper and sometimes even undercut bank, with the possibility of debris or trees toppling into the river.

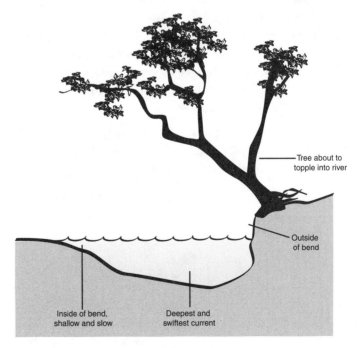

Obstructing the Flow

Rocks—either submerged or visible above the surface—are the most common obstructions in a river. Shallows or bars can form where two rivers join, or where the velocity of the current slows markedly. Bridge piers, dams, rock walls, and other human-made structures obstruct the flow of the water and may also be a hazard to paddlers. Each of these change the flow of the river.

Eddies: The Paddler's Friend

Eddies are the calm areas just downstream from a visible rock or other obstruction. They create a temporary parking place for the canoeist or kayaker. The obstacle deflects the main current, leaving a depression in the water, which is filled in by a reverse current flowing from downstream back into the sheltered area. The line, clearly visible between the eddy and the main current, is called the eddy line.

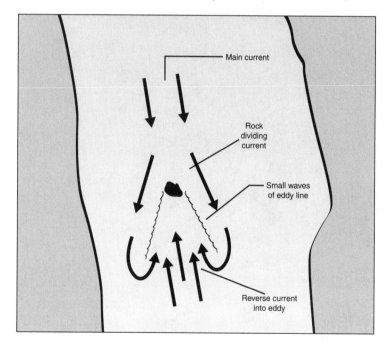

Main current

Rock
dividing
current

Small waves
of eddy line

Reverse current
into eddy

Think of an eddy as a parking place protected from the flow of the river current. You can pause in the calm water of the eddy while figuring out your course downstream to the next resting spot.

Waves, Pillows, and Holes

Water pouring over a submerged obstruction creates a *hole*, also called a *hydraulic*. If the obstruction is large enough and the current is flowing fast enough, that hole will be filled with aerated (and thus white) water. If the force of the current is less and the

Paddlin' Talk _____

A **hole** or **hydraulic** is the usually turbulent depression in the water formed as a current flows over a submerged rock or other obstacle.

obstacle is less blocking the water pouring over the obstruction will not circulate back onto itself. Instead, it will create a series of waves (paddlers call them a *wave train*) downstream of the rock. The waves will stand in one place on the river, and are called *standing waves*. You can watch the river for clues as to the power of the hole. The more the hole looks like a wave, the more likely it will be a fun place in which to play. The waves will be like a roller-coaster ride.

When a river current bumps into an obstacle totally underwater, such as a submerged rock, part of the current will be deflected upward toward the surface. This will create a raised hump or bump in the water called a pillow. If you see a pillow, you know that just upstream of it lies an obstruction. The size of the pillow depends on the force of the current, how deep the obstruction lies, and the size of the obstruction.

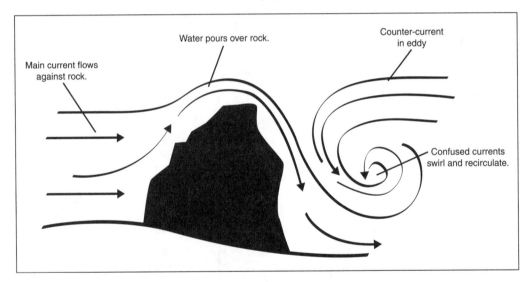

Water pours over rock.

Counter-current in eddy

Main current flows against rock.

Confused currents swirl and recirculate.

A hole or hydraulic is created as a current flows over an obstruction such as a rock. Water flowing over the top of the obstruction joins with water flowing into the hole from downstream (just like an eddy) in an aerated and recirculating ball.

A wave train or a small and smooth depression in the water can be a fun place to play. You can ride through them as if on a roller coaster. You can also use your canoe or kayak like a surfboard, and ride across the upstream faces of the wave or the edge of the depression. If you can see from upstream that the pillow leads into waves, it is probably a good place play.

However, an aerated (that's why the water is white) ball of recirculating energy is not a fun place for a less-experienced paddler. Sharp currents can pull at your canoe or kayak, potentially upsetting you. Downward currents just behind the obstacle can pull you under water and spin you about if you fall from your boat. If you see a well-defined horizonlike line across the water as you approach from upstream and no waves downstream past the line, the hole is probably recirculating and not where you want to be.

A long rock creates a ledge, and water pouring over the top of the ledge can also form a recirculating hydraulic or hole in the water just downstream. For that matter, a human-built weir or low dam creates a water flow just like a natural ledge.

Techniques for Navigating the River

Paddling in a river environment is just the process of linking the basic strokes you learned in Chapter 12 and 13 together in a rhythm. Of course, that's like saying a symphony is just a bunch of notes strung together. If you begin on easy, forgiving rivers and paddle with skilled partners, you'll soon acquire the skills to challenge some very exciting water!

Catch a Ferry

The ferry is the best way to cross a current without being pushed downstream. Start with your bow aimed into the power of the current. Swing your bow so that you are pointed at an angle between the oncoming current and the far bank where you wish to go. Paddle ahead with all your might, and judge where you are in the river. If you're moving upstream, turn a bit more toward the far bank. If you're being pushed downstream, turn your bow a bit more upstream and push on. With a little practice you'll be able to slide sideways across the current to your destination without being pushed downstream.

The ferry is a key technique to learn, particularly for launching. If you push off from the take-out heading downstream, it will be difficult to work your way out of the shallows. The current will push and shove at you, driving you back ashore. But if you head into the current, ferrying out, the current will move you away from the bank and into the great body of the river itself. Which is not a bad thing.

Ferrying across a current.

Boat angles into a current, crabbing sideways without being pushed downstream.

By using the ferry to launch, you can ferry out a few strokes and easily adjust to the rhythm and flow of the river without being swept into the unknown. Even better, if you have forgotten some precious item—your lunch, your raincoat, your shoes—it's easy to reverse your ferry and land at your put-in. If you rushed off downstream, you would have to battle back against the current to regain your launch site and the items you left behind.

While the ferry gets you out on the river, even more important it can get you out of trouble while on the river. If you are paddling down the river and suddenly see a log partially blocking the channel ahead of you, your trusty ferry will move you briskly to the side. By angling your canoe or kayak across the current, with a few paddle strokes you can slip sideways to skirt the obstruction. By linking ferries, first to one side and then the other, you can move in an S-shaped course through a maze of obstacles.

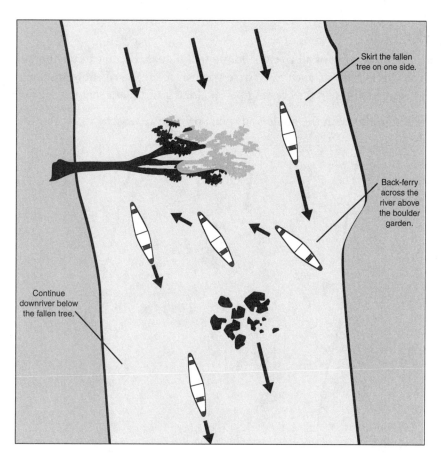

You can ferry your way around obstacles.

Skirt the fallen tree on one side.

Back-ferry across the river above the boulder garden.

Continue downriver below the fallen tree.

You Can Back Against the Current

What if you don't want to spend the time, and take the distance, to turn your boat around and ferry across the river with your bow upstream? You don't have to. Just point your stern in the direction you wish to go, and back-ferry. It works exactly as a forward-ferry, other than that you have converted every stroke into a back stroke and you're proceeding stern-first into the current. Adjust your angle to maintain your position relative to the river bank, and glide across the current in reverse.

Back Paddle for Reverse

What happens when you approach something, anything, you don't quite understand? Put your canoe or kayak in reverse. With a few well-placed paddle strokes in reverse, you can halt your forward progress and hold yourself in mid-river as you scout out what to do next.

Turning in an Eddy

The eddy turn is the most basic of all river-paddling techniques. If you can turn in and out of an eddy, you can rest there, and from there you can scout the river ahead, planning how to hop from resting perch to resting perch along a turbulent segment of river.

Getting into an eddy begins with the angle and speed of your approach.

Approaching the eddy.

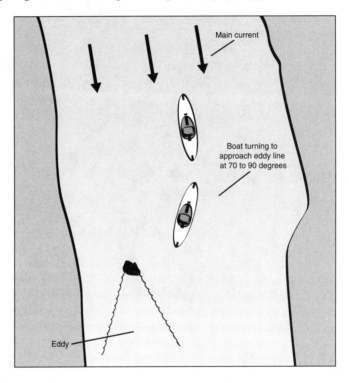

To turn into an eddy, aim to cross the eddy line close to the rock creating the eddy. If possible, you should cross the eddy line at almost a right angle, somewhere in the range of 70 to 90 degrees.

As you cross the eddy line, place a high brace stroke with the paddle blade at right angles across the current flow within the eddy. The current will grab your paddle and pull your bow toward the rock. At the same time, the main current will push your stern downstream and pivot you briskly about. It may be a good idea, in a tandem boat, to make a low brace or a stern sweep stroke off the stern to accelerate your turn and help balance as you cross the currents forming the eddy line.

If all goes well, you'll come to an easy stop with your bow inches from the rock. If you come in too fast, you'll bump the rock. If you come in too tentatively, you might slide right through the eddy to the other side.

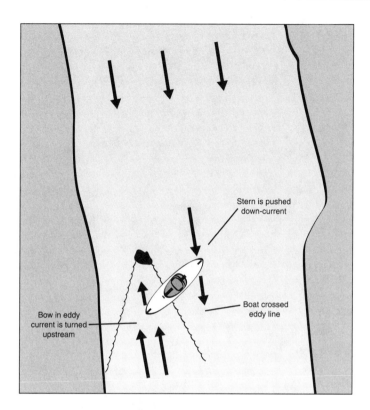

Crossing the eddy line.

If you attempt to cross the eddy line at too sharp an angle, almost parallel to the current, you will find it more difficult to turn your canoe or kayak about so that its bow is pointed upstream. You'll probably just slide right through the eddy and out the other side.

If you are nervous about approaching the eddy-creating rock and enter the eddy well downstream you'll have to paddle very hard to get into the shelter of the rock. You will have to battle against the main current of the river.

Coming out of an eddy is almost the reverse of coming into it. Accelerate up the eddy toward the rock, lean and drive across the eddy line with a slight downstream lean (keep your body vertical, and lean your canoe or kayak with your hips). The main current will grab your bow and spin it downstream while the eddy current pushes against your stern to complete the turn. Some paddlers use the term *peel out* to describe the action of leaving an eddy.

Completed eddy turn.

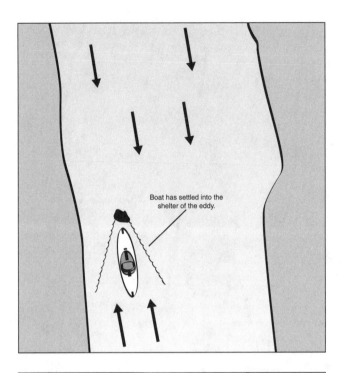

Boat has settled into the shelter of the eddy.

Boat accelerates up the eddy toward the rock, to gain momentum to cross the eddy line.

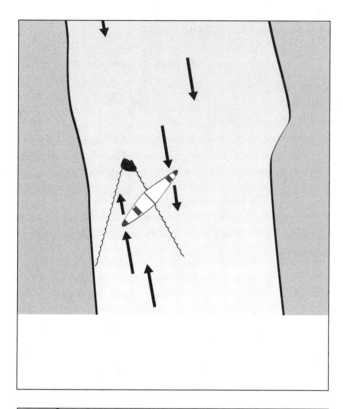

Boat turns to cross the eddy line at 70 to 90 degrees. Both paddlers brace, with the main current pushing the bow downstream, and the eddy current pushing the stern toward the rock in a tight turn.

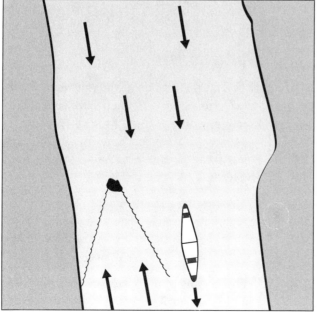

Boat completes turn out of eddy and heads downstream.

Reading the River

When you first look at a river, it appears to be chaos in motion. Whether small or large, steep or placid, quick or plodding, it is filled with undisciplined and unstructured movement. Remember the first day in high-school French, when you opened your book to a page filled with gibberish? Those French seemed to have a different word for everything, and strung them together in illogical rhythms. The river, like the French, has its own language. With a little study (far less than French), you'll be able to understand it and read the movement of the currents with ease. You'll also discover that you'll soon be able to pick out your route along the river.

The language of the river is rich and complex. You'll soon have a grasp of the basics. You can spend the rest of your life in deep study over the nuances and subtlety and still be surprised by the river and its capricious moods.

The Old Paddler Says

Having trouble seeing a vee? Lean over the river, to where you can reach moving water, and stick your finger in the water. See how the water flow splits around your finger and forms a vee shape behind your finger? That's what an obstacle in the river creates.

Rocks and Shoals

Don't be fearful of the upstream vee! It marks an obstruction, to be sure, but it also creates an eddy within the arms of the vee where you can rest out of the flow of the main current. The line of the vee is created by the difference in direction of the main current and the counter-flowing current within the eddy, and can be upsetting to cross for the unwary and unprepared.

Sailors use the terms port and starboard to show direction, without the confusion of someone calling "Over there!" Paddlers also have terms for direction. *River left* always means the left side of the river as seen when you are looking downstream. *River right* always means the right side of the river as seen when looking downstream. If a trip leader suggests that you stay river right, you always know what side of the river he or she means.

Upstream Vees

Look on the surface of the river, and you'll most likely see a clearly defined vee shape etched in the surface, with the apex of the vee pointing directly upstream. It may be a faint line smaller than a ripple on a placid stream, or it might be a foaming line of waves in a turbulent river.

You're seeing the movement of the river current around an obstacle. The obstacle might be visible above the water's surface or it might be out of sight, but that's what creates the vee.

What should you do with an upstream vee? Don't run into whatever created it. If the obstacle protrudes above the surface, skirt it to the side. You might see a bump or pillow of water bulging up on the surface just upstream of the vee. That's formed by water colliding with the obstacle and flowing over it. Again, go around the pillow.

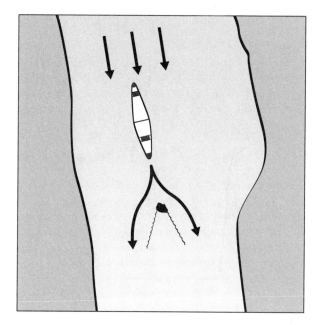

A vee pointing upstream, like the wake of a speedboat, indicates an obstacle above or below the surface. Pass it on whatever side looks clear.

Downstream Vees

A vee in the water with its apex or point aiming downstream usually indicates a clear passage between two obstructions. (Mother Nature doesn't recognize this as an absolute rule, so you have to use a lot of common sense when navigating them.) The downstream vee is really the converging lines formed by the current moving around two separate obstacles, and marks a chute or channel between them. The obstacles, usually rocks, might be visible or might be submerged.

On occasion, you might see what appears to be just half a vee, or one edge of a vee, in the river. This doesn't normally indicate an underwater obstacle. It is a seam, created by two currents meeting at an angle. You'll normally find a seam just below an island, where two river channels converge, or at the confluence of two streams.

A seam can be tricky. One current can dive under the other, creating a zone where the clashing currents can be difficult to read or predict. Try to cross a seam as close to perpendicular as possible, with a good deal of speed.

A vee shape pointing down-stream usually indicates a clear passage between two obstacles.

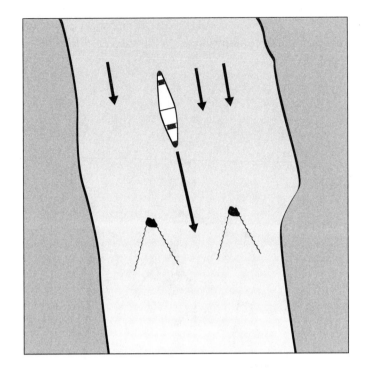

Where the Water Turns White

One obstacle, one upstream or one downstream vee, will not confuse you. If you venture into a boulder garden (just a bunch of rocks sticking up out of the water, like plants growing in a garden), with multiple route possibilities leading into some-times blind passages (a dead end, a channel that is completely blocked), you'll need a longer and clearer look at the river.

Beach somewhere up above this confusing drop and walk down the shore for a closer look. This is not excessive caution but merely good seamanship. See if you can pick out a reasonable course through the white water. Take it one element at a time. Ignore the overall chaos and look for a pattern. If you see the route, great. Take it, with someone down below to catch you if you miscalculate. If you don't see a good route, one in which you are confident you can maneuver through, pick up your canoe or kayak and carry around. That, too, is seamanship of a high order.

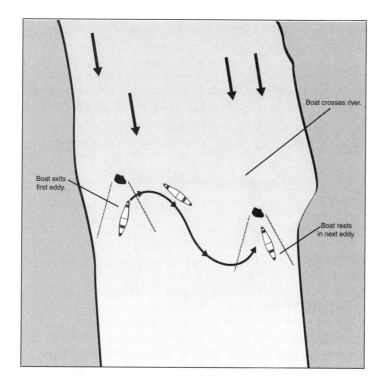

Boat crosses river.

Boat exits first eddy.

Boat rests in next eddy.

When encountering more than one obstacle, take your time and hop your way down river.

Running Through Turbulent Water

White water can be created in either of two ways in a river. The current may collide with an obstacle in its flow, and as the water in the flow splits and flows around the obstacle it can become very turbulent, bouncing and twisting about. Hollow spaces can actually form in the water, creating the air bubbles that turn the water white. Water moving quickly through a number of rocks will bounce back and forth between the rocks, creating waves and froth. That's a classic rapid. One current can collide with another current to create the same thing.

White water can also be created by a change in water flow. Water gains energy as it accelerates—down a steep slope or when constricted in a narrow channel. It yields up that energy when sagging into a horizontal pool or spreading out in a broader channel. That energy turns into waves.

Changes in Water Velocity

Waves grab your attention when you first look at a river. They are not the biggest nor the most difficult of the challenges you'll find on the river, but they are the most visible.

First of all, waves are created as the river attempts to shed excess energy. If the river accelerates down a steep slope, it gains energy. When it slows at the pool at the bottom, it loses energy. It sheds this energy by humping up into waves.

The same thing happens when a river is constricted. The current speeds up, to keep the water moving through the narrower area. Further downstream, as the river expands, this energy is dissipated in a series of waves. Since these waves stand in one place on the river, they are called standing waves. You already saw one example of them when we looked at the wave train formed downstream of a hole. The first wave in a train is the largest, with each following wave a little smaller.

Some paddlers love to knife bow-first into the waves, going for a theme-park ride. Others, attempting to avoid burying their bow and drinking up gallons of foaming river water, like to angle into the waves, at an angle of 30 to 60 degrees, to avoid the sheer climb and the long plunge.

Hazards You May Encounter

Rivers can be dangerous places to paddle. There are hazards in and around the water, and you should be prepared to meet them. We suspect, however (hard evidence being close to impossible to find), that driving to the river is far more dangerous than the river itself, and that crossing the street in front of your house rates as a far more hazardous action than most things you'll encounter with a paddle in your hand.

Logs and Trees Strain Your Safety

A tree toppled into a moving current may well be the single most hazardous object you'll find in a river. The tangle of limbs normally allows the water to flow unimpeded. Any object floating in the current can be swept into the limbs and held there by the force of the current.

Such a fallen tree, called a strainer by river paddlers, is as like as not to be found on the outside of a river bend. That's where the current is strongest and erosion takes place the fastest—and where any object drifting on the current is likely to end up.

Some paddlers, coming into a bend where they cannot see the river ahead, will back-ferry toward the inside of the bend. The water there is normally slower and shallower, and less likely to be barred by a strainer. Other paddlers prefer to angle across the current flow with their bow toward the inside of the turn, and to power ahead if the situation requires.

We already saw how you can ferry around any obstacle. We do the same around a fallen and partially submerged tree, taking extra care because the fallen tree is just a nasty obstacle.

Rocks

Unless they are so closely spaced as to bar your passage, visible rocks are not one of the major challenges on the river. The current forms a pillow of water along the upstream face of the rock, which tends to deflect you off to one side or the other. Unless you manage to hit the rock sideways at the midpoint of your canoe or kayak (that's a *broach* or a *pin*), you'll be flushed downstream with the rest of the water.

Your first and best option is to guide your canoe or kayak away from the rock. Go around it.

Your second option, if you can't avoid thumping sideways into the rock, is to lean toward it. By shifting your weight and leaning, lift the upstream side of your canoe or kayak, so that the current flows under your boat rather than snagging your gunwale or chine and pulling you over. It feels wrong to lean toward the rock, and most of your instincts will cry out that you should lean away from it. Your instincts are wrong. Push yourself around the rock until you can break free and glide away on the current downstream.

Rocks and Shoals

Remember that behind every rock is an eddy, and that the line between the main current and the eddy can be strong and turbulent.

Shallows

Shallow water can be your friend, or it can prove to be a false friend. Generally speaking, the current is slower over shallows, creating a resting zone, either on them or just downstream of them.

On the other hand, a bar or ledge can extend completely across a river, with the current speeding briskly along from bank to bank. If you get turned sideways, the river bottom could snag your canoe or kayak at the keel line and send you tumbling over.

Swimming in deep, unobstructed water is as difficult as swimming in a pool at home, other than that you're wrapped in clothes and footwear and supported by a personal flotation device. Swimming in shallows—including rapids, bars, or anywhere else the water is thin—is another kettle of fish. The major problem facing you is catching your foot under an undercut rock and being pulled underwater. Swim on your back, feet first, with your head upstream and with your feet at the surface. This position enables you to fend off rocks or obstructions without bashing your head. By swimming on your back you can keep your feet close to the surface. If you swim with your feet deep under the water you run the risk of catching them under rocks, an accident that ranges from painful to very, very serious. If your foot becomes trapped, the river current can push you totally under water. Ferry your way across the current to the nearest beach. Swim until your fanny starts bouncing off the bottom. Don't attempt to walk until the water is no more than knee deep, if not shallower.

Abrupt Changes in Height

An abrupt change in river elevation is a fancy way of describing a waterfall. Basically, if the water is falling vertically, avoid it. Yes, there is a whole niche-sport built around shooting over the lip of a waterfall, and it can be done with great élan by the greatly skilled. But you can also break your boat and your body into several pieces by doing it, and that's not any fun.

> ### In the Wake
>
> With a lot of experience and training under your belt, you might try to play in a rapid with a sharp downhill slant and a chain of big waves at the bottom. They can be fun to play in if you've had a fair amount of white-water practice. Be careful, however, as many of these rapids will have a recirculating hole at the base of the drop, which can imprison you in a washing-machine-like turbulence.
>
> The bottom line? Unless you really, really know what you're doing and you're with a party who's highly skilled in white-water rescue, walk around any falls.

The Least You Need to Know

- Trip leaders and sweeps are necessary components of any paddling trip.

- Grab a ferry when you want to cross the river, or move yourself sideways out of difficulties—it's a technique you can't do without.

- You can use an eddy as a temporary parking place out of the current when paddling down a river.

- Fallen trees, rocks, waves: Learn the potential hazards on the river and how to avoid them.

- Trip leaders and sweeps are necessary components of any paddling trip.

Paddling Oceans, Seas, and Lakes

In This Chapter

- Figuring your course
- Finding the best launch site
- Paddling in a current
- Paddling in the wind
- When things get upsetting

Touring with a paddle in your hand is a contemplative activity. You reflect upon what you'd like to do on the water, plan a course of action, and follow that course until you locate your landing at the end of your voyage. We suspect that a big part of the pleasure of the trip comes in the planning. You know the rise and fall of the tides and take them into account, you predict the flow of currents using detailed and uncannily accurate tables, and you locate your route and study your charts. You plunge into guidebooks, swap stories with other paddlers who have ventured there before you, and use your own growing store of experience to translate the printed lines and numbers into predictable experience.

That's not to say that your goal while venturing out onto big water should be to have everything so planned out that you're bored. Rather, the goal is to predict the circumstances most likely to arise during your time on the water, and to establish alternative courses of action to deal with those circumstances.

Launching on Your First Voyage

Every new boater—canoeist or kayaker—should carefully heed two words of advice when making ready to launch his or her boat: Keep calm. That doesn't refer to the boater's emotional state, although that is also good advice. Keeping calm means finding the most protected launch site available, with only ripples sliding up on a gentle sandy beach. Waves even a foot high sloshing up the beach complicate getting in your boat and getting your boat off the beach. Most, but not all, public boat-launch sites are sheltered in bays or behind spits and points. These normally are usable no matter whether it's high or low tide. Many will have a low dock, to aid in launching trailer boats. If the beach is unsuitable—steep or coated in jagged rocks, for example—you should be able to board your boat from this floating structure. In built-up areas, launching areas might even be behind the sheltering arms of a breakwater.

The Old Paddler Says

Build your own guidebook by clipping or copying information from club newsletters, websites, magazines, and books. Then, when you want to venture into an area, you'll have a foundation to build a good trip plan upon.

Sheltered and exposed areas within a bay.

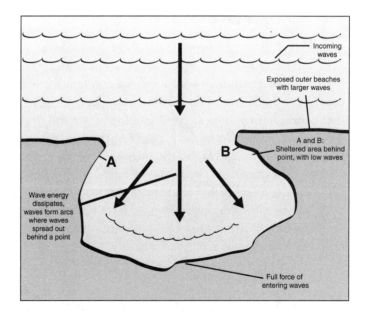

Incoming waves

Exposed outer beaches with larger waves

A and B: Sheltered area behind point, with low waves

Wave energy dissipates, waves form arcs where waves spread out behind a point

Full force of entering waves

In a worst-case scenario, you'll be faced with launching in 1 to 1½-foot-high waves. Larger than that, and you'd be better off roasting marshmallows ashore. Bring your boat to the edge of the water, with the last run-up of each wave coming past your bow and almost to your cockpit. Board, and fasten down your spray deck. Let a couple of the more experienced boaters go out ahead of you, just in case you run into difficulties. As a wave runs under the fore part of your boat, have an experienced paddler give you a healthy shove out into the wave's retreating backwash. Paddle like mad through the waves until you join the others just outside of the surf line—the narrow band of breaking waves or surf between the smooth waves of deep water and the shore. You're going to be pumped! The experienced boaters still ashore will launch in sequence behind you.

Rocks and Shoals ___

Your first instinct will be to stop paddling if a wave splashes over the bow and slaps you in the face when you are paddling out through waves during a launch. Resist that instinct! Keep that paddle stroking to power through a wave and to keep your canoe or kayak more stable.

In Search of Land

Staying calm is never more important than at the end of a day on the water, when you're a little tired and your mind is a little fogged from the weight of the sun and the stimulus of all the things you have seen.

Landing back on the shore requires the same amount of planning you put into preparing for your day on the water. Search out a protected bay with a gently sloping sand or fine gravel beach for your first landings. Even with little wavelets, watch for the pattern of larger and smaller waves to emerge. Charge in to the beach with the onset of the smaller waves, timing your approach to land on the back of the wave as it slides up the beach. You're practicing for a more challenging landing at some future date.

For your first landings, let a more experienced paddler lead the way. As you come ashore, he or she can grab your bow loop and pull you up from the waves. She or he can also help balance you during your exit.

If you miscalculate as you land and the wavelets turn you sideways, lean your boat into the wave (with the boat's bottom toward the beach) and use your paddle to brace on the wave. You can either ride sideways into the beach, using your paddle brace to balance yourself, or once you have regained your balance you can turn your bow to the beach with a forward sweep stroke.

Rocks and Shoals ___

Beware of power-boat wakes. They may well sneak up on you right at the shoreline, when the power boat itself is long past.

Surfing sideways into the beach can be hazardous! If you're being pushed sideways, and your boat grounds and sticks for a moment, you and your boat can be rolled over. It is neither safe nor wise to be bounced off the bottom as a wave twirls you over.

Understanding Currents

Most cruising paddlers will at one time or another ride two kinds of currents: the outflow of streams and rivers into lakes or seas, and the lateral movement of water as a result of tides. Let's consider each in turn.

Rivers Flowing into Seas and Lakes

For most touring paddlers, a river current is something to cross rather than to ride.

When a river enters a lake or salt water, it forms a bay or inlet. It also creates a bar across its mouth. The river current can carry sand or dirt. When the current slows, as the river enters the flatwater, the material falls to the bottom and mounds up into the bar. Waves coming from offshore can crash into this bar, creating a nasty surf. You're more likely to encounter this surf at low tide rather than high (if you are on salt water), or when a wind is blowing toward the shore rather than offshore. Avoid the surf by crossing the river either well offshore beyond the surf or upstream of the bar.

If waves are not breaking at the bar, a river mouth can be a sheltered place to launch. Waves from offshore will lose much of their energy as they spread out in the bay, and you'll find comfortable launching beaches tucked away in the bay.

The river current may force a way through the surf, like the cowcatcher on a railroad locomotive. If the wind and weather conditions let this happen, enjoy it and ride a smooth path out to deep water. If the waves are breaking at the river mouth, launch somewhere else.

The river flow doesn't stop at the mouth. You may be paddling along the shore, beyond the waves, but as you cross the river mouth you may find yourself pushed well offshore. Expecting it, you can ferry into the current for a crossing without a long offshore detour.

You may also find that as you approach a river mouth your apparent speed drops. You are paddling into the current. As you leave a river mouth behind you may find your speed higher than expected. You're being pushed by the river current.

Accommodating the Tides

Time and tide, they say, wait for no man. But the tide does wait upon the passage of the sun and the moon. At its most basic, the tide is merely the vertical movement of water as it is pulled by the gravitational forces of the sun and the moon. The movement of the tide is created as the earth rotates under those same tugs. The water doesn't move (well, at least not as much as the earth), but the earth moves under the bulge of water.

A flood tide means the tide is coming in, or rising. An ebb tide means the water is going out, or receding. Slack is that brief time between the tides.

When the sun and moon pull in the same line, at the full moon and at the new moon, the attraction is greatest and the tides are the most extreme. These are spring tides. When the sun and moon are at the greatest angle to each other, at the waning quarter and the waxing quarter (when the bright face of the moon looks as if it has been lopped in half), the combined pull is at its weakest and the tidal range is at its smallest. These are neap tides.

What's so neat about water going up and down like an elevator? For the cruising paddler, the vertical motion of the tides opens and shuts the door on a wide variety of tidal landscapes.

The state of the tide affects where and how we can land or launch. We may land at the very top of a beach at high tide, bumping our way through drift logs. Six hours and a few minutes later, as the tide has ebbed away from a long, shallow mud beach, we may have to slog through a half mile or more of gooey slop before reaching dry ground. A sheltered passage behind an island that's passable at high tide may dry well before low tide, leaving an alternative course of miles of open sea with waves crashing against sheer cliffs.

Let's get practical. From a tide table we know, to the minute, the time of the high tide, as well as the low. Tide tables are the predicted times and heights of the tides in a region for a year in advance, compiled by the National

The Old Paddler Says

If you want to be spot-on accurate, convert the time span between low and high tide into minutes, and divide by six for the six time periods. Each period will be somewhat longer than 60 minutes, as the tides take a bit longer than six hours to flow or ebb.

Rocks and Shoals

The Rule of 12 predicting water height during any part of the tide fails on those rare places on Earth where the tide comes rushing in as a wall of water, such as Canada's Bay of Fundy or Alaska's Cook Inlet.

Oceanic and Atmospheric Agency (NOAA) and sold for a dollar or so in most marine stores and paddling shops. But how do we know when the tide has crept far enough along to allow us passage over a thin spot? We invoke the ancient Rule of 12.

For a close approximation, note on a piece of paper the vertical distance that the tide will change. The tide will rise one twelfth of the total rise in the first hour, two twelfths in the second hour, three twelfths in the third hour, three twelfths in the fourth hour, two twelfths in the fifth hour, and one twelfth in the sixth hour. As you've probably figured out by these calculations, the tide doesn't move very much in the first and last hours, and it rushes briskly in the third and fourth hours.

The rule works just as well on an ebb tide.

Navigating Tidal Currents

Tidal streams, reversing their direction with every turn of the tide, can carry us effortlessly over vast distances if we harness them. For us paddlers, the tides are a great machine that offers us a choice of repeating, consistent, and predictable currents. Booklets, called Current Tables, available in most marine stores describe the direction and speed of currents during the ebb and flow of tides.

Since the rise or fall of the tide starts slowly, accelerates through the middle of the cycle, and then tapers off, you might assume that the velocity of a tidal current does the same. You'd be right. The current increases from zero at the change of tide, to one third of its maximum predicted speed in the first hour of the tidal cycle, to two thirds of its maximum in the second hour, and reaches three thirds—or, more simply put, all—of its maximum in the third and fourth hours. The velocity will ease to two thirds of maximum in the fifth hour, and in the final hour, will decrease from one third of its maximum to zero at the slack. Again, if you want to be more precise, divide the total time between the two slack tides into six equal increments, each being a bit more than 60 minutes long.

> **In the Wake**
>
> Jot down your distances covered and your time spent paddling over a number of trips—tossing out the days when you practice your sprints and the "take three strokes and then a picture" kind of days. You'll soon see a pattern emerging with your average paddling speed during both your loaded and your empty boat trips.

Calculating Your Speed in a Current

Most touring paddlers cruise at around 3 nautical miles per hour, or 3 knots (3 knots equals 3.45 miles per hour). You can sprint faster than that, for a while, but you will soon sag back to a pace you can hold for hours. A tidal current may flow along at 1 to 2 knots (and paddlers can find currents of 8 to 10 knots, with fierce rapids and waves). If you paddle *with* the current, you'll average 4 to 5 knots over the ground, but you'll only work as if you were paddling your normal 3 knots. You paddle 3 nautical miles in an hour, and the current carries you on another 1 to 2 miles. If you paddle *against* the current, you will only average 1 to 2 knots over the ground, although you will be paddling as if you were covering 3 nautical miles each hour. You paddle 3 miles in an hour, but the current sweeps you back 1 to 2 miles. You can cover 1 nautical mile in an hour, measured from your put-in, or you can cover 5 nautical miles in that same hour just by choosing when in the tidal cycle you want to launch your boat. You might launch at 6 A.M. and fight the full force of the tide for six hours and cover little distance. Or you might launch at noon, and ride the next cycle of the tide over many miles to your planned destination. It's up to you.

Rocks and Shoals _____

In the north, along Puget Sound in Washington and the island-spattered Maine Coast, as well as the Pacific and Atlantic coasts of Canada, the tidal range between low and high tide can be 15 feet or more. If you camp on a gravel beach at low tide, you might be swimming a few hours later.

We've sort of assumed that we'll either have the current pushing us from behind or shoving right into our bow. That's not what happens most of the time. For instance, if we launch from an island and paddle across a channel to our lunch spot, there will likely be a current pushing down the channel, running perpendicular to our desired destination as well as to our boat.

Rocks and Shoals _____

Being swept a mile and a half away from your planned destination can be a half-hour paddling's worth of aggravation. If you're heading for an island only a mile long, it can be a serious problem.

We'll assume that we have started off paddling due west, and the current is pouring due south. If we kept paddling due west, for every foot gained crossing the channel we would be pushed to the south. Even though we kept on the same compass course, we would end up landing well south of our destination.

If we can see our destination, we might simply paddle directly toward it. Each minute we paddle, we'll cross a few more feet of channel, but we'll be swept a few feet to the south. If we keep paddling directly at our destination, we'll be pushed far enough south so that we'll end by paddling almost due north to reach the beach.

The better answer is simply to take a ferry.

Ferrying Across a Current

Let's make another couple of assumptions. The southward flowing current in the channel is 2 knots. We estimate that it will take us 1 hour to cross the 3-mile-wide channel.

In 1 hour, we would be swept 2 nautical miles to the south. We get this number by multiplying the velocity of the current, 2 knots, by the duration we'll be in the current, 1 hour.

Mark your chart right at your planned destination. Measure 2 nautical miles directly up-current from the destination, and make a mark there. Now, draw a line from our put-in to the second, up-current mark. Transfer that line over to the compass rose and determine the course heading along that line.

When you launch, paddle so that your bow is right on that compass course. We're neither heading for, nor plan to arrive at, that upstream mark. Instead, we're crabbing into the current. Our upstream progress should be canceled out by the current pushing us downstream. Because we are at an angle to the current, we are going to glide sort of sideways to the other side without going upstream or downstream.

In the real world, the current will not be the same the whole way across the channel, and we will also be affected by any wind. We will, though, ferry-glide right across to our destination.

The Old Paddler Says

There are two kinds of distances and two kinds of speeds while paddling: one measured against the ground and the other measured against the water. The ground distance between Point A and Point B might be 2 miles. If you're paddling into a current, you might have to paddle across 3 miles of water to cross those 2 miles of bay bottom. If you're paddling with a current, you might only have to paddle across 1 mile of water to cross the 2 miles of ground between the two points.

Because we are heading a bit up-current, it will take us a tad longer ferrying. If we are paddling at 3 knots (close to the average for most touring kayaks) and the channel is 3 nautical miles wide, we will have to paddle about 3.6 miles over the water to cover the 3 nautical miles between our put-in and take-out. And you thought that math in school would never have a practical application!

We found that distance on the same diagram we used to find the compass heading we needed to ferry across the channel. If we measure the distance from our put-in (A on the accompanying drawing) to our destination (B) (using the mileage scale on our chart) it is 3 miles. The line we drew from our destination north to compensate for the tidal current (to C) was 2 miles. We measured that when we drew it. If we measure the line we drew from C to A, the one we used to figure our compass heading, we'll find it to be 3.6 miles long.

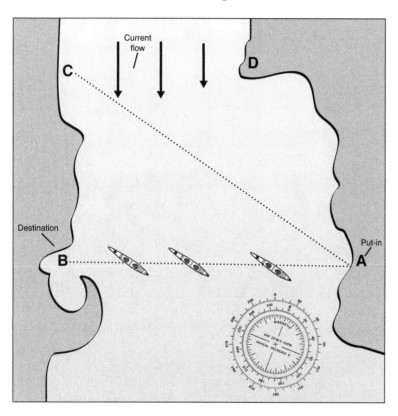

If you try to paddle directly from A to B, you'll be swept well to the south. A reasonable option is to estimate your crossing time and, from that, deduce how far the current will push you. Then measure up-current on your planned landing side of the channel that same distance, here at C, and mark your chart. Draw a line from A to C, and use the compass rose to measure that course. Launch at A and keep your bow pointed on that heading. Your up-current paddling and the down-current flow will cancel each other out, and you'll glide directly from A to B.

Ferrying across the channel is a good solution, but not necessarily the best. In the right conditions, in that same channel, you may be better off to ride the *eddies*, the counter-currents behind the points along the put-in side of the channel north for about 2 nautical miles. Then you can swoop out from the shore and angle across the current, with the current adding to your speed as it pushes from behind. The currents in the eddies will push you from A to D, and the main current will boost your speed from D to B. In many cases, the longer course assisted by following currents will be quicker than a direct course ferrying across a current.

Take advantage of the eddies and current to make a channel crossing easier. Sneak up the shore about 2 miles (how far you'd be pushed down current by a 2-knot current) on the A (Put-in) side of the channel, taking advantage of the counter-currents in the eddies. When you reach D start across the channel getting a boost from the following current to your destination at B.

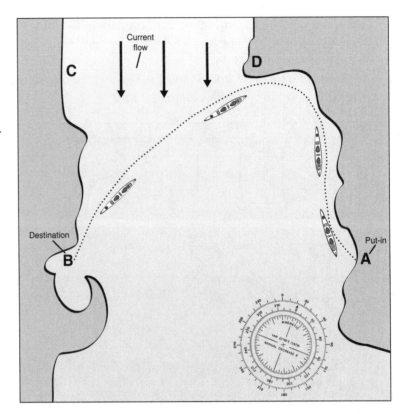

Hopping from Eddy to Eddy

If there are islands or visible rocks spattered across the channel, you don't have to make the entire crossing in one jump. Ferry your way out to the first islet (or go up-current and glide back) and then pop into the eddy behind the islet for a breather. The tail of an eddy reaches farther down-current than you might expect. It will provide shelter from the main current for quite some distance, allowing you to reach the island without fighting the main current. When you hop from one islet over to the next islet, don't be concerned if it is far up-current. Work your way into the tail of the eddy and let the eddy current help you reach the islet.

Paddlin' Talk

Eddies are relatively calmer areas just down-current of a rock or other obstruction, with a current flowing counter to the main current.

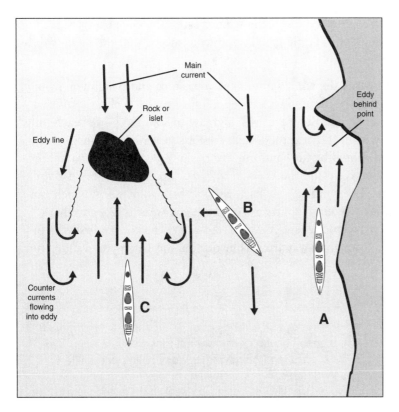

Learn to use the natural and predictable features in the water for easier paddling. Rather than fighting the current the whole way across, duck into an eddy for a breather. Sneak up the shore at A, taking advantage of the eddies formed by the point. Then ferry out, at B, in a glide to the eddy at C, behind the rock.

Paddling in the Wind

Plan on wind being a constant companion while you're on the water. At its friendliest, it will cool you on a warm day and will blow the nasty biting bugs away from you. At worst, it will throw spray in your face, kick up waves, and chill your hands and face.

A wind greater than 10 knots is probably too strong for most inexperienced paddlers. It becomes harder to stay on course. Your boat will feel unstable and wiggly, tensing you up and tiring you out. That force of wind will generate waves a foot and a half high, which not only makes it harder to paddle (and land) but also will hinder any assistance if an inexperienced paddler runs into difficulties.

If the wind blows from straight ahead, right over your bow and in your face, you're in for a few lessons in character building. It will keep pushing, and you'll keep slogging along into

In the Wake

If you're headed into the wind, you'll have an easier time paddling with a feathered paddle. The upper blade slicing edge-forward will cut through the wind much more easily than the broad face of a blade.

the force of wind as well as into the waves the wind creates. On the positive side (we have to look for that), most of the time paddling upwind means that the waves will be getting smaller and less powerful.

If you're paddling downwind, the wind will grab at your stern and twitch you from one side to the other. It can be unnerving, even in a light breeze. It also means that you're going with the waves, and the waves will increase in size and power each mile you paddle. (You'll see why in the next section, as we look at waves.) Riding waves, even little ones, can and should be fun, but only after you've acquired the paddling experience to brace instinctively and the skills to roll back up if your instincts didn't kick in at the right time. The wind at your back will increase your speed, which can be good or bad. It can hurry you on your way to where you want to go, and that's good. It can push you far beyond where you expected to go, during the first part of a day, and can leave you a long, long way from your destination when you want to turn about and head home.

The Old Paddler Says

On one trip we were paddling across a series of open crossings, hopping from islet to islet, with a fresh breeze coming at us from just forward of abeam. We had almost nothing in the kayaks, and one paddler was fighting constantly against his or her boat's tendency to turn downwind. In the shelter of an islet we took a couple of filled water bottles from behind his seat and stashed them as far forward as possible in his or her bow. Just this little weight sank the bow enough so that the lateral resistance of the deeper waterline countered the force of the wind and let him or her paddle straight and with far less energy.

What Makes Waves?

Waves, for the most part, are the children of the wind. They are created by the friction of the wind blowing over the surface of the water. Think of a wave as a cylinder of energy rolling through the water. Individual molecules of water move up and down as the energy passes but are not significantly laterally displaced.

The size of the energy cylinder, and thus the size of the wave, is determined by three factors: the force of the wind, the duration of the wind, and the length of the surface of water (the fetch, in nautical speak) crossed by the wind.

Touring paddlers should understand this wave-making threesome, in practice if not in theory. If you start paddling down a long, narrow fjord with the wind at your back and with small waves helping you along, you may be assured that the waves will keep increasing in size as you paddle along. As long as you are in deep water, this is of academic interest. As you approach shore, or a landing at the end of the fjord, you'll have to contend with significantly bigger waves crashing up on the beach.

> ### CAUTION Rocks and Shoals _____
>
> Bouncing through a train of short, steep waves can be teeth-jarringly annoying. Your bow soars skyward, and then crashes down in the next trough. Your bow plunges into the next wave and, as it rises, throws a face-full of water at you. These waves could even come from the wake of a passing powerboat on an otherwise calm day. Instead of meeting the waves directly bow on, turn so that you cross over them at a slight angle. You'll ride up and over each wave far more smoothly and gently.

If you can find a gentle beach on the far side of an island or behind a sheltering point, you're fine. If such a shelter doesn't exist, then you'll have to land in big waves and foam. For a skilled boater with plenty of experience in *surf*, that's a fairly routine chore (depending on the kind of surf, but we'll get to that in a minute). If you haven't had good surf lessons, you can be in a peck of trouble.

This is a great case for "Know before you go." You can predict an increase in the size of the waves, you can eyeball your chart for safe harbors, and you can estimate roughly how long it will take to reach your destination. If your forecast says "Big waves, hard surf," it's time to exercise caution and stay on the beach.

 Paddlin' Talk _____

Surf is a wave, usually breaking. Surf is also the ability to ride the face of a wave.

Surf's Up

The shape of the sea or lake bottom approaching the beach determines the kind of surf you will encounter. You can get a pretty good idea of the bottom profile by looking at your chart, which marks out depths. Also, look at the colors. On a chart, a sort of dingy green outlines the intertidal area. At high tide, this area is covered by water. At low tide, it is exposed to air. A narrow intertidal area may indicate a steep shore. A wide green band might point to a gradually sloping bottom profile.

The blue on a chart indicates shallow water. If the blue band is wide, the bottom looks to be gently sloping. If the band is narrow, the average gradient looks to be steeper.

Gentle beach and slumping or spilling waves.

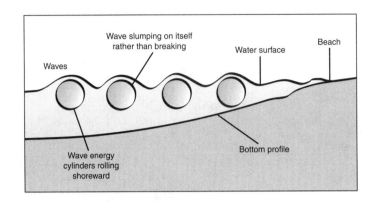

You might also look at the tide tables. As a rule of thumb, the bottom profile is steeper near the high water mark and becomes less steep as you head out into deeper water. If your beach conforms to the rule, you'll have a less steep slope and a better chance of finding friendly slumping surf at a low rather than a high tide.

Avoid Breaking Surf

If the energy cylinder rolling through the water creating your waves runs up against a very steep beach, it will rear out of the surface of the water, but, in doing so, will run out of a reservoir of water that supplies the wave pattern. The back of the wave will arch over the collapsing front, and the wave will break with a huge explosion of energy. Breaking waves make more dramatic pictures. If at all possible, avoid landing in breaking surf without lots of training and experience.

Steep beach, breaking surf.

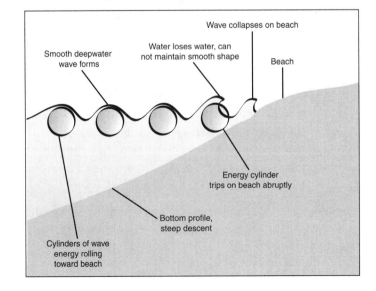

For most casual recreational boaters, figure that a foot to a foot and a half of high surf is about as much as you want to experience, even if it is a gentle, spilling surf.

There's one nasty example of breaking surf that challenges a lot of our expectations. If the wave-energy cylinder rolls up a gentle beach but collides with a large underwater obstacle (a house-sized rock, for instance), it can create a vertical explosion of water called a boomer. Yeah, they truly boom, and the sound and sight can send shivers running up and down your spine. Most nautical charts will mark these reefs and rocks, but some might not be properly identified or even marked. Stay clear of these!

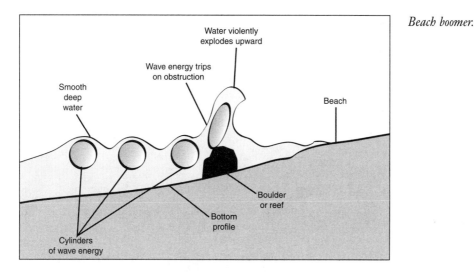

Beach boomer.

Ride the Spilling Surf

If the cylinder of wave energy rolls up on a long, gradually sloping bottom, friction will slacken the wave formation's headlong rush. The wave will slump or spill lower and lower as it progresses. It will dissipate in long, even forms that slosh up on the beach. Gliding up to the shoreline on the backs of one of these friendly waves is a great experience.

It can be hard to see if the waves marching up to a beach are breaking or spilling if you are bobbing in a kayak on the open water. You can sneak toward the outside of the surf line, where the waves start to mound, and look along the upper edge. If you see spray and foam above the lip of the wave (as seen from the back, it is a horizon line), then you can be pretty sure the waves are breaking and should be avoided.

The Old Paddler Says _____

Generally speaking, paddlers on navigable waters use compasses that have a floating disk marked out with all 360 degrees, and the disk rotates to point its north mark at magnetic north. The vast majority of marine charts have a compass rose (a drawing of the compass card) with an outer circle of numbers oriented toward true north, and an inner circle of numbers oriented to magnetic north in the area covered by that specific chart.

Finding Your Way

Learning to find your water across the water with chart and compass is a combination of common sense and the accretion of the skills previous mariners so carefully developed.

On your first few voyages, you should follow in the wake of a more experienced paddler. You should also carry a chart in a waterproof case on the deck ahead of you, as well as a compass. Watch how the trip leader plans the course and predicts the time your party arrives at each of the landmarks, and then duplicate what he or she is doing on your own chart. Write down the compass headings, the distances, and the estimated times for each leg, and make note of currents or the possible effects of wind.

In the Wake

Pick up a copy of Chart No. 1 (in the United States), which is not a chart at all but a dictionary of all the symbols and abbreviations used on a marine chart. The booklet is published by NOAA, and is available anywhere charts are sold.

First, get yourself a chart of the area you plan to paddle. A chart is a detailed sketch of a waterway, including navigation aids, water depths, obstructions, and distinctive shore features. For kayaks and canoes, the largest scale you can find is usually best, as it gives you the most detail. Add in a guidebook, written by a paddler, for a waterside perspective. Also have on hand a compass, a watch, tide tables, current tables, and a waterproof transparent map case.

Piloting starts by pointing at a clearly seen landmark, and saying, "Let's head over there." That works pretty well. You can expand that by saying, "Let's paddle over to the point with the big tree, and then go around the point and land on the beach on the other side." That's a two-segment course.

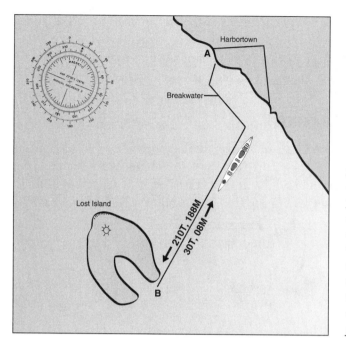

Laying a course from Harbortown to your planned campsite on Lost Island is easy. Draw a line from A, at the entrance to the Harbortown breakwater, to B, the mouth of the bay where you'll camp. Transfer that line over to the compass rose, and read both your magnetic and true courses. Write those above your course, with an arrow for direction. Note the reciprocal course, the other way, and write those down below the course line with an arrow noting direction. If your trip carries you on beyond, just keep drawing those straight lines from landmark to landmark.

If every paddle voyage was along a straight line, figuring your course would be easy. Fortunately, every voyage is in a straight line—if you break down a complex route into short segments, that is. Draw a straight line on your chart from your put-in to the first point on your planned voyage where your direction has to change. Using the scale on your chart and the compass rose, figure your heading and your distance. Write these next to the penciled line you drew.

Now, draw a straight line from that point to the next place where your direction has to change. Repeat these steps, straight segment by straight segment, to your final destination.

> **Rocks and Shoals**
>
> Some folks regard charts as pristine and hate to write on them. Don't be one of those folks. Charts are tools, and you improve them with the information you add to them.

Ranging Ahead

Aiming at a single point has its drawbacks. You can be swept far to the side of your planned course but still have your bow pointed at the same landmark. Your actual course might look like huge curves, which means you're probably paddling greater distances than necessary. If you are aiming along a compass course, you can also be swept sideways and, although you're proceeding in the right direction, you might entirely miss your destination.

Try paddling along ranges. A range is any two clear landmarks (well separated is best) directly along your planned course. As long as you keep the two in line, you're on your planned course. The range marks could be natural—a tree and the peak of an island, say—or might be man-made such as a buoy and a smokestack on the shore.

Think Backward To Find Yourself

You can locate your position accurately by thinking backward. The reciprocal of a compass bearing is its opposite, just 180 degrees different. For instance, if you aim your compass at a landmark and find that it is on a bearing of 270 degrees from you, then the reciprocal—the compass bearing from that landmark back to you—is 90 degrees.

You don't have to have a clear view of where you're headed, as long as you've figured your compass course and can see where you've started. As long as your put-in is at the reciprocal bearing of your planned course (the exact reverse, just 180 degrees different), then you have not been swept off your planned route.

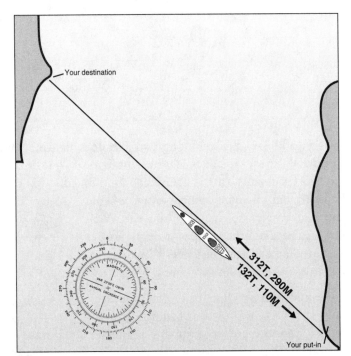

Your destination

312T, 290M
132T, 110M

Your put-in

In the Wake

We divide the compass circle into 360 degrees. To find the reciprocal of any compass heading, either subtract 180 from any compass bearing of more than 180 degrees or add 180 to any compass bearing of less than 180 degrees. You can also place a ruler over a compass rose, with the edge bisecting the center mark and your indicated compass bearing. The reciprocal will be right across the compass circle from your heading.

To use the reciprocal of a compass bearing to locate your position, sight on a landmark—anything you can see clearly. Draw a line along the reciprocal bearing from that landmark back toward you. Write the compass bearing and the reciprocal right on your chart. You're somewhere along that line.

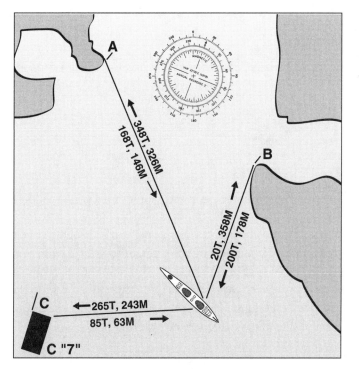

By using your compass backward, by taking reciprocal bearings, you can locate your position if you can see two or more landmarks.

Look off to the side, at a fairly broad angle to your first landmark, and identify another landmark that you can see and that is on your chart. Sight a compass bearing to that landmark, and then draw a line from that landmark along the reciprocal heading back toward yourself. The two lines you've drawn will cross, and that's where you are.

Let's try it in real life, using the accompanying drawing as a chart. From your kayak, take a compass bearing on the black No. 2 buoy at C. It is 265°T (true north). The illustration also shows the magnetic north bearings—use either true or magnetic, depending on your compass. Draw the reciprocal of that heading (the exact opposite, 180 degrees different) from the buoy toward where you might be. In this case, it is 85°T.

Do the same with the point at A, with a bearing from your kayak of 348°T and a reciprocal from the point to your kayak of 168°T. You should be where those two lines cross.

Since you're bobbing around and might not be spang-on accurate, take a sight on the point at B, on a bearing of 20°T and a reciprocal of 200°T. The three penciled lines might cross perfectly, or might mark out a small triangle. You're inside that triangle.

> **The Old Paddler Says**
>
> Most marine compasses, the kind with a disk that rotates rather than a needle that points to magnetic north, have a mark or a line on the body (the nonturning part). This is called a lubber line, and there are usually two. Align those marks parallel to the keel line of your boat. When you do this, one mark will show just what direction your boat is heading and the other mark will show the reciprocal of that course.

Look Back To See Ahead

Usually, you'll paddle toward something you can see. Sometimes you'll paddle in a little low haze, or perhaps right into a bright sun, and you won't be able to see your landmark. Then just keep an eye on the rear-view mirror. You're looking down the reciprocal bearing. If your planned course from your put-in to your destination is 90 degrees, then the reciprocal is 270 degrees. You can read that right off your compass. Every little while, sight back over your stern. If your put-in is still at 270 degrees, then you're right on your planned course. If it is off, say to 250 degrees, then you've been swept off course a bit and need to correct your heading.

When Wrong Is Right

Being wrong is sometimes the right thing to do. If you want to reach a specific spot that you can't clearly identify from the water, and you don't know just how much you're being swept off course by wind or current, your best bet might be to go the wrong way.

Your overnight trip to Foggy Island in the accompanying drawing shows the wisdom of going wrong. You drove to the beach, parked your car, carried your boat to the water, and paddled to Foggy Island for a night's camping. In the morning you looked at the shore through low haze and fog and realized you couldn't see your car.

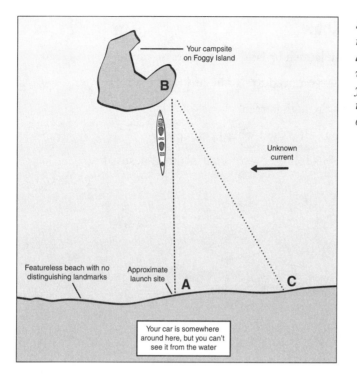

Sometimes, going wrong is the best answer. By deliberately heading to one side of where you hope to land, you'll know which way to turn to find your destination once you reach the land.

You could paddle a compass heading back, but you suspect there is a current of unknown velocity or direction. If you paddle a compass course from B to A, from the island to the beach near your car, you might end up anywhere. If you land just a bit away from your car, you could go the wrong way and spend hours hunting for it. Do you flip a coin? Naw. You go the wrong way. If you paddle from B to C, you'll miss your car way to one side. However, you'll know which way to walk to find it. Are you going to paddle from B to A and trust to luck, or paddle from B to C, walk a bit further, and know where your vehicle is parked?

Piloting a canoe or kayak by finding your way from one landmark to the next is as simple as keeping your eye on where you want to go and heading that way. It is also an art with a huge number of tricks and techniques, the subject of many books and magazine articles. Look in your favorite paddling magazine, look under "Navigation" at your local library, or consider taking a class from your local paddling club, paddling shop, U.S. Power Squadron, or U.S. Coast Guard Auxiliary. Many community colleges also offer piloting and navigation classes.

The Least You Need to Know

- ◆ Where should you launch or land your canoe or kayak?
- ◆ The paddling skills you need to paddle in wind or waves.
- ◆ Finding your way through currents.
- ◆ You can rescue yourself if (and when) you upset.
- ◆ The techniques of paddling toward your planned destination.

Part

Go Paddling

Now it's time to really polish up all those skills you've started to acquire.

Part 6 gives you the nitty-gritty on where you can buff up your paddling techniques, plan a paddling trip, follow into new waters in the wake of a professional guide, enjoy a day on the water with kids, and even build the very boat you dream about paddling.

From your local paddling club to national organizations, a university of paddling instruction is at your fingertips. You can sample an introductory course, or dig in for post-graduate study.

Chapter 16

Jump-Starting Your Paddling Skills

In This Chapter

- ◆ Developing your paddling skills
- ◆ Tapping into clubs
- ◆ Making the grade in school
- ◆ Getting the most out of symposiums
- ◆ Guiding your way to better skills

"Belladonna" is a plant that yields up the deadly poison atropine, at least if you're speaking English. If you're speaking Italian, you're referring to a beautiful lady. It helps to know the language. When you first venture out on the water in a canoe or kayak you'll also have to learn a new language, not only of the names of things but also of the skills and attitudes required to go forth in safety and comfort.

If you really wanted to, you could reinvent all of paddlesports by yourself. By trial and error you could rediscover what paddle strokes worked, which hull shape was best in any particular set of circumstances, how to make clothes that provide protection from sun and cold, and even what waters are the most fun to paddle. You could, but why? A half-dozen excellent options already exist for teaching you the language of paddling. Each will surround you with other paddlers, eager to share their knowledge and equally eager for your companionship on rivers or touring waters.

How do you choose which of the many resources to take advantage of? Do a little looking around, keep an open mind, and remember that paddlesports is way too important to be taken seriously. That's right—it's meant to be fun, and if it isn't fun, it's not worth doing. Golfers take lessons, card players join bridge clubs, dressage riders gather at horse stables. They're all looking for ways to increase their enjoyment of their favorite activity. Paddlers are no different. Here are the key steps in choosing the course you want to follow to paddling proficiency.

Join a Club, Join a Club, Join a Club

Clubs are the backbone of paddlesports in North America. Some are large, spanning many states, with a codified structure. Others are a loose bunch who meet in members' houses or in the back room of a paddling shop to swap stories and plan the next few weeks' adventures. Whether or not they issue membership cards and collect dues, collectively they speak for the more than 20 million paddlers on the waters of North America.

The Old Paddler Says

Paddling is flat-out fun. To increase your fun, increase your knowledge of what you'd like to do and how to achieve it.

Rocks and Shoals

Paddlesports do carry a certain amount of risk, but the risks can be balanced by knowledge. The paddler who is aware of potential hazards can avoid them, but the person who forges ahead without knowledge or care is paddling into danger.

For openers, clubs offer great paddling and technique instruction. Some groups offer members structured classes, but many others provide instruction far more casually, through an informal exchange of tips and techniques among club members during trips and workouts. If you join a club, you'll be exposed to a variety of paddling styles, and by osmosis you'll begin to develop and refine your own style based on what you learn from others.

Second, you'll learn practical boating safety. For instance, if you join a club trip, one of the first things you'll learn is that the absolute safe minimum number of boats—canoes or kayaks—on a river trip is three, and most paddlers will argue that five is a better number. An organized club trip will put at least that many on the water. On the trip you'll learn more than you can possibly imagine. You'll find out that one boat carrying a skilled paddler or paddlers always goes first, and that a designated *sweep boat* always brings up the rear, making sure that no boats lag behind. The sweep paddler is skilled in rescue, in the event of an upset. This system enables new paddlers in the group to focus their efforts on learning to always watch for the boat just behind, the manners of playing in a wave or hole, what rescue and emergency gear should be carried by every boat, and what is required for the group as a whole.

Paddlers like to joke that you're not learning anything if you don't end up swimming on occasion, and every person in a club gains valuable experience assisting paddlers from the water and recovering boats. Perhaps needless to say, they also gain experience in being assisted from the water! Members also have an opportunity, as they progress from a club member to assistant trip leader to *trip leader*, how to plan and organize for a safe trip.

The same holds true whether you're a touring kayaker, flatwater racer, surfer, or marathon paddler. The club provides a nurturing environment for developing paddling skills.

Each club becomes an encyclopedia of detailed knowledge on local rivers and river conditions, based on simple experience. That's a source every new paddler needs to tap in to. The rock almost invisible in the waves at the base of a tongue might have the local name of Ruthie's Rock, and you'll be warned of its lurking presence the first time you line up to descend the current closed in by rocks on each side. One part of a river will be known as an easy float, while just a couple of miles upstream the river is a foaming exercise in high-level boating skills.

Paddlin' Talk

On a river trip, the **sweep boat** is the last boat in the group, which serves as a broom, sweeping all boats in front of it.

The **trip leader** is the person who organizes a trip, decides who may paddle with it, and assigns tasks within the group.

Don't feel left out if a trip leader discourages you (again, using the river paddlers as an example) from participating in a particular trip if he or she worries that the water will offer challenges greater than your skills. However, in many cases a very strong party of skilled paddlers might open ranks to a less-experienced paddler. The less-experienced paddler can follow more experienced members through the technical stretches. If a mishap occurs, the skilled group can make quick work of a rescue.

Paddling with a club, you'll meet paddlers who share your interests and your paddling habits. For less-experienced paddlers, they are an opportunity to learn more about the sport while having a good time. For more experienced paddlers, clubs give members a chance to share the pleasure of the sport with others and to increase its popularity.

Make the Grade in a Paddling School

What's the flat-out quickest way to improve your paddling skills? Immerse yourself in a dedicated paddling school.

What kind of paddler do you want to be? Do you seek out a lonely island on a wine-dark sea? Do white water and foaming rapids fascinate you? Do you yearn for a winding stream penetrating deep into the wilderness? Do heart-pounding effort and the thrill of perfect teamwork stir your juices? Maybe you've never had your feet wet, but still the grace and precision of a canoe or kayak pulls on your soul like a magnet.

The Old Paddler Says

A paddling school immerses you completely in the sport, letting you paddle, talk paddling, watch paddling, and even ruminate on paddling as you eat. You're isolated from all other distractions.

Then there is a paddling school just for you. It doesn't matter if you're a raw beginner trying to learn how to hold a paddle, or a grizzled veteran wanting to hone cutting-edge skills—a week-long paddling school vacation will open your eyes to new possibilities, instill new skills, and possibly make you aware of muscles that you haven't thought about for years.

To get the most out of your paddling vacation, and the most from your instructors, you'll have to ask yourself a set of serious questions:

♦ **What's your passion**? White water, wilderness tripping, sprint racing, or open ocean touring are among the possibilities. You don't have to push for the outer limits of the sport. Many schools open their doors to beginners in every discipline and provide paddlers with a solid foundation in the basic skills for that kind of paddling.

Your passion doesn't have to be, nor probably even should be, the paddling you're most familiar with. Let's assume that you like canoeing on small ponds and placid streams. Then consider a white water kayaking school to open your mind to new pleasures. If you've been kayak-touring for a couple of years and can competently handle your kayak, then explore river canoeing. You'll meet new people and have fun acquiring new skills.

♦ **How would you rate your paddling skills (or lack thereof)?** If you're a beginner, say so. If you're reasonably skilled in one kind of paddling but not necessarily the one you want to learn more about, be upfront about it. If you're really good, don't be shy about saying so. This has nothing to do with modesty. Most schools will have a fairly small ratio of students to instructors. A paddler whose skills are a long way from the norm in that group won't be getting his or her money's worth.

♦ **When can you schedule at least a week of your vacation?** If you're looking for a white-water school, the best of the run-off flows down the channels in late spring and early summer. By late summer and early fall, rivers that were booming in the spring may be reduced to mere trickles. If you want to practice touring skills along either of the Canadian coasts, keep in mind that spring comes late in the north, and it can be downright cold when areas farther south are already have summerlike conditions. On the Texas Gulf Coast, temperatures can be scorching after the summer solstice. The big lakes of Montana, Wyoming, and Colorado offer good kayak-touring water, and they stay relatively mild even during the peak of summer. Don't, however, rule out any area as implausible without checking it out.

Why take a week for a paddling school? Because, for one glorious week you can completely focus on developing new paddling skills. Over breakfast you'll talk about what the day will hold. All morning long you'll paddle, and each hour will unveil a new skill, a new technique, or a correction on a lesson you haven't fully grasped. Sitting on the beach for lunch, you'll go over the morning's successes. Back on the water for the afternoon, and from dinner on into the evening, you'll review what you covered that day. You won't even have time for a lesson to fade from your mind before putting it into practice again the next morning.

You won't have to worry about meals, about shuttling your boat to a new route, about finding water that is neither above nor below your skill level. That's all part of the program.

How good can a school be in jump-starting your paddling learning curve? A basic river/white-water kayaking course can open day-one with complete neophytes gathered on the beach, and by the end of the week, have everyone competently paddling real white water. Some folks could even be starting a self-rescue *river roll*. It probably won't be a bomb-proof works-every-time roll, but you have to start somewhere.

Paddlin' Talk

A **river roll** is the combination of paddle strokes and balance shifts that enable you to turn a capsized canoe or kayak back right side up.

Finding a School

Finding a paddling school is easy. Read the paddlesports magazines: *Canoe & Kayak*, *Kanawa*, *Paddler*, and *Sea Kayaker*. Surf the paddlesports websites: www.acanet.org, www.boatertalk.com, www.canoe-camping.org, www.crca.ca, www.gorp.com, www.paddlingcanada.com, www.outdoorplay.com, or www.paddling.net.

Finding a paddling school that meets your desires and needs takes a little longer, but isn't all that difficult. Ask your local paddlesports shops for their recommendations.

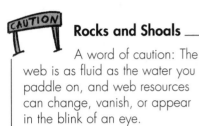

Rocks and Shoals

A word of caution: The web is as fluid as the water you paddle on, and web resources can change, vanish, or appear in the blink of an eye.

Check out the opinions of local paddling club members, especially paddlers whose interests are close to your own.

With a handful of choices gleaned from those resources, ask for brochures from the schools that might interest you. They might look good, they might discourage you, or they might open up new directions for you.

With your list pared down to a manageable size, start asking the hard questions:

- How long has a school been in business? An established business has learned to deal with the quirks of customers, a wide range of unexpected problems or difficulties (even finding lost luggage), and has references you can check. A start-up can bring passion, enthusiasm, and new ideas (as well as new paddling waters), to its students.

- What's the total cost? A bare-bones instruction program might cost $165 per day. Add in lodging, boat use, most meals and the price approaches $2,000 for a seven-day package.

- What, exactly, is being furnished? Accommodations, number of meals, boats, paddling gear, daily transportation, even rental of clothing such as wet suits or dry suits should be figured into your budget.

- What's the ratio of instructors to students? A 1:4 or 1:5 ratio is good.

- What are the certifications and experience of the instructors? Instructor certification by the British Canoe Union is accepted world-wide. Also good are certification from the American Canoe Association, the United States Canoe Association (for marathon racing), and the Canadian Recreational Canoe Association.

- Ask for references from students, especially from near your home.

- What cancellation penalties could you face if you have to opt out?

- What refund guarantees will you have if the school changes dates or cancels a particular class? After all, you may not be able to change your dates.

When you pack your gear to head for your chosen school, remember to include the proper attitude. It's your vacation, you're there to have fun, and you'll come away with greater proficiency in a sport that will offer up more enjoyment because of your time in class.

Close to Home with Local Lessons

You don't have to cross the country in search of competent paddling instruction, and you don't have to carve a week out of your busy life in order to develop your paddling skills. Odds are that you can find evening, day-long, or weekend classes within a short drive of your home.

Where can you mine these little gems? Start with your local paddlesports shops. Many stores offer paddling classes, ranging from basic paddling techniques to some pretty cutting-edge skill development. It's good business for the shop, showing folks how to make best use of their products, and it also showcases the expertise of the staff. Read the bulletin board while you're at the shop. Even if your shop doesn't offer classes itself if may allow local instructors to advertise courses there. Other shops will link up with groups or organizations offering paddlesports or paddlesports-related instruction.

Every paddling club in North America prides itself on offering new members (and prospective new members) a basic introduction of their favored discipline as well as formal or informal instruction in more advanced paddling skills. This can be as structured as the coaching, physical-fitness training, and scheduled workouts of Olympic flatwater sprint kayak and canoe clubs, or as free-form as taking new paddlers under the wing of more experienced paddlers and nurturing them into trip leaders.

The Old Paddler Says

Look for off-season mini-classes offered at indoor swimming pools. The warm water and protected environment make these outstanding venues for learning rolling and other rescue techniques.

Fee-wise, local clubs can be the least expensive way of acquiring paddling knowledge. Each club lesson, though, comes with the unstated obligation of giving at least that much time back to the club and to the sport. You'll find that you'll learn more as a teacher than you ever did as a student.

Check out local park and recreation districts and councils, as well as your local Red Cross, YMCA, YWCA, and community college/adult education catalogs for paddling classes. Most of these tend to be fairly introductory overviews, but that should be enough to give you a good foundation for paddling on local waters.

Go with a Guide

Following the prevailing winds east along Hawaii's Little Na Pali Coast is one of the great kayak-touring routes in North America. You'll see everything from sea turtles to porpoises in the clear water, you'll glide over reefs, you'll bask in the tropical sun, and, as you paddle along, you'll realize that paradise is on your left and Antarctica on your right.

Unless you live on Kauai, how will you know where to launch, to find camping spots? How will you move your gear from one camp to the next? Where can you rent kayaks for the trip?

For your first trip along this tropical treasure trove, bypass these challenges by signing up for a guided trip. You'll also get great meals, an insider's view of local history and sites, and a private paddling instructor coaching you in everything from surf riding to paddle-stroke efficiency.

You don't have to travel to Hawaii to enjoy this level of personalized attention. Touring kayak guides can lead you to up-close-and-personal views of Alaskan glaciers calving icebergs (as well as massive bears), white-water rivers through the canyonlands of the American southwest, the mangroves and shallows of the Florida coastline, and the rocky headlands of Maine.

Rocks and Shoals

A new guide brings energy and passion to the water. An outfit with a longer history most likely is familiar with the challenges associated with moving folks on the water, and has coped with them.

The one thing you won't be is a passive passenger isolated behind a glass wall. Your guide, usually with such a light touch as to be nearly unnoticeable, will raise your paddling skills to a much higher level. It will be an unstructured classroom, in which you won't even notice how he or she nudges you into making the right decisions and choices.

Sample a Symposium

Paddlesports symposiums are a something-for-everyone package shoehorned into a (usually) long weekend and crammed with a variety of speakers, classes, boat-and-gear displays, and try-a-boat demos.

Rocks and Shoals

Do you hanker after an in-depth examination of a focused paddlesports niche, with speaker after speaker covering the same points from different perspectives? Then you'll be disappointed in the vast majority of symposiums. They represent the other side of the introductory spectrum, with speakers addressing as many different topics as there are hours, and with as broad a collection of manufacturers, suppliers, and dealers as can be shoehorned into the facility.

Most symposiums start with a defined topic, which could be regional kayak touring, competition cruiser racing, or waveski competition, just to open the door on the possibilities. Organizers assemble a solid core of experts who talk about significant opportunities, challenges, or questions impacting that particular facet of the sport. For a touring kayak symposium this might include small-craft navigation or deep-water rescue techniques. For marathon canoe competition, this might be the proper blade/shaft angle for a bent-shaft paddle.

In the Wake

You won't have enough time (and energy) to take in every speaker, every event, and every demo opportunity at a symposium. How can you make best use of your time? Start by figuring out in advance what speakers or clinics you'd really like to see. With those time blocks marked out, schedule your shorter available times with look-sees at the shops and displays, and save longer free-time periods for trying out boats and gear.

Building on that focus, organizers invite manufacturers with the latest boats, paddle gear, and related equipment to set up their displays and make their products available for on-the-water demonstrations. You'll find the boats lined up along the nearest beach, ready for you to admire, compare, take for a paddle (and perhaps to buy).

Expect to see, back of the beach, a coterie of shops and suppliers displaying the gear, the clothing, the classes, the guides, and the books you'll feel the need to have after listening to the talks and paddling the boats.

Don't expect to just walk out on the beach and start kicking figurative tires. You'll pay an entrance fee admitting you to the symposium, the speakers, and the displays, usually reduced for a multiday package. Be sure to sign up early, because you may well find that all the slots are filled if you wait until the last day before seeking tickets. Entrance fees range from around the price of a movie admission to well over $100 for a multiday event with international speakers and classes.

Many manufacturers and dealers offer a special symposium price. If you're reasonably interested but want some extra time to make up your mind (and to balance your checkbook), then go ahead and ask for a price extension. Be honest, admit you haven't made up your mind, but make it clear that you're very interested.

Keep in mind, however, that the manufacturers are going to have to pay to get their boats back home, or at least back to their nearest distributor. They also will have to buff and polish each of the hulls back into salable condition. If you buy a boat off the beach with delivery on the last day of the symposium, you could end up getting a real bargain.

The National Organizations

Get involved with one of the national organizations offering a collective voice for North America's 20 million-or-more paddlers. The American Canoe Association is the umbrella organization (with U.S. Canoe/Kayak) for United States Olympic and international sprint and slalom paddling as well as recreational paddlers. The Canadian Recreational Canoeing Association offers similar services in Canada. The American Whitewater Affiliation is a treasure trove of information and support for white-water paddlers. American Rivers addresses river protection and conservation. North American Water Trails pushes for the development of designated water trails across the country. The United States Canoe Association is the parent organization for competition cruiser and marathon racing. You'll discover how to contact these and more organizations in Appendix B in the back of this book.

When you get involved with your local club, you'll be introduced to the spectrum of regional and national bodies speaking for your particular facet of paddlesports.

The Least You Need to Know

- Your paddling pleasure increases with your paddling skills.

- Paddling clubs offer instruction as well as new places to paddle and new people to paddle with.

- Paddling schools range from week-long schools to an evening at a local swimming pool, all of which can jump-start your paddling education.

- Try a guided trip for a great vacation plus the opportunity to improve your paddling skills and knowledge.

- Symposiums are good places to find out more about particular aspects of the sport and to try out new products.

Chapter 17

Planning Your Own Paddling Trip

In This Chapter

- ◆ Learning to plan your trip
- ◆ Determining how far can you paddle
- ◆ What to do if your boat breaks
- ◆ Great places to paddle

A paddling trip, for a day or for a multiweek vacation, isn't necessarily about the repetitious process of paddling your canoe or kayak. In truth, the canoe or kayak is merely the magic carpet that carries you nearly effortlessly into some of the most beautiful corners of North America. It is a trip into history, into nature, and into stunning beauty.

You can camp where Lewis and Clark camped, paddle along the shores where the first Polynesians discovered Hawaii, drift through clouds of birds in Florida, Connecticut, and North Carolina. Best of all, it is quite easy to plan a trip that satisfies every member of your paddling family.

Planning Is Half the Fun

Knowledge is the coin with which you buy a fun and successful paddling trip. That's true for a day, a weekend, or a month on the water. The more you know, the better the trip becomes—and the easier your course between potential shoals and whirlpools.

It's easy to build the foundation of a great trip. Read your favorite paddling magazines. Browse through outdoor and travel publications and the travel pages of a good newspaper. Get your partner involved, adding a pair of eyes and a new viewpoint. You're not looking for a detailed route, but rather a feeling for a general area. Some paddlers clip out articles and neatly file them. Others jot down a few rough notes. Still others tuck ideas away in the back of their mind.

> **In the Wake**
>
> Keep a log of places you've paddled, and places you'd like one day to see. That way you can slip odd bits of information about future trips into a slot where you can find it again.

As you muse, and this is something you should be doing months in advance of your trip—perhaps on Sunday mornings over coffee, or in the evenings with a glass of wine—you'll discover that certain things attract you and certain areas sort of feel right. Without really meaning to, you'll find yourself concentrating on first a broad and then a narrower geographic area.

Buy Books, Maps, and Charts

Once you have a general idea of the region you want to paddle, start searching out guide books covering the waterways and routes within the area you've selected. Some guidebooks are great, presenting detailed and accurate information. Some are, well, haphazard at best and, as often as not, painfully outdated. Get on the phone to paddling shops in the area of your potential trip and ask for their suggestions on good books. As a thank you, order a book from them rather than from an online discounter. Odds are you'll find one book won't be quite enough, and you'll end up with several on your planning shelf. The writers don't follow in each other's wake: One will paddle one stretch of waterway, and a second will hopscotch to the west and paddle another. One likes spring, a third seeks fall colors. One is an awesomely skilled paddler to whom all waters are easy, while another cautions the reader at each wave. "Best" becomes a very subjective standard.

Find as many maps and charts as you can: topographic maps showing the contours of the land as it is carved by water, charts laying out the visible and hidden faces of the waterways. Add the journals and reports of historians and explorers. Contact state and provincial tourism offices. Ask paddlers from your home club if they have paddled there. Contact paddling clubs in and around the region you've chosen for your vacation. Paddlers like to chat and will share their knowledge willingly with you.

Ask the Locals

Talking to local paddlers can steer you out of disaster. What if the only road to your put-in washed out in a spring flood? What if an unusually dry summer reduced your river to a trickle? What if …? Well, you get the idea. Conditions change hourly on the waterways, and the most current information you find can rescue or founder your planned trip.

Surf the Web

The American Whitewater Affiliation offers an amazing encyclopedia of rivers across the continent. The National Water Trails Association marks out dedicated paddling routes. Both the American Canoe Association and the Canadian Recreational Canoeing Association have extensive libraries. Thousands of websites provide information on rivers, lakes, and saltwater routes. In the United States, the National Park Service, the U.S. Forest Service, the Bureau of Land Management, and the U.S. Army Corps of Engineers compile water recreation information. Most electrical utilities with hydro-electric projects develop recreational programs along the reservoirs behind their dams.

Use the web to fill in the blanks in your travel plans: How are you going to get your canoe or kayak to the put-in? How are you going to *shuttle* back from the take-out? Would it make sense to rent boats from a shop or *livery*, and let them arrange drop-off and pick-up? If you're heading for a big lake or the saltwater, would it make sense to catch a ride on a commercial boat out to your cruising area? What would the costs be for rental or rides? Will you need cash, check, or plastic?

Finding information becomes easy. Shutting the spigot on the flood of information pouring over you becomes the hard part.

> **Paddlin' Talk**
>
> To **shuttle** means to move boats, people, and gear between the take-out and the put-in.
>
> A company that rents canoes, kayaks, and related gear such as paddles, personal flotation devices, and safety equipment is called a **livery**.

How Far Can We Go?

The question of how far you can paddle on a trip hinges on a huge number of variables. How long will your trip be? How many hours a day do you want to paddle? What conditions do you expect to encounter? How physically fit are you? What kind of boat will you paddle (a high-performance sleek rocket or a beamy freighter)? How strong is your party?

Paddling by the Numbers

All that considered, most paddlers cruise at no more than three knots or so, and most think that a four- to five-hour day with paddle in hand is more than enough. Do the numbers, and that translates into a 12- to 15-mile day. That assumes that you want to bend your paddle for that many hours each day, and that weather and conditioning enable you to do so. The hard truth is that an average, typical day with paddle in hand is rarely even close.

Despite your best hopes, nature well could have spaced your launching site and your first available take-out 25 miles apart. That's well within the limits of a somewhat skilled paddler and an efficient canoe or touring kayak. In fact, a proficient touring kayaker with a light load can cover 40 nautical miles in a day. After a very long day of paddling most paddlers will haul out on the beach for at least one and often two days of rest. Factor rest days in your planning, especially after what you see will be a hard day. A rule of thumb on many multiday trips is an average of two days paddling and one day of rest or shoreside exploration. If you're comfortable paddling 15 miles a day, your average then drops to 10 miles. A 12-mile-a-day clip comes out to a 3-day average of 8 miles per day.

Go over your calendar and mark out just how many days you can spend on this particular trip. Then subtract the days you'll spend getting there and getting back. For example, if you plan a one-week trip, you have two weekends plus five days for a total of nine days. If it takes a day to get there and a day to return home, then you have seven paddling days. Multiply the number of days left, your on-the-water days, by your average miles per day. Let's say you can comfortably paddle 8 miles per day. If you have 7 on-the-water days, that's 56 miles. Now deduct between 10 percent and 20 percent for bad weather or minor emergencies. In round terms, you can comfortably paddle between 45 and 50 miles on this week-long trip.

Rocks and Shoals

Never, ever, put yourself in the position of having to paddle in conditions near the upper limits of your skill just to make a deadline. Add in a reserve of time for the unexpected. Be safe and sit on the beach.

After a few paddling trips, you'll be able to adjust these distances to the kind of paddling you really enjoy. Some folks think the best definition of fun is dawn-to-dark high-energy paddling in a straight line. Others like to poke and snoop in every bay, behind every rock, and, when possible, around every historical remain or natural attraction. Everyone knows the photographer who will wait hours for the light to play just right, or the birder who totally loses track of time when observing a kingfisher fishing.

One-day trips can be mapped out more casually, depending on the waters you are paddling. You won't be shore-bound by weather—if the weather is bad, don't launch—and you won't be confined by the need to build a new campsite each evening. All you have to do is get to the put-in and return home from the take-out, and in between, load and unload boats, eat lunch and snacks, plus take in the sights.

With good weather, a light load, and plenty of energy, you certainly can paddle 5 to 6 hours a day, covering between 15 and 20 miles. Realistically, set your goals down to the lower end of the range. Give yourself extra time for foul winds (it seems there is always a head wind on the last bit to the take-out), a current not to your liking, or even road work and a detour when shuttling between the take-out and the car(s) left at the put-in.

> **In the Wake**
>
> Many paddlers use the rule of thirds when planning (and paddling) on any paddling trip: One third of the time and resources are used from the put-in to the mid-point; one third from the mid-point to the take-out; and one third kept in reserve for when things don't go according to plan.

A Word About Efficiency

Paddlers throw around the word "efficiency" quite a bit, as in "an efficient paddling stroke" or "an efficient hull." Although efficiency is something most paddlers seek, don't confuse efficiency with speed. Instead, think of efficiency as the wisest use of the power in your canoe or kayak. Being efficient isn't a boast that you can paddle faster or farther. Rather, it is the ability to cover the same distance, or paddle at the same speed, with less effort. Look at a group of paddlers at a take-out. Some are excited, energetic, ready for more. The next morning they won't have sore muscles. Others will be knackered, exhausted, barely able to lift their boats from the water and carry them to the top of the beach. The difference lies in the efficient use of energy.

> **The Old Paddler Says**
>
> Remember that when you measure distance there are two scales to use: the distance you travel over the ground, and the distance you travel over the water. You may paddle 4 miles in 1 hour over the water, but if you are paddling with a 3-knot current, you will cover 7 miles over the ground.

Efficiency can translate into speed, when it is needed. Although at first blush you wouldn't consider the difference between three knots and four as "big," it certainly becomes so on the water. That's a one-third gain in speed, the highway equivalent of driving at 45 mph or 60 mph. The four-knot paddler can cover 12 miles in three hours. The three-knot paddler will cover 9 miles in that same three hours, and will have to paddle for a full hour more to match the 12 miles of the faster paddler.

Surprisingly, the difference in the speed is often not due to increased effort by the faster paddler. Rather, it comes with developing a more efficient paddling stroke. The energy output per hour of paddling is often the same.

Signaling Your Intentions

When the wind is blowing and the water splashing, no matter how much you want it to, your voice just can't be heard from any distance. To communicate, you need a set of clearly understandable signals. You and your friends can make up your own, but these are accepted and understood by experienced boaters all across North America

- **Stop.** Hold your arms straight out from your shoulders or hold your paddle over your head with the shaft horizontal. To attract attention, you can quickly raise and lower your hands a few inches, or can raise and lower your paddle. Means just what it says: *There is a potential hazard ahead. Wait for further signals, but don't proceed.* Wait for the "All Clear" signal (see the following). If you see the "Stop" signal, repeat it for those following you.

Extend your paddle horizontally over your head, raising and lowering it a few inches at a time repeatedly, to warn paddlers to stop because of a potential hazard ahead. You can also make this signal with your arms held straight out from your shoulders.

(Suzanne Stuhaug)

- **Help.** Wave a paddle, helmet, or PFD over your head, while giving three long blasts with your whistle. You can just make the motions if you don't have a whistle (though you should have one on a lanyard attached to your PFD). This is an urgent call for immediate aid, and whoever spots it should come to the signaler as soon as possible.

- **All Clear.** Hold your paddle or your arm vertically over your head. Hold the paddle blade so that the upper blade faces the people you are signaling, for better visibility. It means: "Come on" or "Come this way." If you want to signal a direction or the preferred course, first make the "All Clear" signal and then tilt your paddle or arm about 45 degrees in the direction that the oncoming paddlers should head.

Hold your paddle vertically or stretch one arm straight over your head to signal "All Clear."

(Suzanne Stuhaug)

If you want to direct upstream paddlers to a preferred route on one side of a river, first hold your paddle or arm vertically, and then tilt the paddle to around 45 degrees in the direction that they should go.

(Suzanne Stuhaug)

♦ **This Way.** This signal advises the viewer to head in a particular direction. First make the "All Clear" signal, and then lower your paddle to about 45 degrees, aimed at the direction to which the paddler should go. Never point at or toward an obstacle, only in the preferred direction in which to paddle.

♦ **I'm All Right.** Face the oncoming paddlers, hold your elbow out to the side so that it may clearly be seen, and repeatedly pat the top of your head. You're signaling that you are all right, not hurt, and do not require assistance.

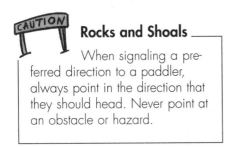

Rocks and Shoals

When signaling a preferred direction to a paddler, always point in the direction that they should head. Never point at an obstacle or hazard.

A whistle is a great signaling tool. A Fox 40 or a Storm can be heard a quarter to a half mile away, and can blast right through the crash of water or the whine of wind. While most paddlers know that the call for help is three long blasts, you might want to expand that vocabulary. If you have children with you, emphasize that one blast of a whistle is a call for attention, and that a person hearing it should reply with a similar blast. It is far easier to locate a whistle than the faint sound of a child's piping voice.

Gathering the Equipment You'll Need

You don't need all-inclusive survival, first-aid, and repair kits in your boat if you're just going to paddle a few hundred yards down the lake to visit a friend. Likewise, the gear you pack along for a day's fishing on a pond wouldn't at all be suitable for a four-week, totally self-contained expedition along a remote stretch of northern Canadian coastline. Match the gear you carry to the waters you'll be paddling.

The Old Paddler Says

A cell phone in a waterproof bag can summon aid to an accident site or can allay worries if you're detained. But they don't work everywhere. For years, paddlers have carried EPIRBs, small radio beacons that can signal a location worldwide if assistance is needed. They're pricy. Some folks have started renting satellite phones for deep wilderness trips. They offer worldwide communications and connection, but expect to pay for the privilege in coin, weight, and batteries.

You'll need certain basics even for a quick trip along the shore. You must have a good-fitting life jacket (PFD) for each person aboard your canoe or kayak (see Chapter 6). You should have a method for removing water from inside your boat (scoop or bailer, or a portable or fixed pump), a whistle that can be heard over a great distance, a spare paddle, drinking water, energy bars for a quick pick-me-up snack, a minimal first-aid kit, and a big yard-waste garbage bag.

The purposes of the first items are obvious. As for the garbage bag, you can use it as a raincoat/poncho, as a tent, and sleeping bag during a totally unexpected overnight bivouac, and to pack trash out. Even though others may be thoughtless enough to litter, we owe it to nature and our fellow citizens to clean up what we can in our passing.

It's a good idea to include a throw line (usually stuffed into a fabric throw bag) for towing and rescue, and a waterproof bag or two to keep personal items from getting wet.

Your First Paddling Trip

A bit of common sense is all it takes to build a list of what personal items you'll need for a one-day trip on placid water:

- A map, chart, or sketch showing where you'll start, where you're going, and where you'll end up. In case you have to abort the trip along the way, the map should include the direction and distance to the nearest roads and towns.

- Two complete sets of clothing from skin out, one to wear and the other to change into if you get wet. Pack the change of clothes in a waterproof bag, or at least in several heavy-duty garbage bags securely shut. Bring along a lightweight windbreaker/raincoat as well as a fleece pullover or sweater. If the weather is chancy, add rain pants. Ponchos can be a hazard if you end up in the water. It is difficult to swim while in a poncho.

The Old Paddler Says _____
Plan to stay dry if you will, but expect to step into deep water, get splashed, or even just sweaty. Wet clothes will suck heat out of your body, so a dry change is as much for safety as a fashion statement.

- Wear a pair of lace-up tennis shoes. Some paddlers like mid-calf rubber boots. These can be sweaty, uncomfortable, and are difficult to swim with, but they do keep your feet dry. Good water sandals offer support and protection to the bottoms of your feet, but no protection from sun or cold without socks.

- If you have delicate hands or get cold easily, you may want to bring along a pair of cycling gloves made of synthetic material.

- Sunglasses are a necessity, and the polarized ones with UV protection are best. You'll protect your eyes from the glare, and you'll be able to see the water as well as obstacles. Wear a retainer strap with your sunglasses or corrective lenses. Glasses do fall off. If you wear corrective lenses, or contact lenses, carry along a back-up pair.

◆ Sunscreen. Even on a cloudy day, the sun can burn you. Look for a waterproof lotion (if your paddling shop doesn't carry any, check out a dive shop or a surfer store). Add some lip balm.

◆ Top it off with a big old hat. Sunburned ears hurt! So does a scorched scalp. A comfortable chin strap will keep the wind from snatching it away. A baseball cap is a minimum, but it won't protect your neck.

◆ Fasten your car keys to a snap hook inside a PFD pocket, and give a second set of keys to someone else to carry. You could also hide a set of keys around your car. You don't need your wallet, credit cards, money, or photographs of your family. Lock your valuables away (such as in the trunk) and don't bring along what you don't need.

◆ Drink some water before you are thirsty. Eat an energy bar or other food before you get hungry. Make sure you have plenty of water and food with you, including a lunch.

The Multiday Voyage

There are as many kinds of multiday canoe and kayak trips as there are colors of boats on the water. Fortunately, all of them are fun.

You can paddle from lodge to lodge in Maine or Florida, beaching each night at the edge of a well-kept lawn with a four-star dinner waiting for you. The hot bath and soft bed are no small inducements, either.

You can paddle essentially empty boats, lugging all your gear in a larger power boat or raft. You can hire the raft/power boat crew, or you can rotate the duty among the paddlers.

Or you can do what the majority of paddlers do and pack all your gear into your boats, surviving comfortably with what you carry along.

One of the great advantages of a touring kayak or an open canoe is its ability to carry gear. As a broad rule of thumb, either kind of boat will carry a paddler and the equivalent of about three loaded backpacks. Their ability to carry sizable loads is also their disadvantage, because people tend to fill as much space as they have. There is no paddling rule that says you have to completely fill your boat with everything you own. If you can manage without it, leave it behind.

Everyone's needs differ. The following checklist is a good foundation, well tested by touring kayakers and wilderness trippers, upon which to build your collection of camping essentials.

Remember, though, that you must keep in mind your destination. Is it frigid? Add warm clothes. Is it rain-swept? Increase the size or number of rain flies. Is it swampy? Remember bug juice. Use a little common sense and forethought. The following list is intended as a guide only:

- **For your boat.** A paddle for each person, plus a spare for each boat; heavy line for lining, securing, throwing; bailer and sponge or pump; appropriate boat and gear repair kit.

CAUTION

Rocks and Shoals

There can be no universal checklist for a canoe or kayak voyage. Any list has to take into consideration your needs, your desires, your paddling habits, and most important, your destination.

- **For your camp.** Tent with rain fly, extra rain fly (10 x 10 lightweight tarp); 50- to 100-foot parachute cord; sleeping bag, mat, pillow; folding saw (or a hatchet or ax); trowel or folding shovel.

- **For cooking.** Stove (two is better) with twice the fuel you think you'll need; nesting pots and pans; serving utensils; heavy-duty *sharp* knife; plates or bowls and eating utensils; cups; matches; steel wool; biodegradable soap; paper towels or equivalent; 2-liter water/juice container; water filter; two 2-gallon collapsible water jugs; coffee maker (optional); fire starter; aluminum foil; collection of spices, seasonings, oils; a container for all kitchen supplies.

In the Wake

Stoves are a contentious issue. Some paddlers abjure any form of campfire, citing charcoal rings and the use of driftwood as environmental no-nos. Others say that utilizing high-tech stoves and depleting irreplaceable natural resources is wrong. Unless you're going to eat cold, raw food, you'll go one way or the other. If driftwood is plentiful, then it's a fuel source. If it is rare, then preserve it. In some areas, and in some parts of the year, fires are banned. In others, fires may be restricted to already constructed stoves or pits. In other places you might be required to pack out any ashes. When it comes to fire rules, know before you go.

- **Clothing.** Hat with brim, long pants, shorts, warm long-sleeve shirt, lightweight long-sleeve shirt, fleece pullover, fleece vest, hooded raincoat and rain pants, sandals (or tennis shoes, but they dry slowly) or rubber boots, bandana, underwear, towel.

- **Miscellaneous.** Sunglasses, extra corrective glasses, sunblock, lip balm, Swiss Army knife, whistle, signal mirror, insect repellant, first-aid kit, snake-bite kit (if you'll be traveling in an area known for poisonous snakes), camera and film, notebook, personal sundries. Don't skimp on whistles for everybody, especially children. A whistle can be heard over greater distances than a voice. Musical instruments, games, books, and the like, as you desire.

Planning for When Things Go Bust

Planning for the unforeseen is a lot like scheduling time to be spontaneous: good in theory but difficult in execution. That said, anyone who ventures aboard a canoe or kayak should be able to rig serviceable repairs on all pieces of important gear. Important? Use your common sense. What's "important" when you're lolling 50 feet off the beach in front of your cabin is far different than what's important in the wilderness when the next take-out is five day's paddling downstream.

You have to live with the truth that all manufactured items will eventually fail—the only question is when. Murphy's Law dictates that failure will happen at the worst

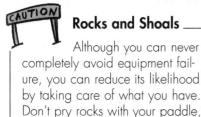

Rocks and Shoals

Although you can never completely avoid equipment failure, you can reduce its likelihood by taking care of what you have. Don't pry rocks with your paddle, jump up and down on a tent pole, or pitch your tent immediately downwind of an open fire.

possible time. And Murphy was an optimist. You face the challenge of figuring out just what you're going to do when any critical piece of gear gives up on you. Your first step is to assemble the tools and materials that will give you the best shot at making those repairs.

Start your repairs before you go. In other words, go over each piece of equipment when you're in the comfort of your own home with a store and parts close at hand. Service what needs to be serviced, repair the weak and worn, and replace the worn-out or irreparably damaged.

Luckily, you can cram an entire workshop and parts inventory into a small bag that will weigh in at 3 pounds or less. Similar bags have been packed along sub-Arctic rivers, remote coastal islands, and tied inside a decked boat playing on close-to-home white water. Think of your parts bag as a work in progress rather than a complete package, evolving with each trip and each destination. It grows and shrinks with each trip on the water, depending on need and exposure. It's no more than a jumping-off point for what you may need down the waterways:

- **Waterproof bag or box** to carry everything in, along with smaller waterproof bags (use zip-top freezer bags) to store and separate tools and materials.

- **Multipurpose tool.** This combines pliers, wire cutters, a file, and a selection of screwdriver bits in a small and sturdy package. Quality and durability are essential, and a flimsy one is trash just waiting to be thrown out. Go for a Gerber Multi-Plier, Leatherman, or the like. Uses range from retrieving a hot pot to cinching down a wire wrap.

- **Knife.** A basic Swiss Army knife, with scissors, tweezers, awl, and bottle and can openers. Mine has a small magnifying glass, which I seem to find more uses for as the years go by. Learn to sharpen the blades, and do so.

- **Tweezers.** If your knife doesn't have tweezers, include a pair for picking up small parts and snatching at slivers.

- **Utility knife.** Small size, and super sharp. Cut a line, feather a hull patch, trim a plug, sever a tape. It doubles as part of your first-aid kit.

- **Scissors.** Sturdy, foldable, and small. You'll use them for cutting gaskets, trimming patches to size, snipping threads. The scissors on your Swiss Army knife should be your fall-back pair.

- **Small flashlight,** with an extra set of fresh batteries and a spare bulb. You *will* need a light.

- **Epoxy repair kit.** Epoxy resin and hardener, a couple of graduated mixing cups, a small roll of 2-inch-wide Kevlar tape, squeegee, waxed paper, and gloves. That, a healthy respect for the chemicals, and prior experience mixing and using them. Use it to patch a cracked fiberglass hull, fill a gouged Royalex hull, refasten a coaming on a touring kayak—the list is endless. Collect the patching materials needed for your particular boat: composite lay-up, plastic, fabric, or aluminum.

- **Several sheets of sandpaper,** from 100 to 220 grit. For cleaning an area prior to patching, smoothing up a repair, eliminating a rough spot.

- **Alcohol swabs** for cleaning parts before glassing, gluing, or sealing. Doubles in the first-aid kit.

- **Gardener's coated tie wire.** Zipper pulls, eyeglass hinges, bag ties fail at the worst possible times. A small coil of coated wire is great whenever you want to quickly and temporarily secure one thing to another. Dental floss, hygiene aside, works just like gardener's wire.

- **Baling wire, snare wire, stainless steel wire** ... for holding things together. Repair a cracked thwart, a cracked paddle shaft, loose or missing rivets along a gunwale, or whenever you need a tight wrap. Stronger but more bulky than gardener's wire. Twist tight with your Multi-Plier.

- **Duct tape.** The great repair essential. Comes in all sorts of quality—go to a real hardware store or sheet metal supply house and find the really sticky, reinforced kind. Tape a broken hull back together, seal a water bottle or ripped tent, or use to hold a compress in place when the going gets wet.

- **A stubby lantern candle.** Melt cord ends, glue stick, or light a fire when the wet closes in.

- **One or two sticks of glue-gun glue.** Melt over a candle to seal small holes and cracks. A small tube of Superglue is a good substitute.

- **Small tube of Barge cement,** from a cobbler's shop. It's a hell-for-stout glue that can reattach a flopping sole to a shoe or just about any other two items.

- **Urethane adhesive/sealant.** Use it to repair a wet suit, glue a shoe sole in place, patch a leaking hull, or seal a patch over a ripped tent

- **Light lubricating oil** (such as Tri-Flow). To reduce friction any place two pieces of metal stick instead of slide, including nuts and bolts.

- **Sewing kit,** with stout threat, a selection of needles with large eyes, a couple of leather needles, assorted buttons, and a metal thimble. For a large group, consider a sewing awl.

- **Diaper pins.** Half dozen or so, large size. A quick way to hold two pieces of fabric in place, including bandages.

- **Hose clamps.** Large enough to splint a paddle shaft, a tent pole, or anything else that might break. Flex-ties also work. A small flex-tie can even substitute for a single-use emergency shoelace.

- **Assorted nuts, bolts, washers, and gaskets,** sized to fit all through-hull fittings, gunwales, thwart hangers, or whatever you have in your gear.

- **Paper and pencil,** for notes or messages.

- **PakTowl.** Great for cleanup, doubles as a work surface, and can buff up a hull. A PakTowl is a synthetic fabric which packs very small and soaks up amazing amounts of water.

- **Lighter.** More reliable than matches. Back up with waterproof matches (which usually aren't, and are hard to light in a wind).

- **Cord.** A 50-foot hank of ⅛-inch braided nylon cord. You'll eventually have to tie, lash together, or support something.

- **A small coil of 50-pound test fishing leader.** For tying things down, together, or apart.

- **Spare 10-foot tiedown strap** from a boat carrier, with buckle.

- **Six-inch square of heavy nylon pack cloth,** to patch tents, packs, bags, jackets, and so on. A small roll of self-adhesive nylon tape.

- **Six-inch square of mosquito netting,** to repair tent netting and keep out the detested biting bugs.

- **Six-inch square of leather.** Thin enough to use for an emergency stove-pump gasket, strong enough to patch any worn or abraded fabric.

- **A small roll of Velcro** or other hook-and-eye tape, the kind with adhesive on both pieces.

- **Condoms.** You can transport water with one (support it in a cap or sock), or waterproof watches or photographic film.

- **Neoprene patches** for wetsuit and sprayskirt holes.

And for when you're camping:

- **A 3- to 4-inch metal sleeve** that will slide over a crimped or broken tent pole.

- **Stove repair and maintenance kit** for your stove model.

> **In the Wake**
>
> Paddling a boat with a rudder? Don't forget the spare rudder cable, swages or cable clamps, and end fittings to match your system.

When People Need a Little Patching

There's no such thing as a perfect first-aid kit. Someday, you'll need something your kit won't have, and just as surely you'll pack along some item that you'll never end up using. And you'll always wish you knew a little more about first aid.

Here's one foundation for a basic first-aid kit: Put everything in a waterproof container or bag. Here are some first-aid kit essentials:

- **Simple painkillers** like ibuprofen or aspirin. For sore muscles, headaches, fevers, or most painful discomforts. Just a few tablets, and not a big bottle of every brand on the shelf.

> **In the Wake**
>
> A great first-aid kit is useless if you don't know how to use it. A very basic kit is great in the hands of a trained person. Take first-aid classes before you need to know how to use your kit!

- **A mild antihistamine,** such as Benadryl. Helps with allergies, insect bites, and some cold symptoms.

- **Remedies for insect bites/stings or food-allergy reactions.** See your doctor for these, and make sure everyone in the party knows of potential allergic reactions and the proper treatment.

- **Meat tenderizer.** We all hate mosquito bites and other chewing things, and meat tenderizer works to alleviate the discomfort of some insect bites.

- **Sunscreen, lip balm, and a powerful hand cream.** Protect your skin—it's the only thing that keeps your insides from being outsides.

- **Anti-diarrhea tablets** such as Imodium.

- **A small tube of antiseptic ointment** for treating cuts.

- **Eye wash** or irrigating solution.

- **A few adhesive bandages.** The 3-inch size is best, and the "waterproof" ones will stay in place a little longer.

- **Sterile gauze.** The 4-inch × 4-inch size covers larger areas and can be cut down for smaller spots. Use them to cover an injury, clean a dirty injury, or use as a pad. You can pack along a larger trauma dressing, but wilderness medicine expert and writer Buck Tilton once told me that an individually wrapped sanitary napkin makes an equally good compress for badly bleeding wounds.

- **Spenco 2nd Skin.** Two pieces at 3 inches × 13 inches. Use it to cover an irritated area before it becomes a blister or to protect an already blistered area. Hold it in place with Spenco's knit bandaging. 2nd Skin works well on small first- or second-degree heat burns, with professional care advised for second-degree (blistered) or worse burns. Moleskin also helps in the treatment of friction blisters, protecting irritated areas from blistering, and the blister itself.

- **Waterproof adhesive tape.** One-inch × 5- to 10-yards or so, on a metal spool. Hold a compress, protect irritated skin, and lots of other uses. Athletic tape can also help support a stressed joint.

- **Elastic bandage.** The 3-inch-wide size is pretty versatile.

- **Triangular bandage.** Support, sling, wrap.

- **Wound closure tapes.** Does just what the name says, and the better ones can be removed and reapplied. Butterfly bandages don't work as well, but are an alternative.

- **Three or four diaper pins.** Better than regular safety pins, and *much* harder to inadvertently pop open. Secure an elastic bandage or a triangular bandage.

- ◆ **Tweezers and scissors.** If they're part of your pocket knife, they're handy. If not, add them to your kit. A magnifying glass is a handy accessory, too.

- ◆ **Ingredients for replacement fluid.** Small containers of a powdered sweetened drink (Gatorade, Tang, or the like); salt and baking soda; one liter of dilute (about half the recommended mixture) drink mixed with ⅓ teaspoon salt and ⅓ teaspoon baking soda is a good replacement fluid for dehydration triggered by shock or burns.

- ◆ **Condoms.** Can be used to hold purified water from a filter or chemicals when supported with a sock.

- ◆ **Vinyl gloves.** They'll last longer in a kit than latex ones.

Making a Float Plan

A float plan is the simplest safety tool known to any paddler, and unfortunately, one quite often ignored. It is no more than a note left with a responsible friend or family member outlining where you are going, when you are going, when you expect to return, who is in the group, and a description of your canoes or kayaks as well as your car(s). Don't attempt to file your float plan with the Coast Guard or with local law enforcement. They have other duties. Check back in with the person holding the plan when you're off the water.

If you are late, the float plan is a quick collection of information that can dramatically assist appropriate search and rescue agencies in locating you. It removes the potential confusion as to when you are expected back, and how to contact the families of the people paddling with you.

For an in-depth look at the information you should include in your float plan, refer to Appendix C in the back of this book.

> **Rocks and Shoals**
>
> Don't forget to contact the person holding your float plan when you return or if you change plans. It is embarrassing—and potentially expensive—to be the subject of a massive search if you're not missing.

Where to Go

Every part of North America has great paddling possibilities. Just open your eyes and look around. White water, serene ponds, vast reaches of ocean, lakes … it is all within your grasp. A note of caution: More and more recreation areas now require permits. Check before you go. Here are just a few places to whet your appetite:

Adirondack National Park, New York. Some 120 miles of waterways, criss-crossed by a network of trails that link more than 2,800 ponds, creeks, lakes, and rivers. Half-mile-high mountains overlook the scenic waterways that have been prime canoeing routes for more than a century. Paddle here and you'll learn the true meaning of "portage."

Alaska, LeConte Bay. A great bite slashed out of the land just north of Wrangell, Alaska, with LeConte Glacier spawning great chunks of ice into the tidewater.

Algonquin Park, Ontario, Canada. Some 120 miles of waterways located east of Ottawa. The park information office is in Whitney.

Allagash Wilderness Area, Minnesota. Nearly 100 miles of lakes and rivers surrounding the Allagash River, one of the nation's first Wild and Scenic Rivers, a federal designation citing the beauty and recreational importance of the waterway. The Minnesota Bureau of Parks and Recreation, which administers the Allegash Wilderness Waterway, is in Augusta.

Buffalo River, Arkansas. The 125-mile run from Ponca to White River through wilderness areas is safe for beginners in all but the highest water.

California: Santa Cruz Island, Channel Islands National Park (www.nps.gov/chis). Santa Cruz is the largest of five islands in the park, 17 miles off the southern California coast, with a dramatic and remote coastline. Lots of wildlife ashore and in the water, archeological sites, paddling in the lee of the land as well as on the exposed and turbulent weather side. About a quarter if the island, the east end, is owned by the National Park Service, with a seaside camp at the Scorpion Ranch. The rest is owned by The Nature Conservatory, with a campground near Prisoners' Harbor.

Everglades National Park, Florida (www.nps.gov/ever). This is a 1.4-million-acre tangle of mangrove islands which has some outstanding paddling areas preserved, such as the 100-mile Wilderness Waterway. Anticipate plenty of biting insects, fantastic birds, and warm paddling during the winter paddling season.

Hawaii, Kauai. In the summer, paddle the north shore, Na Pali. In the winter, head east along the southern shore, the Little Na Pali Coast, for a ride as close to Paradise and you can find.

Lady Evelyn-Smoothwater Wilderness Park, Ontario, Canada. Four beautiful lakes set in the Temagami Wilderness in northeastern Ontario, with the charming Lady Evelyn River the most popular canoe route in the park. Photogenic waterfalls, rapids, placid rivers, plenty of campsites, and good swimming.

Long Island Sound, Connecticut. Great Island is a mile-and-a-half long salt marsh off the mouth of the Connecticut River. While you can paddle around it in an hour, you could spend days poking through the channels in the marsh watching an amazing collection of birds. Part of the island is designated the Roger Tory Peterson Wildlife

Area. Look for a lot of boat traffic around the island in the summer. Waves from the Sound can also kick up over the constantly moving sandbars, so keep a good watch.

Maine Island Trail, Maine. More than 375 miles of saltwater trail along the scenic, rocky Maine coast from Casco Bay to Machias, with more than a 100 designated campsites. Join the Maine Island Trail Association (www.mita.org), and more than half the campsites (the ones on private property) will be open to you.

Minnesota: Boundary Waters Canoe Area. A million-acre wilderness located in northeast Minnesota, stretched out along 150 miles of the U.S.-Canadian border. About 1,200 miles of canoe trails link and cross 1,000 lakes, with more than 2,000 designated campsites. Quetico Provincial Park in Ontario is a million-acre park across the border from the BWCA, with 1,500 miles of canoe trails. There are so many lakes that many haven't even been named.

New Jersey Pine Barrens, New Jersey. A paddler's dream, with 2,000 square miles of streams, swamps, and marshes for easy paddling within 100 miles of Manhattan. Whaton State Forest, Hammonton, New Jersey.

Niobrara River, Nebraska. Spanning 450 miles from its birth in eastern Wyoming to its confluence with the Missouri, the Niobrara is the prettiest prairie river in North America. Habitat, in just a few miles, changes from Rocky Mountain pine forest to prairie grassland. A 76-mile section centered around Valentine was declared a National Scenic River in 1991.

Pea Island National Wildlife Refuge, Pamlico Sound, North Carolina. An endless variety of bays, inlets, and little holes, creating 30,000 acres of National Seashore along the 130 miles of the Outer Banks of Cape Hatteras fame. Avoid the tourist-crowded Atlantic shore and paddle on the Pamlico Sound side. You can drive down the Outer Banks and launch all along the island chain for great day trips.

Robson Bight, Johnstone Strait, British Columbia. A remote and beautiful channel on the northeast corner of Vancouver Island, marked by the cruising pods of orcas. With the proper permits from the First Peoples, you can visit the nearly abandoned villages of the totem-pole people.

Upper Missouri River, White Cliffs section. 51 miles from Fort Benton to the Charles M. Russell National Wildlife Area, Montana. Sandstone spires, vertical walls, and gargoyle-like formations jutting out of the hillsides. Lewis and Clark came here during the spring runoff, lining six dugout canoes and two 35-foot pirogues against the current.

Voyageurs National Park, Minnesota. On the border between Minnesota and Ontario, the park covers 217,892 acres of which 83,789 acres are water. Choose from an estimated 1,600 islands. You can enjoy a two-week paddle with the only carry from your car to the water. Voyageurs National Park headquarters is in International Falls, Minnesota

Wisconsin: The Apostle Islands, Apostle Islands National Seashore, Wisconsin (www.nps.gov/apis). Wrap 21 craggy islands around 12 miles of protected shoreline on the west side of Lake Superior, and mix in sandy beaches, dense forests, sea caves and arches, and postcard-pretty lighthouses. The archipelago ranges from close against the mainland to 25 miles offshore, resulting in crossings of from a few minutes to several miles. Near-shore islands are popular in the summer, offshore islands are remote and limited to wilderness camping. Currents and cold water temperatures (rarely over 60 degrees in the summer), challenge experienced paddlers heading for the remote areas. Incredibly sculpted cliff faces, eagles, and wildlife.

Wyoming: Yellowstone Lake, Yellowstone National Park, Wyoming (www.nps.gov/yell). Crystal-clear water, 110 miles of pristine shoreline along large and small arms and inlets, and outstanding views come together in this imposing, remote, and yet readily accessible high-country lake. Amazing wildlife, including bears (plan on bear-proofing your campsite). Shuttles are available to a few drop-off points on the lake. Paddling here can be in the present or could be 200 years ago when Jim Colter first brought back tales of what would eventually become the first national park.

A great paddling trip lasts for far longer than the days you spend on the water. It begins, like an appetizer before a meal, with the delights of selecting where to go with all the possibilities opening before you. It extends through the selection of a route and a time frame, and builds as you assemble the gear you want for the trip. And then there are the days paddling, the days you've mapped out and are now experiencing. Finally, long after, there are the quiet conversations as you share your memories and photos of the trip with your fellow paddlers. And, as you talk, you start the planning process all over again.

The Least You Need to Know

- When you first begin planning a trip, let your mind go wild with the possibilities. Once you've narrowed the options down, start doing serious research.

- You should take certain gear with you no matter how long your trip is going to be: PFDs, a scoop or bailer, a loud whistle, a spare paddle, drinking water, snacks, a first-aid kit, and a garbage bag.

- To determine an appropriate length for your trip, multiply the number of paddling days by the number of miles you can comfortably cover in a day; then deduct 10 to 20 percent to arrive at an approximate number of miles you should plan on traveling.

- You can—and should—assemble your own repair kits for your canoe or kayak.

- Great paddling awaits you in every corner of North America.

Enjoying a Guided Trip

In This Chapter

- ◆ Finding the guided trip you really want
- ◆ Selecting the level of luxury you want—and deserve
- ◆ Learning to ask for the services you require
- ◆ Defining who does what on a guided trip

Spray flew in a warm mist from the bow of the sit-on-top kayak, burbling and hissing as the bright red boat accelerated along the face of the small wave. Fragments of sweet scents broke through the gentle breeze eddying off the shore 100 or so meters away, just past the beginning of the small surf. Riding the march of the waves was a new art, learned in the shelter of a tiny bay at the put-in that morning under the skilled eye of one of the two guides shepherding a party of eight quasi-novice paddlers during a week-long voyage along the southern Na Pali Coast of Kauai in Hawaii.

Earlier that morning we stowed our beach clothes in our bags by our tents, and wandered over to a breakfast of cereal, absolutely tree-fresh fruit, juice, coffee, and hot-out-of-the-oven muffins. There had been no takers the night before for pancakes. As we ate, the outfitter struck the tents and loaded the entire camp into a van and headed down to the night's landing spot. Lunch was already packed in a waterproof hamper, to be shared as we rafted together somewhere down the coast.

The world was strangely reversed. Big sea birds looked like they were swimming against the wind high overhead, while a sea turtle crossing under our kayaks appeared to be flying in transparent green air. Turning to the left we'd glide over a low surf onto shimmering beaches. There was nothing to the right, nothing but the Equator and, beyond that, Antarctica.

The whole world was paddling across the gentle rise and fall of the sea, with all our other cares stripped away for a week of hedonistic paddling.

If you desire that level of pampered paddling, then a guided trip can be just the thing for you. Read on to find out how you can enjoy one.

How to Select a Guide

Some paddlers so like a particular guide that they will book a trip with that guide with little regard as to where they will be led. That works, but for most people who want to enjoy a paddling vacation with the skill and support of a trained guide, the process works the other way around: They decide where they want to go, and then find a guide who will take them there.

Your best bet is to daydream. That's right. Just lean back in your most comfortable chair, stretch out your legs, and imagine the kind of conditions you'd like to paddle. At this point, don't even think about specific locations. Do you want to paddle some-place warm? Meander through untouched wilderness? Want to paddle, but don't want to camp? All you're doing is setting the stage.

When one dream starts looking more appealing than the others, start refining it. What time of year, for instance, do you have available for a voyage? You'll find nice paddling along the Texas Gulf Coast, but you'd want to avoid it during the height of a hot summer or in the depths of hurricane season. Newfoundland is beautiful in the summer and early fall, but not during winter storms. Rocky Mountain white water booms in the spring and early summer runoff, but slows to a trickle after a long, dry summer.

Paddlin' Talk

An **outfitter** is a company that assembles the outfit—the boats, equipment, supplies, and sometimes even the guide and cook—for a paddling party.

When you've identified the kind of paddling you'd like, the environment you'd like to do it in, and the time you can go, you've automatically narrowed your options down to a manageable size. Thumb through the pages of your favorite paddling magazine and you'll find many listings for *outfitters*, guides, and liveries.

Check out the locations offering the kind of paddling you'd like to do, and then note the names of the guides and outfitters offering trips in those areas. They advertise in the paddling magazines described in Appendix B. Look for their specialties. If you don't want to sleep in a tent, then look for the Maine outfitters who offer lodge-to-lodge trips, or the Florida outfitter putting you up in a single guest house with day trips leading you along the shore or up local rivers. If you want a tropical paradise, study up on Hawaii, Costa Rica, or Belize. If remote, tree-dark islands and the traces of totem-pole villages set against a stormy sea lure you, consider the Queen Charlotte Islands off Canada's west coast. On the other hand, if picture-postcard villages nestled in tiny rocky bays are your thing, look at Nova Scotia. These locales just scratch the surface of the possibilities, and the best choice among all of the possibilities is the one that works for you.

The Old Paddler Says

Don't rule out something completely different. If you're a dedicated river runner, try kayak touring. If you concentrate on saltwater and surf, look to the Boundary Waters Canoe Area or Quetico Wilderness Provincial Park (both along the Minnesota-Ontario border) for a mix of small streams, lakes, and portages in open canoes. Many paddling skills are very portable, and you just might find out how much you enjoy a different paddling venue.

Contact the local guides and outfitters, asking for information brochures. Some just won't mesh with your plans—if you want a lily-dipping float through ponds, a company that specializes in jump-starting your racing skills will be off the mark. You might want white water and plenty of it, while an outfitter concentrates on kayak touring along Lake Superior's North Shore. Sort out those who seem to meet most of your desires, and follow the steps in the rest of this chapter to pick out the two or three that could suit you best.

Once you've narrowed the field down, find out if the outfitters offer the trip you want at the time you want to take it. Also, start checking costs to see if you can fit the trip within your budget.

Costs

The cost of a guided trip involves many variables. The bottom line is that you'll pay for what you get. If you want four-star meals, vintage wines, someone to pitch your tent and air out your sleeping bag and to provide plenty of on-water instruction, it is within your grasp. You'll also spend more than a couple thousand dollars for your week's vacation. If you bring your own tent, sleeping bag, and boat, as well as share the cooking and clean-up chores, you'll get by for a fraction of the cost.

Decide what you can afford, the level of support you want, and the time you want to go, and then determine whether it's a feasible trip.

> ### In the Wake
>
> Expect the prices of some popular trips to vary like airplane tickets do. If you go during the peak of the season, you'll pay peak prices. If you choose less popular times, when fewer paddlers are seeking the same stretch of water, you'll find lower prices. Some outfitters will also offer group rates for larger parties.

Cancellation Penalties

Be fairly certain that you not only want to go but are committed to go on a particular trip before putting a deposit down. Most outfitters require a deposit, beginning at about 10 percent of the total cost of the trip, when you make your reservation. Total payment is often required before the start of the trip. Many outfitters have a justifiable policy of keeping all or part of a deposit if you cancel. The closer to the trip date the cancellation is, the larger the cancellation fee. If this concerns you but yet you want to nail down a specific date, look into trip-cancellation insurance.

> ### Rocks and Shoals
>
> Cancellation insurance can be expensive (10 to 12 percent of the trip cost), and may be very restrictive. It may only pay if you are sick or injured, not if your reasons for not going are optional (such as a change of mind). Understand what cancellation options the outfitter offers and read the fine print of a proposed insurance policy before making up your mind.

What Equipment Will the Guide Furnish?

The question of what gear will be supplied by the guide should be at the top of your list.

The Bare-Bones Option

At the bare-bones end of the scale, the guide will show up with his or her clothes and possibly a paddle. You've hired him or her for his or her expertise and local knowledge, and that's all that he or she will provide. You'll need to make arrangements for boats, paddling gear, camping gear, supplies, transportation, and whatever local fees and charges accumulate.

Bare bones isn't necessarily a bad way to go, depending on the logistics of assembling your gear and the destination you have in mind. Friends paddling in western Brazil found that it was not only the best option, it was the only option. In addition to furnishing a seat in a canoe and a canoe paddle (the guide was amazed at what he regarded as very long paddles—and what to most North American paddlers would be a standard length) and the guide's food and camping gear, they were also obligated to pay his way back upriver home.

The Old Paddler Says

All guides, whether or not they set out to be, are de facto instructors. You copy their moves and style to solve every paddling situation. Take advantage of their expertise.

Paddling in Style

On the other end of the scale is a fully outfitted ride. For instance, in one guided tour down the Dolores River in Colorado, everything other than clothing, cameras, and personal effects are ready in waterproof bags on the beach at the put-in. The outfitter even supplies bright tee-shirts embellished with his logo for all the participants. The guide and his staff erect the tents, spread out the sleeping bags on pads, place clothing bags in the tents, and pour sundowners for the paddlers at the first night's camp. Following a four-course dinner that would garner multiple stars in any restaurant guide, the group leans back in their (outfitter-supplied) chairs for a selection of early Italian music from the accompanying string quartet.

Over the top? Hey, they don't leave a mint on each pillow. What they promise, and what they deliver, is a luxury vacation sited along a bouncy river in the middle of some of the most fantastic scenery on Earth.

Most guided trips fall somewhere in between luxury and bare bones. It's up to you to find out where, specifically, on the spectrum the trip you're interested in will fall. A typical (if there is such a thing) guided trip comes with canoes or kayaks, paddles, PFDs, basic safety equipment, and guides. Tents are usually furnished, and the guides handle the cooking with company cookware. Wetsuits, drysuits, sleeping bags, and pads can usually be rented for the duration of the trip.

If you're really hot to paddle your own canoe or kayak, most trips can accommodate your wishes. Don't expect a reduced rate, but you quite likely will be able to use the guide shuttle to haul your boat back to the put-in. Consider the pros and cons of using your own boat before committing to it. One of the advantages of a guided trip is that you get to leave behind the hassle of transporting your own boat. Also, it just might be fun to slip behind the paddle of a new or different boat.

In the Wake

A big raft can serve as a pack elephant on a river trip, carrying all the gear and cargo while enabling the paddlers to sport in empty, light boats. Likewise, a power boat can serve as a mother ship for kayak touring parties. In addition to packing gear, it can also pick up tired or otherwise incapacitated paddlers.

A number of Western river guided trips are built around big rafts that carry all the gear and as many folks as don't want to paddle alone. Some of these offer solo boats, which may include inflatables, sit-on-tops, or traditional hardshell canoes or kayaks. Many, if not most, of these anticipate that guests will bring and paddle their own boats.

Ask for a Written List

You best bet is to ask the outfitter to send you a written list of what gear is involved, including …

◆ A detailed list of the gear and equipment deemed necessary or advisable for the trip planned.

◆ The gear and equipment furnished to each paddler, and to the group, by the outfitter.

◆ The gear and equipment to be furnished by the paddler.

◆ An itemized list of fees and charges for equipment and gear rental above and beyond that which is covered in the basic fee.

Outfitters and guides are in business to make money, and continued profitability depends on happy customers. Most will be more than happy to supply such lists, just to keep unpleasant confusions from rearing their ugly heads at the end of a trip. It's sad but true that the memory of an unexpected charge at the end of a trip can stay with some folks far longer than the joy and pleasure of the trip itself.

What Equipment Will the Paddlers Furnish?

Obviously, the gear you bring on a trip will depend on where you're going and how long you're going to be gone.

For a warm-weather, warm-water paddling trip, start with paddling shorts of a quick-drying synthetic material and with a mesh liner, with a mesh-lined pocket that won't hold water and that will seal with a flap and a zipper. You'll want a pair of long pants, offering protection from wind as well as sun. Short-sleeved, quick-drying synthetic shirts are comfy, but long-sleeve sun-block shirts with a high collar offer more protection. Polarfleece sweat pants and a Polarfleece vest are comfortable for when the sun goes down.

Some paddlers are more comfortable in a lace-up paddling shoe with quick-draining vents. Others prefer a good guide sports sandal for boat, beach, and light hiking wear. With sandals, consider a pair of breathable, waterproof socks. Add in a pair of light wool socks for beach wear or for light hiking. Don't forget to pack t-shirts, underwear, and socks.

Rocks and Shoals _____

When cotton gets wet, it stays wet for a long time, as do tennis shoes. Synthetics dry quickly. Remember that you'll spend all day on or near water, so the likelihood of getting wet is high.

If you're worried about (or prone to) blistered or chafed hands after several days paddling, consider purchasing a pair of lightweight paddling gloves. You may find that a pair of fingerless synthetic cycling gloves, with gel padding, will protect your fingers and palms.

Rocks and Shoals _____

A hat isn't always appropriate gear. On a whitewater trip, especially in kayaks, remember your helmet. Your personal helmet is likely to fit better and offer more protection than outfitter-provided helmets.

Layer up with a paddling jacket and rain/paddling pants for when the weather turns sloppy. It's a paddling truism that having rain gear on hand keeps rain away.

A hat may be the most important item in your wardrobe. Make that a hat with a big, floppy brim that will keep the sun out of your eyes and off your neck and ears. Find one with a chin strap, to keep it from turning into a kite.

The number of changes of clothing you pack depends entirely upon how long you'll be on the water. Don't forget that you can always rinse your clothing out and hang it up to dry overnight. And trust me, you won't get raised eyebrows if you show up in the same outfit more than one day.

If you wear corrective lenses or contact lenses, bring at least one spare pair with you. If contacts are your vision du jour, you'd be wise to pack prescription glasses in your case just in case you need them. Dust, glare, and an unfamiliar environment can give you the itchies in a hurry! You *will* need sunglasses. Polarized, UV-protection glasses slung around your neck with a retaining cord are a must.

The guide should have a complete first-aid kit. However, if you have allergies or sensitivities that could require medication, make sure that you have the meds clearly labeled with instructions as to dosages. At least two other folks should know where the meds are and how to use them, and the medication should be easily accessible.

CAUTION

Rocks and Shoals

Paddling presents few insurmountable difficulties for most physically challenged folks. Technology and technique have opened the door wide for river running and kayak touring, sailing, and just plain messing around in boats. If your challenge requires medication, let the trip leader and guide know so that they are prepared to assist you if it becomes necessary.

If each paddler is responsible for his or her own camping gear, start with a synthetic-fill sleeping bag (dries quicker than down and costs less), a good sleeping pad, and a pillow. Crazy Creek, among others, makes a pad cover that transforms into a chair in seconds. You can find inexpensive inflatable pillows at most outdoor shops. Extremely small *bivvie* tents, only inches bigger than your sleeping bag, are handy if you're crunched for space, but you'll probably be far happier with a tent large enough to comfortably sit or kneel in and with plenty of room for all the occupants and their gear. A tent with plenty of ventilation mesh panels and a rain fly will be the most comfortable.

If you have a special paddle that you must take, first make sure it will work with the outfitter's boats. If you paddle a skinny kayak, for example, and the outfitter will have you paddling a beamy double kayak, your favorite paddle will probably be too short.

Rivers, lakes, and saltwater just don't mix well with high-tech electronics or delicate camera innards. Leave your top-of-the-line camera at home unless it's truly waterproof. For your first paddling vacation, play around with a one-time-use camera, which comes in water-friendly models, or splurge on a water-resistant camera and a waterproof carrying case.

Save some room in your bag for a journal, reading material, a game, or a deck of cards. You won't spend all your time paddling.

Transportation: Getting There, Getting Back

Getting around on the water is simple. Just aim the pointy end of your canoe or kayak at your destination, following your guide, and paddle. Getting to the water may be a little more complicated.

Start by figuring out just how you are going to get to your paddling vacation. If you are driving, map out the best route and give yourself plenty of extra time. Ask for a sketch map clearly marking where you are to meet. Find out well ahead of time what arrangements you can make for parking your car. If you have concerns about security, ask whether alternative parking arrangements can be made.

If you will be arriving via air or rail, can you be picked up at the terminal? If not, how will you get from the terminal to the meeting place? What will this cost? Double-check the size of your bags well before checking in, to avoid oversize or overweight charges (check with your carrier) as well as potential baggage delays. You really don't want to arrive at the put-in without your luggage. Although lost luggage isn't all that common, what recourse might your carrier offer? Explore insurance options, and detail each item you packed aboard. Don't leave that list in your luggage!

And don't forget to plan for the return journey. You'll be tired, probably a little grubby, and your gear will be packed in waterproof bags with a little sand and dust. How will you get it from the outfitters to the terminal? If you're driving, how will you retrieve your car? If you brought your own canoe or kayak, where will you stow it while you're getting your own vehicle?

> **In the Wake**
>
> Alaskan and some Canadian trains understand and appreciate canoes and kayaks. Other trains and airlines really don't know how to deal with paddlers and appear not to want to. You might want to avoid a lot of hassle by simply letting your outfitter get a canoe or kayak for you on your trip.

To the Put-In

Well, you've made it to the nearest city and you've linked up with your guide and outfitter. How are you going to get to the put-in? In most cases, you'll ride in the outfitter's van, so that's one problem solved. But you need to find out how you're going to get to the outfitter's van. Assuming that you arrive the night before, will the outfitter pick you up at your motel? Will you camp somewhere, and if so, how will you get there? Will the outfitter expect you to make it to his or her shop first thing in the morning (better know what time that should happen) for a ride to the water? Will your paddling trip begin at the actual water's edge, and if so, how will you and your gear get there?

When you first really focus on selecting a particular outfitter and guide, you should bring these questions up. An answer of "Hey, we'll make it work" usually means just what it says, but it's up to you to nail down the specifics as tightly as your comfort zone demands.

From the Put-In to the Take-Out

A week after the put-in, give or take, you'll haul your boat up the beach for the last time at the take-out. Unless you've made a loop (assuming that you're on a flatwater trip where you can go out somewhere and return to the same place), you'll be miles away from where you started. You may not be in the same state or province, and you may not even be in the same country. But you knew that when you signed on for the journey.

How are you going to get back to where it all began? In most cases, you can just help load the canoes and kayaks on a trailer, pile your gear in the back of the guide's van, and either swap stories or snooze while someone else handles the driving. That's the low-pressure way. What if your particular outfitter doesn't offer such services? Most do, but you should ask.

> **In the Wake**
>
> Travel arrangements can be very flexible, and so can pricing. A good travel agent can come up with good prices, if you give him or her and the carrier plenty of advance time. Last-minute hurry rarely works to your advantage.

Look at a map, and see if it makes more sense to depart from a different city than the one where the trip began. After all, you've paddled a whole bunch of miles, and why backtrack if you don't have to. Look at the alternatives, ask, and don't forget to get things in writing.

What About Meals?

Eating may not be the primary reason paddlers paddle, but the pleasure of a good meal certainly can be a highlight of any paddling trip. In most cases, the outfitter/guide will handle the cooking chores as well as gathering together all the necessary supplies. For most outfitters, that's just part of the fee. On Idaho's Salmon River, you're likely to find a sommelier pouring a rich Northwest wine complementing your gourmet evening repast. He might be sporting river shorts and sandals, but he'll know his wines. Not on every trip, or with every outfitter, but you will find touches of four-star elegance even on a river bank. You'll probably also eat three meals and two snacks a day, plus take in more liquid than you thought you could.

> **In the Wake**
>
> Figure out what you eat at home in three meals. You'll need at least one more meal every day to have a paddle in your hands. You're also going to drink a *lot* of water. Drinking two bottles of water each morning and afternoon is skimping; three would not be out of line.

Will the meals suit you? If you're a picky eater, ask ahead for sample menus, and for the final menu not long before you depart. If you have specific dietary requirements, or if you really dislike a specific food, most outfitters can offer alternative menus.

Meals on the beach simply taste better. It might be that you're hungrier, it might be the fresh air and the scenery, it might be the skill of the cook. For whatever reason, you're going to dig into whatever is on your plate. And you'll save room for the hot apple pie served for dessert.

If the meals and meal planning are in the hands of the outfitter and you have specific extras you want included, expect to pay extra for them. You might, for instance, want wine with dinner; if this isn't a normal part of your outfitters meal, you will have to pay to have that as an add-on, or you can bring your own.

Tips for mealtime?

- Find out ahead what's on the menu.

- If you have specific dietary requirements, make them known well ahead.

- You *will* be hungry—enjoy!

The Old Paddler Says

Even if the guides are responsible for the cooking, it isn't out of line to offer help with the wash-up. Your help will be appreciated.

Asking for References

When you're still in the planning stages, ask prospective outfitters for a list of references. A reputable outfitter and guide will be glad to supply such a list. Although they won't send you a list of unsatisfied clients, the people on the list should still be able to give you a good sense of the outfitter. Call one or two on the list and ask them about the overall trip experience. Inquire if they plan to or have booked a second trip with the same company.

If you're booking with a newly created company, locate clients who have paddled with the owner-guide in the past and chat with them.

Asking for Company History

Finding a guide company with a history is important, but not absolute. A great guide might decide to form his or her own company, and you might end up on that company's initial voyage. This is not bad. A new guide company brings excitement, passion, and pride to the water. He or she is out to prove him- or herself in a competitive world, and will strive to offer more stories, better scenery, and better food than anyone else.

On the other hand, an established company has already run over many of the bumps and difficulties that come with the territory of taking a party of strangers down a particular stretch of water. They've already honed the process of packing and unpacking gear, delivering brochures, and arranging parking and shuttles. For that matter, they already have faced making coffee in the morning on the beach, while at the same time heating water for tea or cocoa. At best, they maintain the same passion for their profession and for their clients.

There is no right choice between the two.

Asking for Guide Qualifications and Certification

Your safety, your well-being, and your vacation are in the hands of the outfitter and guide. It behooves you to find out your guide's qualifications. On the paddling side, just what are their certifications? Are they instructor-certified by the British Canoe Union (BCU, and really top drawer), the American Canoe Association, the United States Canoe Association (the marathon and fast-paddling canoe set), or the Canadian Recreational Canoeing Association?

What first-aid or medical-response training do they have, from where, and how current is it?

On the company side, are they insured and bonded, and if so, with whom? You'll most likely be riding in their van, so what kind of vehicle insurance do they have? Does their home state require special driver's licenses for those vans, and do the drivers/guides have such? Are the guides certified/tested by the state as food handlers, if so required? Is the company licensed or permitted to serve wine or other alcohol with meals? Does the company belong to any of the outfitter/livery trade associations, and if so, which ones? Belonging to a trade association doesn't automatically make someone a good person, but it indicates that he or she is keeping abreast of what's happening in the industry.

What If the Route Is Changed?

Because you thought ahead, and planned ahead, you chose where you wanted to go and when. In January you signed up for a specific guided trip calendared in May, had your vacation plans approved at work, and even found a kennel for Bowser. What happens, come May, if Mother Nature doesn't cooperate and your chosen river is in flood, or that drought choked it down to an unrunnable trickle?

The best solution is having an outfitter with a comparable Plan B. If the Dolores River is unrunnable, for whatever reason, a great section of the Green is a fall-back choice. If you're not happy with the switch, how forthcoming will the outfitter be with your refund? Will you face a cancellation fee, perhaps a pretty hefty one? In some cases, maybe yes. Your initial agreement with the outfitter may give the company the right to change the planned route. In most cases, the outfitter wants to keep you—the paying customer—happy and will do whatever is possible to keep you smiling. But he or she has only a limited number of slots open on each of his or her limited number of trips, and if you bail out at the last minute for whatever reason, that perhaps is an irreplaceable revenue stream.

There may be reasons, and good ones, that the dates of a particular trip are changed, rather than the route. This may be harder for you to deal with, having to change vacation slots, travel tickets, even babysitters for the dog. If you're traveling with a group of friends, these problems are compounded.

Most reputable outfitters will attempt to offer you an equal package in the same time frame. They don't want to lose your business, or have an unhappy client. I even know of some outfitters who have swapped clients to put a person on a desired stretch of water. Keep an open mind.

To prevent any changes from ruining your trip, follow these two tips: First, be flexible. A vacation, and that's what a guided trip is, should be fun. The second is to remember that you're investing a fair amount of money, time, and effort into your vacation. Protect this with a bit of trip or vacation insurance to cover those expenses not under the reimbursement/refund policy of the outfitter. Make dead certain, though, that a description of the refund and cancellation policy and its associated charges are in the contract that the outfitter offers you. Keeping everything written eliminates unexpected surprises.

Additional Charges, Fees, Expenses

When you first talk with a guide company, they should offer you a price sheet with the trip charge or cost. That's good. Any trip, though, may run into other charges. Some Native American reservations, for example, charge a per-person entrance fee, a camping fee, or even a waterways-use fee. Are these covered? If you have specific dietary requirements or needs, are these covered under the base cost? One outfitter I know is an excellent photographer, and offers a memory book of photos from each trip. This comes with an extra charge, if travelers want it.

Find out whether you are expected to tip your guides. Some outfitters say yes, some no. Are the tips automatically included within the bill? Does the base charge include all sales taxes or their equivalent? Do you understand what items are being supplied as part of the base cost, and what items you're renting at additional cost? Talk it out, so that when you put your name on the contract you both understand just what you'll be paying.

Your Contract

Somewhere along the line you'll be asked to sign a contract sealing the deal. It might simply spell out the total cost, the amount of the deposit required, and the due date for final payment. It might be a number of pages specifying the trip route, duration, cost, basic and added expenses, taxes, and the services the company expects to provide. Essentially, this is the agreement between you and the guide company. Anything you chatted about on the phone, anything you assume from reading the brochure, anything you hear from a past client that is not in this document, really doesn't exist. It doesn't exist for the company, and it doesn't exist for you. If you want specific items spelled out, included or excluded, make darned sure it's in that document exactly as you want it. You're paying out money, sometimes a lot of money, for a trip, and the guide company wants to make that trip as close to what you desire as it can—so it behooves both of you to understand what is promised and what is offered.

This isn't high-finance negotiations where fractions of a penny lead to court battles. This is merely an agreement between equals as to the best way for you to have a great time on your vacation. If you don't ask for something you feel you need, and the company doesn't agree to provide it, then don't be surprised if it doesn't happen.

Rocks and Shoals

A trip contract is a legal document, and, yes, it offers both parties certain rights and duties. But far more important, it lets each of you know what is expected of the other in making the trip a great vacation.

Your guided trip is an invitation to have fun, big-time fun! You'll have fun exploring your options on where you'd like to go, you'll have fun on the trip, and you'll have fun reliving the trip in your memories. Understanding the details of your trip is fundamental to its success, and you want to keep the fun in *fun*damental.

The Least You Need to Know

- Once you've decided where and when you want to paddle, selecting a guide becomes far easier.

- Make sure the outfitter spells out exactly what he or she is supplying and what you're expected to bring.

- From hedonistic luxury to bare-bones travel, guided trips come in all levels of comfort.

- You can get trip insurance in case you have to cancel your vacation.

Chapter 19

Paddling with Kids

In This Chapter

- ◆ Turning to the fun experts in your family
- ◆ Determining when they are old enough
- ◆ Shopping for kid-size gear
- ◆ The scoop on kid-friendly paddling schools

You have within you the potential to be a good paddler and a great companion for any jaunt on the water—if and only if you chill a bit and lend an ear to the really good-time experts in your family. Listen to your children. Kids know about having fun, it is their life's work and the path along which they develop an understanding of the world. As a typical adult, you're involved with schedules, risk assessment, mortgages, and bedtimes. It's all too easy to substitute rules for spontaneity, exercise for pleasure, and even distance covered for good time. Kids haven't gotten bogged down with all that baggage, and they understand that a day on the water is all about *having fun*. And having fun is what paddling is all about.

If you have the good fortune of paddling with a child, this nearly forgotten world of childhood can reopen for you. If we can't re-enter it, at least we can look in and remember how it was.

Because you're at the juncture of different worlds, you're burdened with two, and at times contradictory, responsibilities. The exciting world of a child, with its fresh colors and sounds, is terribly seductive. At the same time, the child's world is without responsibility or consequence (we said "seductive"). On one hand, you have to keep that world fresh and exciting and bright with all its allure and fun. At the same time, you must keep in mind hypothermia and sunburn, late nights around a campfire, the sudden pull of a current on an unsuspecting ankle. No one promised it would be easy.

How Soon Is Too Soon?

What's the best age to take a kid paddling? Better you should ask: "How long is a ball of string?" There are too many variables in the question to make it meaningful.

At one end of the scale are canoeists who carry their pre-toddler in an infant seat strapped to the center thwart of their canoe. Before your hackles rise, these folks are outstanding paddlers and backcountry travelers, carefully choosing the water they'll explore and the weather they'll most likely experience. They know what they are doing.

The Old Paddler Says

Young children are very exposed to sun and wind in canoes and kayaks. Rig an awning over them, insist on hats and long-sleeved tops, and slather them up with lotions and sunblock. Don't forget insect repellant suitable for them.

On the other hand, some 12-year-olds are far, far too immature to be allowed anywhere near the water without one or preferably two full-time keepers. If you know the kids you're considering paddling with, you'll be able to decide for yourself whether they are ready to go paddling.

In most cases, a two-year-old or older is a delightful comrade in and around a boat—with planning and an open mind on your part. Before stepping near a boat, however, you should both understand some ground rules:

♦ Fire is hot and is not to be played around.

♦ Everybody carries a loud whistle. It is not a toy, and any time someone blasts his or her whistle, everyone else blows a loud-as-possible reply.

♦ Nobody (no matter how tall) leaves the put-in or take-out alone. Make this a game, and whenever an adult has to leave the beach, have the child be the chaperone escorting them.

♦ PFDs, or life jackets, must be worn when on or near the water. The bother of wearing yours all the time isn't nearly as great as trying to explain why Young Sprat has to wear a cumbersome PFD and you don't. This is a prime example of learning to take the easy way out.

Choosing where to go on that first trip, or trips, is almost a no-brainer. Head for a local pond with a clean (unmucky) beach, a river with an almost unnoticeable current, or a really sheltered bay. In a perfect world you'd locate such a place with an island to explore, with shells to find, with the possibility of a turtle or a heron to spot, and with just enough wind exposure to keep the bugs away but not enough to chill a tiny body.

Logistically speaking, overnight trips more than a few feet from your back door should be put on the back burner until potty training is well along. You'll find little room in a canoe or at a campsite for a diaper pail, and a wet sleeping bag can be anywhere between uncomfortable and a major inconvenience.

> ### In the Wake
>
> Wind, water, waves, and even the blanketing effects of brush, can muffle a child's voice within a few feet. Panic or confusion makes them even harder to hear. A good whistle, such as a Fox 40 or a Storm, blasts through most background sounds and can be blown by even very young children.

Rocks and Shoals

Despite their potential beauty to an adult, there are places to avoid for a kid's initial paddling experiences. Shun ocean beaches exposed to the surf or swept by currents, rivers with serious white water just downstream, or areas adjacent to bogs or standing water with lots of nasty biting bugs. If the weather is turning sour or the wind is picking up, switch your destination or your plans for the day.

To work out these difficulties, try a few full-scale overnight camping trips in your backyard complete with outdoor cooking, tents, and everyone's personal sleeping bags. You'll discover the shortfalls in your planning, and, at the same time, ease Young Sprat's concerns over sleeping in an unusual environment.

Gearing Up, Scaling Down

Kids are not the same size as adults. Obvious? Well, not to the unthinking adult who hands a full-size paddle to a child and expects delight. Let your child spread his or her hand across your open palm. Would you be comfortable hefting a 15-pound paddle while wrapping your hand around a 5-inch-diameter shaft? That, though, is what a young kid faces while attempting to grasp an adult-size paddle.

You can find a full range of paddling-specific personal flotation devices, clothing, and gear properly scaled for a child's needs by manufacturers who take pride in producing quality products. You'll find them in your local paddlesports shop, in catalogs from manufacturers and retailers, and listed in paddling magazines. If you don't want to buy new—and quality gear carries a price tag—check with the other parents in your family-oriented paddling club. Don't stop with your club's membership roster, but link up with parents in other local paddling clubs who may or may not have overlapping interests. Paddling jackets, water/windproof pants, water sandals, and kid-sized sleeping bags can work their way through generations of young paddlers.

> **Rocks and Shoals**
>
> Children grow, but not into a PFD. It has to fit today in order to work today. *Never,* never attack an oversize PFD with your sewing scissors in order to modify it for a better fit! In spite of your best intentions, you'll destroy the integrity of the PFD and place the child at risk.

Your pint-sized paddler probably won't need a pint-size white-water helmet—you weren't really going to start him or her out down a gnarly steep creek, were you?—but he or she may want one to strut his or her style. Likewise with a neoprene wet suit or a dry suit.

Makin' Good Time

Time passes differently in a child's world. That's all too clear, a couple of hours into any car trip, when "Are we there yet?" becomes like the chorus of a song stuck in your head. A kayak or a canoe can be much more confining than a car seat, made even more so by the tantalizing enticements of the shore so close at hand.

Don't let that become a problem, for the adults or for the children. Simply match the duration of the trip to the attention span of the participants. Plan to cover no more than 10 to 12 miles in three hours or so, rather than spending a whole day bending your paddle and shooting for 25 to 30 miles in your wake. Remember to put the emphasis on "good" when you're trying to make good time.

Back-paddle when you see a turtle sunning itself on a log. Pause to watch a heron stalk the shallows for a fishy lunch. Never put off a requested rest stop with a "Can you hold it for a bit?" It is always permissible to drift and munch on a cookie.

The child in your boat is seeing everything for the first time. The water world is new and wonderful and splendid. If you're infected with that terrible adult virus of rushing from the put-in to the take-out without a moment to reflect on your journey, you're going to miss the eagle soaring over the shoreline, the burl bulging out of a tree like a face, the sudden sweet smell of flowers. As one young girl said: "Let's just be quiet and listen to nature."

Pause, and you might regain that ability to enjoy. You'll also pass along the pleasure and lure of paddling to someone who will share miles of waterways and generations of time with you. Force them, harry them from launch to landing, and you'll soon lose the pleasure of their company.

Don't expect most young kids to paddle for two hours or more. Start by putting a kid-sized paddle at hand, and expect it to be more toy than power. Don't get cross when splashing dominates paddling, or when the Sprat unexpectedly explores what happens when he or she back-paddles. He or she is becoming a real-world scientist, running empirical experiments on paddle dynamics.

A good rule with two adults and a child in a canoe is that the nonpaddler can at any time exercise the right to switch seats and become a paddler. No debate. Head for the beach, switch positions, maybe pause for a snack or a sip, and push on. A few minutes of paddling, at least in the beginning and with a younger child, will probably be enough, and for a while you'll spend more time switching than paddling. Your child is testing your commitment to equality on the water, and you're opening the door to the child's participation as an equal.

Comfort in the Kid Zone

Kids don't think about comfort. That's your job: You're the responsible adult. Kids will play in cold water with the rain drizzling down until their lips are blue and their teeth are chattering. When you carry them back to a campfire, they'll complain about being unfairly yanked away from a really fun time. They'll stay out in the full blast of a noonday sun wrapped in an insulating PFD until they are parched with nary a thought of taking a drink.

Think *layering*. Three light layers of water-friendly clothing make a lot more sense than one heavy item of apparel. Add or remove one layer at a time to match changes in temperature. Young skin is delicate. High fashion in or around the water includes big-brimmed hats and long-sleeved tees. Look for a sun-blocking material for both pants and tops.

Lead by example. Layering and sun protection work for adults, too.

Paddlin' Talk

The key to comfort is **layering**, wearing several light layers of garments rather than one heavy layer. This enables you to "fine-tune" just what you might need. In cool weather, layering may start with polypropylene undergarments to wick sweat away from the skin, a fleece top—and depending on temperature—pants, and a windproof and water-repellant jacket and pants.

Avoid cottons. Quick-drying synthetics and fleece are the fabrics of choice, and pack along several changes of each. Wool works, but it dries slower than fleece and retains less of its insulating value when wet. You may plan on everyone staying dry and out of the water, but any kid is going to find a way to get splashed, dipped, and soaked at least once a day. A thirsty towel and a fleece throw are invaluable additions to your bag of dry things.

Rocks and Shoals

Cotton fabrics have their place, but not near the water. Cotton sops up moisture readily, and is slow to dry, leaving you feeling clammy.

Keep the fun in functional. Help pick out bright colors and wild patterns. Vivid hues appeal to a kid's sense of style (shop with them, not for them) as well as making it a lot easier to find shirts or pants left along the beach. Tennis shoes are marginally okay, because they will protect tender young feet, but they dry ever so slowly. Sandals, real outdoor sandals, provide that same protection as well as offering support while walking or running. And they dry quickly.

Kids in the Kitchen

Kids want to be included as valuable members of the paddling team. Kids barely out of the toddler stage get excited about gathering a bit of firewood, although that bit may turn out to be one waterlogged twig. By the time they turn six, most kids are willing and able to help with meals as well as do their bit putting up a tent, unrolling a sleeping bag, or washing dishes. Bring your children into full—to the extent of their abilities—partnership. Use your common sense as to what they can do and the amount of supervision they require.

In the Wake

Paddling, and just being on the water, requires more calories than sedentary life in the city. As a starting point, figure an increase of 25 percent to 30 percent over your normal diet. Practically, figure on eating four meals a day rather than three, or your regular three meals plus mid-morning and mid-afternoon snacks.

Cooking is a very flexible term. Spreading peanut butter on a pilot cracker with a plastic knife is cutting-edge cooking when you're five or six. Shaking up a bottle of Tang (once an adult makes sure that the lid is on tight) is an intensely important task. Combine a kid, a pot, a spoon, and instant pudding, and inside of a few messy minutes you will have your own personal dessert chef. Plan your menus so that the dropped cracker or spilled pudding is nothing more than a moment's inconvenience.

You're introducing a kid to a universe of new things that first time paddling. Pit toilets, the constant rocking of the canoe or kayak, isolation from friends, and the lack of familiar surroundings can add up into something rather scary. Stir a bit of comfort into their lives by choosing (with their participation) the meals they really enjoy. Don't forget the unexpected treats. Try apple pie for breakfast. Learn how to make S'mores (a dessert sandwich with graham crackers, chocolate, and toasted marshmallows) or banana boats (split an unpeeled banana along the inside of the curve and stuff it with squares of milk chocolate. Rest it next to the fire until the chocolate melts and serve with a spoon).

The Old Paddler Says

With older children, let them take their rotation into the cycle of meal preparation—including buying ingredients for *their* day of cooking on the river or saltwater. Instant oatmeal for breakfast, or macaroni and cheese (toss in a can of chili for chili-mac) is within the supervised range of surprisingly young kids.

The Games We Play

Don't let your mouth promise what the environment won't provide. It's easy to get a kid jazzed up over catching fish, but if that was your promise and the fish aren't biting, the day is heading for a downer. Change the emphasis from the goal to the action, from *catching* fish to *let's me and you try to outfox a fish*, and the value of the experience doesn't hang on the outcome. Don't promise a moose around every bend, lest, like the boy in the fable, you'll be branded as a wolf caller.

Unless you preempt the situation with careful planning, any child can back you into a corner over the issue of toys. Kids cling to the familiar, and toys are about as familiar as things get. Their first impulse will be to cart along every toy they might possess. Limiting the number of toys to a set number won't work: Your little one will select a tricycle, a multistory dollhouse, and a life-sized bear.

Start by bringing home boxes, one for each person in your boat, labeling each with his or her name. These are for personal possessions, and it goes for you as well as a kid. Children have had the concept of fairness drilled into them, and if you want them to paddle with you as equals, you better be prepared to treat them as equals. Whatever toys come on the trip have to fit within that box. Hand out the boxes well-enough ahead so that your kid can select and reselect the most important items. Just before you load the car for departure, inventory the contents of the toy box, so the absolutely most valuable thing in the box won't accidentally be left on the beach.

The toy box should be the last thing loaded into your boat. As such, it will be the first thing unloaded and will be immediately available.

Sneak in a few more toys or amusements. Hand a post-toddler some water-soluble colors (test them first!) and let him or her muralize the inside of your boat. Introduce a rousing game of Old Maid or Go Fish on the beach, or, with older kids, Gin Rummy or Hearts. Draw a ring in the sand and shoot marbles.

Open a book at the end of the day, in camp or at a take-out, and read a story or a chapter. Learn a few nursery rhymes and kid's songs for a round-the-fire sing-along. With songs like the Fox, Bill Grogan's Goat, or the Grand Old Duke of York, you don't need a tune, just volume and the willingness to make a funny face. Drop some pebbles into an aluminum pie pan, and tape a second pan on to for a homemade tambourine. Sand or pea gravel in a plastic butter tub makes a great rattle.

Help a little-older kid capture his or her own memories with a one-time-use camera. You and Abe Lincoln can pick one up at most stores. Water-resistant cameras are available for just a bit more.

With crayons and soft paper you can make rubbings. Make a casting of animal tracks found along the beach with plaster of Paris. Learn the names and shapes of the most prominent constellations, as well as the difference between a star, a planet, and a satellite.

Invent the most outrageous tall tale you can, and three sentences into it, point at the person who must take up where you just left off. With older kids, start each sentence of the story with the next letter of the alphabet.

Rocks and Shoals

The damp environment of a river, lake, or bay absolutely eats up delicate electronics. When in doubt, leave electronic games, cameras, and music players at home.

Rocks and Shoals

Rubbings can be a great memento of a trip, but be exceeding careful of the original art. Petroglyphs and cemetery headstones may be fragile and potentially harmed by even delicate rubbings.

Killing the Fun

If you work at it, you can discourage kids from joining you paddling. One way is to drag them along, but then isolate them from any activity. That's the "Shut up and don't rock the boat" concept. How bored would you be if you had to sit in the bottom of the boat while others got to paddle and to decide where to head?

Another excellent way to quash kid participation is to set impossibly high standards, and then constantly criticize them when they fail to meet them. Paddling is not about perfect paddling skills or even keeping your feet dry. It's about having fun. If a kid embraces paddling, technical competence will come as that child develops.

Another course toward paddling by yourself in the future is to insist that every family member go on every paddling trip, and not admit that other activities might also be pleasurable. Forced participation simply doesn't work. When faced with being told that "Paddling is fun and good for you" many kids will automatically reject paddlesports just out of youthful rebellion. Show 'em that it is fun, don't tell them. If they really don't enjoy paddling, don't force it upon them. This just closes the door to future opportunities.

If you present paddling as an adult "grown-up" activity, you may well convince a child that he or she can't paddle.

Honing Their Skills

There are certain things you should just never do: play poker with a man named Doc, argue with your spouse over the right way to read a map, or teach your kids advanced paddling skills. You just bring too much baggage to the table.

We're hard-wired to do everything within our power to keep our children safe and comfortable. Yet we know that learning comes from confronting difficulties—be they physical or intellectual—and that involves a certain amount of risk. Thank goodness for paddling camps and schools with kid-focused programs! They do teach paddling skills, but even better, they place young paddlers in situations where kids have to make decisions based on their skills and learning (sometimes swimming) from their experiences.

Throwing a kid onto the water to sink or swim is criminal, no argument about that. Giving that same kid the appropriate skills for that same patch of water along with the right equipment and surrounding him or her with proficient instructors offering advice and a safety net creates a good learning environment. If you will, paddling becomes a metaphor for life.

Finding the paddling school that best meets your standards and desires will take you more than a couple of minutes. Fortunately, others have been down this same channel before you, and have established the kinds of questions you should ask:

> **In the Wake**
>
> A kid whose paddling skills are far less than his or her peers will not be a happy camper, or a willing participant. But as a novice among novices, he or she will bloom and progress rapidly. That's one of the strengths of taking the child from your group of skilled adults and placing him or her within a circle of equal paddlers.

◆ **What's your safety record?** Compare the number of accidents/incidents with the number of students for the past several years. It might be fairer to make those student/days, multiplying the number of students by the number of class days. If there were significant (major injuries, a misplaced student, or worse) incidents, how did the school respond?

◆ **What's your instructors' certification and experience?** British Canoe Union (BCU) certification is outstanding on both flat and moving water. American Canoe Association (ACA) certification is the standard for any paddling discipline, but it is probably a bit more common in white water and flatwater than in kayak touring. Canadian Recreational Canoeing Association (CRCA) coordinates instructor certification through 10 provincial and 3 territorial associations. Ask about instructor experience, especially for those leading on-the-water trips.

◆ **What are your itineraries and backup plans?** Does the school have an itinerary for multiday trips or day trips during the duration of the school? Are there provisions for mishaps or evacuations in case of a problem on the water? How does the school contact parents in case of an incident? How can parents contact the school if needed?

◆ **Can the school supply a list of student references?** Good programs are more than willing to have happy and satisfied students talk up their programs.

◆ **Can I see the liability waiver form?** They're horrifying to read, with their implications of disaster, and there are more than a few questions in courtrooms all across the land as to whether they have any legal standing when applied to minors. They are, however, a strong indication that the school is contracting with reputable insurance companies for coverage. The waivers may shield the school and its insurance carrier from frivolous claims.

◆ **How complete is the package of information describing the school and the program?** Does it include a breakdown of costs? Are there optional cost items? Does it clearly state the goals, and map how it expects to reach those goals? What are the housing provisions, including chaperones? Can they accommodate special dietary requests? What nonpaddling activities are on tap for the kids? Does it include a history of the school and its principals?

Launching your canoe or kayak with a young child aboard is frightening. You'll study first-aid techniques you pray will never be needed, you'll downsize routes and destinations, and you'll teeter along that thin line between fun and responsibility. Your tongue will hurt from clamping your teeth down on it to prevent snapping out orders rather than suggestions. You'll learn the weight of being a role model. And you'll never be able to describe the pride as you see the new skills each kid so nonchalantly acquires.

Sound daunting? It ain't. With a child along you will resize your paddling adventures to a more manageable level. That doesn't mean reducing them. Seeing through a child's eyes—and that's what you're learning to do—will magnify all the magic and excitement of a trip that your more jaded adult eyes gloss over. You'll gain far, far more than you give.

The Least You Need to Know

◆ Paddling is an all-ages sport.

◆ Kids and toys: Preplanning makes for a better compromise.

◆ You *can* discourage young paddlers, if you try hard enough.

◆ Paddling schools can really boost young people's skills while treating them to a good time.

Chapter 20

Building Your Own Canoe or Kayak

In This Chapter

- ◆ Building your boat from anything
- ◆ Three levels of boat-building challenge
- ◆ Three technologies to build your canoe or kayak
- ◆ Building a boat at school

Building a boat, whether canoe or kayak, is a project of passion and personal need. Logic rarely enters into it. Even a cursory look around your local paddlesports store or through the pages of your favorite paddling magazine's buyer's guide will convince a nonbeliever that the materials you'll need to build your dream boat will cost more than most comparable craft—without taking into consideration your time, your tools, and the space it will take up for far longer than you predict.

With that off our collective chests, we concede that building your very own canoe or kayak is almost as great as going paddling. The alchemy of transforming a mixed pile of raw materials into floating perfection (if only in the eyes of its maker) stirs at the very soul. The delight of launching your own boat and setting out on your first trip is indescribable.

Not only that, if winter blizzards or summer droughts keep you off the water, you can retreat to your shop and shape and sand as a surrogate for paddling.

What's It Made Of?

Canoes and kayaks have been constructed from paper skins over frames, from milk cartons, and from sheets of aluminum hammered into shape and riveted together. One of the most popular classes of Hawaiian outrigger competition is the koa, hollowed out from a log. Native Americans and First Peoples from the Northwestern United States and western Canada carve big dugout canoes for competition and for tribal ceremonies. Workshops along the Eastern Seaboard and the Upper Midwest of the United States occasionally offer classes in traditional birchbark canoe construction.

These aren't practical for most paddlers, but show that you can make a seaworthy boat out of just about any material that comes to hand.

> ### In the Wake
>
> An 11-year-old can build a beautiful and efficient kayak, with just a little supervision. They've done it. Can you imagine a better way to share paddling with a child than to build a boat with him or her, or to build family boats together? It's truly a case of many hands making light work.

The most popular materials today are resin/composite lay-ups, carefully shaped plywood planks that are "stitched" together and glued into complex rigid shapes, thin strips of flexible wood bent around forms and edge-glued into a rigid shape, and frame-and-stringer frames covered with fabric skins. A few skilled boatwrights still craft traditional canoes with thin planking arced around bent ribs and with the hull protected by a layer of paint-impregnated canvas. Here and there you may run across a kayak built by bending planking around frames.

Choosing How to Begin

It is, they say, easy to sculpt a statue of an elephant. Just take a big block of marble and cut away anything that doesn't look like an elephant. You can approach canoe or kayak building the same way. Just start sticking random pieces together until you have something that looks like a canoe or a kayak. There are easier ways, involving far less time, energy, and materials. They also predictably result in better boats.

Kit Boats

Think of a kit as a boat in a box. The kit should contain all the materials and all the hardware needed to build your boat, along with detailed instructions. Complicated or critical parts should be cut to shape, leaving you with only minor or simple trimming. The instruction manual should have step-by-step instructions, leading you from how to unpack the box to how to tie the last knot on the rudder lines. Follow the directions, and you'll create the promised boat. This is the most expensive option, but you're hiring the company's expertise in fabricating the shapes that come together in your boat. For a first-time builder, the bottom line is that this could end up being the least-expensive alternate.

In the Wake

With a kit boat, you get the items you'll need to build a canoe or kayak that will meet the designer's and your expectations.

Plans Plus Materials Packages

Plans give you the dimensions of each part of your canoe or kayak, and tell you how each part fits into the overall boat. The materials package contains the right amount of material to shape each of the parts. Many include the hardware, from screws to cleats, required to complete your boat. The plans may indicate a sequence of steps you should follow in putting the parts together—for which you should be thankful—but they don't always. This option tends to be less expensive than a kit boat, but requires more time and skill in the building.

Plans

A plan is an accurate and detailed sketch of each component and part of your canoe or kayak, and an exact perspective of how each part fits into the whole. It's up to you to find the materials and shape the parts. In a plans-plus-materials package, you're paying the supplier for finding the materials and shipping them to you. If you're building a boat from plans, you're spending time and energy locating the materials and your gas in driving around to pick up what you need. You'll probably forget an item, or make a bad cut, and you'll get to drive back for a second or third time before the boat is complete.

Fiberglass Boats from Club Molds

With a few caveats, laying up a composite hull in a mold is about the easiest for most amateur builders. First, the caveats: You'll need a mold, and a good mold represents a lot of labor and the intellectual skills of a good boat designer. In some cases, you may be able to rent a mold from a small boatbuilder. More likely, you'll find that a larger paddlesports club acquired a mold for a club-popular design and allows members to use it. In either case, you'll be working with a design a few steps back from today's cutting-edge boats. That's not necessarily bad, if you admire a particular design.

Molds are intellectual property. Plan on paying the designer for the one-time use of that design. From a legal standpoint, you're buying a license for one use of the design as created within the mold. Some folks will stoop to making a mold from an existing boat, effectively stealing the time and talent of the designer. If you respect the designer's work, make sure you're working with a legal mold and that you've come to an agreement over the licensing fee.

The Old Paddler Says

Don't expect most designers to license out their designs and molds before they have come up with a newer boat for the commercial marketplace. Only after commercial sales have slowed to a trickle are you likely to see a mold enter the club universe.

The other caveat is that you'll be working with volatile chemicals, some which may cause instant reactions, and some of which you may become sensitized to while working with them. You'll also be working with materials that can cause permanent injury.

Rocks and Shoals

One of my less-brilliant moves was to build a decked canoe in a basement garage. I sealed off the doors with duct tape and plastic sheeting, brought in a fan to keep air circulating, and stored the fiberglass cloth and resins well away from the sealed door. Then I mixed the resin and catalyst right in front of the air intake vent for the furnace. The house was permeated with the stench of resins setting up!

This isn't meant to frighten you, or cause you to drop your boat-building project. It's only meant to encourage you to heed the warning labels on all the chemical jugs, to wear gloves, to use a respirator or dust mask, and only to work in a well-ventilated area. Pay attention to fire regulations and hazards.

The actual process is as complicated as baking a cake. First, coat the mold surface with a release agent. Think of butter slathered on a griddle, to keep the pancakes from sticking. The first coat on the interior surface of the mold, which is the outermost coat on the hull when it is popped from the hull, is a (usually colored) gel coat that offers ultra-violet protection to the resins and support cloth as well as serving as a watertight wearing surface to protect the inner hull layers from scratches and abrasion.

Lay a full-length layer of support cloth in the mold, smoothing out any wrinkles. Wet this with your chosen resin. Repeat until you have three layers in the hull, along with pieces needed for reinforcement. The deck is formed in the same way, usually with only two layers of cloth.

Bolt the two halves of the mold, the bottom or hull half and the top or deck half, and place a wide ribbon of support material tape along the seam between the two. Wet it out with resin, and when all is set, you can pop your basic boat from the mold.

Basic is the key word. You still have to fabricate and install the coaming, seat, foam walls, hardware such as foot braces, and grab loops, but you can look at what you've built and see a boat.

A canoe will have a single hull mold.

Boatbuilders have a choice of resins with which to work. It's important to match the resin to the cloth. Resins also come in various mixes, to cope with differing temperatures.

The least expensive support media is fiberglass cloth. Lighter, stronger, and more expensive is Kevlar, a modern synthetic woven material also used for military helmets and bulletproof vests. You can mix other cloth into the composite sandwich for specific characteristics, or you can embed designs.

An advantage of working with a legal club mold is that you can call upon others who have made boats for their advice and input. If someone worked out a neat stick with a flattened hook to place the seam tape smoothly in the far end of the hull, borrow that stick, or idea, rather than reinventing it yourself. The same holds true for resins and cloth. Go with what has been proven to work.

The Old Paddler Says

Wear a shower cap when you stick your head into the cockpit hole to place the seam tape between the two halves of your mold. You *really* don't want to inadvertently fiberglass your hair to the boat or to your scalp.

The Old Paddler Says

One of the primary benefits of joining a club is the chance to learn from people sharing your interests. If you're stumped or even mildly puzzled when facing your not-yet-done canoe or kayak, remember that "Let Me Show You" are the four most popular words in English. Tap into the experiences of your friends.

Stitch and Glue Construction

Stitch and Glue is a relatively new and very elegant way of shaping a beautiful hull quickly and accurately. You simply "stitch" the edges of carefully shaped plywood planks together with short pieces of wire, and then glue the planks into a whole. A protective layer of fiberglass cloth is wrapped around the hull and sealed with resin.

The accuracy of the hull depends entirely upon the accurate shaping of each plywood plank. In a great kit, such as from Pygmy Boats or Chesapeake Light Craft, the planks are cut by computer-controlled machines to super-accurate specifications. If you're working from plans, it's up to you to transfer the dimensions exactly to sheets of plywood, and then to perfectly cut each piece out. With care, you can do it.

Stitch-and-glue construction delivers beautiful touring kayaks, canoes, rowing boats, and outrigger craft.

Strip-Built Hulls

Strip-built construction is very similar to old balsa-wood-and-paper model airplanes. A series of forms exactly creating the cross section of a canoe or kayak at specified distances along its keel are cut from a rigid material such as ¼-inch plywood, and then are mounted exactly perpendicular to a strongback or building form. Thin strips of flexible wood, often cedar, are bent from the stem (the front edge of the boat) to the stern, beginning at the gunwales and working toward the keel. The strips are edged-glued, holding each in place and creating the rigid shape of the completed boat. The hull is covered with a protective layer of fiberglass and resin, lifted off its forms, and a second fiberglass coat is applied inside.

> **In the Wake**
>
> How do you measure the soft, complex curves in a canoe or kayak hull? By eye! By sighting along a seam or a keel, you can usually see a bump or a dip of as little as $\frac{1}{32}$ of an inch, and can correct them with a little padding or a little carving away of the underlying form.

The resulting boat is very strong, quite light, and can even have complex curves and shapes. It may well be the easiest type of hull construction for the amateur wanting to build from scratch. Cost is relatively low, and the technique works equally well for open boats as well as for deck boats. For a decked boat, such as a kayak, the deck is made separately and then placed atop the hull and attached.

Frame and Fabric Hulls

In the old days, kayaks were made by creating a shape of ribs (at right angles to the keel) forming the desired cross section of the hull, and *stringers* bent from the bow to the stern on the outside of the ribs, or the shaped forms that create the cross section. This shape was then covered with a flexible waterproof fabric or hide.

It worked then, and it works today. The ribs, or frames, may be made of solid wood, plywood, aluminum tubing, or rigid plastic. The bow to stern stringers may be wood or aluminum tubing (or for that matter, possibly even plastic pipe). Hides have fallen out of favor; most builders today experiment with canvas, synthetic woven materials, or sheet materials such as urethane. Frames may be lashed together, and screwed, bolted, or glued to the stringers.

Sewing a tight skin is a challenge for most of us. Some builders, evolving with today's materials, are adopting heat-sensitive skins that shrink to a taut fit when heated.

Part of the attraction of frame-and-fabric boats lies in their return to what we fondly imagine as the roots of paddlesports. An equal attraction is their supple flexing as you work through wind and wave. They have a soft and comforting ride. And they are surprisingly easy to build. Frame and fabric should work equally well for canoes as well as kayaks, although the overwhelming majority of these boats are touring kayaks. Big open canoes, called umiaks, were the freight and household boats of much of the Canadian Arctic for generations of First Peoples' life.

Paddlin' Talk

Stringers are long strips, which may be round or rectangular, stretched from the bow to stern of a canoe or kayak over the outside of the ribs or frames. They create the shape of the hull and give it strength.

Schools and Workshops

You're not alone in wanting to build your own canoe or kayak. Lots of people have the same desire. And you're not alone in building your boat. Like you, though, many paddlers are a little concerned about attempting to build their first canoe or kayak.

Fortunately, schools and workshops are available. Start by reading the pages (and looking at the advertisements) in your favorite paddlesports publications. That's your fastest way to keep abreast of the schools and workshops offered. Keep in touch with the major paddlesports associations such as the American Canoe Association and the Canadian Recreational Canoeing Association, and link up with the Wooden Canoe Heritage Association. Find them in Appendix B in this book.

Some programs will extend over many weeks. Others may be a week or less. One frame-and-fabric builder recently offered a week-long workshop for $1,000, which included the single kayak you'd build in his shop under supervision.

Amateur builders with a few hulls under their belt and all the parts prefabricated can show you how to construct a basic strip-built 16-foot canoe in 4 or 5 days.

Because of time spent waiting for glues to dry and resins to set up, you'll spend close to a month building a stitch-and-glue solo or tandem touring kayak.

The Least You Need to Know

◆ You can build a canoe or kayak out of a wide variety of materials.

◆ Choose how difficult you want your boat project to be: from a kit, from plans and materials, or from just the plans.

◆ Clubs can also help you build your canoe or kayak.

◆ Schools and workshops offer boatbuilding knowledge.

Appendix A

Glossary

abeam   Perpendicular to the keel line of a boat at the midpoint or amidships.

aft   Toward the stern of a canoe or kayak.

amidships   The middle portion of a canoe or kayak.

asymmetrical paddle   A paddle blade in which the left and right halves of the blade are different sizes and different shapes. In the water, however, the force on each side of the blade is equalized.

back face   That side of the paddle blade that has no power applied to it during a forward stroke.

back-ferry   Paddling backward at an angle into a current, to edge or crab sideways across the current without being swept downstream. A great way to pause briefly to observe your down-current course.

backpaddle   To paddle a canoe or kayak backward, often against a current.

bailer   A scoop for dipping accumulated water out of a canoe or kayak. You can easily make one by cutting the bottom off a plastic jug.

bang plate   A wearing surface applied to the bow and stern of a canoe or kayak and along the keel line(s), to protect the outer skin from abrasion and wear. Also called a skid plate.

bank   The margins or sides of a river. Banks are called right or left as viewed when facing in the direction of the flow.

bar   A shallow obstruction, made of sand, gravel, or small rocks.

beam   The maximum width of a boat.

big water   Rivers with large volume or wicked hydraulics.

bilge   The transition from the bottom to the side of a canoe or kayak.

blade   The wide and flat surface at the end of a paddle, which transmits the power of the paddler to the water.

boils   Ascending currents unpredictably rising to the water surface.

booties   Neoprene socks or slip-on soled boots for cold-weather comfort.

boulder garden   A rapid formed with many boulders. Also called a *rock garden*.

bouse   To hoist or lift, with a tackle.

bow line   A short painter or rope attached to the bow of a canoe or kayak.

bow paddler   The front paddler in a canoe or kayak with more than one paddler.

bow rescue   A rescue in which the capsized paddler grasps the bow of a rescuing bow and uses it in conjunction with a hip snap to right the inverted boat. More common on white water than in touring, because of the lesser maneuverability of the touring boats. Also called an Eskimo rescue.

bow seat   The seat or position for the front paddler in a canoe or kayak.

bow sweep   A paddle stroke in which the paddle is inserted near the bow of the boat and is pushed away from the boat in a "C"-shaped arc back toward amidships. This turns the bow away from the paddle side.

bow   The front part of a canoe or kayak, the leading edge that parts the water when moving ahead.

brace   A paddle maneuver assisting stability: A low brace pushes you up away from the blade; a high brace pulls you up toward the paddle blade.

break in/break out   British Canoe Union lingo for eddy turn and peel-out.

broach   Pinned or stuck against a rock or other obstacle, at the middle or at the ends. A canoe or kayak pinned or stuck sideways against a rock or other obstacle by the force of a current.

broadside   The position of a canoe or kayak that is perpendicular to a current, wind, or waves, thus presenting its broad side to potential obstacles.

bulkhead   Partitions or walls inside a kayak; usually waterproof in a sea kayak to separate the sitting area and coaming from the dry storage and flotation areas in the ends; occasionally foam in a white water boat to aid structural integrity and rigidity.

buoy   A floating device identifying a location, obstruction, or channel.

C-   A letter indicating the paddler capacity of a canoe, most often a decked canoe, followed by 1 for a single paddler, 2 for a tandem, and so on.

capsize   To turn over, to upset. *See* huli.

carry   Same as portage, the act of carrying a canoe or kayak over land from one waterway to another.

catch   The beginning of a stroke, where the blade enters the water.

centerline   The direct line from the bow to the stern.

channel   An open conduit, either naturally or artificially created, that periodically or continuously contains moving water, or forms a connecting link between two bodies of water. River, creek, run, branch, anabranch, and tributary are some of the terms used to describe natural channels. Canal and floodway are some of the terms used to describe artificial channels.

chart   A detailed sketch of a waterway, including navigation aids, water depths, obstructions, and distinctive shore features.

chine   The meeting of the bottom and sides of a canoe or kayak.

chute   A narrow, constructed portion of a current.

clean   A description of a river route free of obstruction.

coaming   The lip or edge around a cockpit.

cockpit   The place where a paddler sits or kneels in a closed (decked) canoe or kayak.

creek boating   Paddling small, very steep, and turbulent streams, with big drops and often waterfalls. Also called steep creek boating.

creek   A small stream of water (a relative measurement that varies by region and environment) that serves as the natural drainage course for a drainage basin of small size.

cubic feet per second (CFS)   A measurement of water flow representing one cubic foot of water (7.48 gallons) moving past a given point in one second.

current rips   Small waves formed on the surface at the confluence of opposing currents.

current   Moving water.

cutwater   The sharp edge of the stem, which cuts the water.

deck   The upper surface of a canoe or kayak.

depth   The distance between the gunwale and the bottom of a canoe, or the deck and the bottom of a kayak, at a specified point such as amidships.

downstream vee   Smooth water created as a current flows between two obstacles, indicating a usually safe passage. The apex of the vee points downstream. *See* tongue.

draft   The vertical distance from the waterline of a canoe or kayak to the deepest point along the keel.

draw or **draw stroke**   A paddle stroke in which the blade is extended out from the side of the canoe or kayak parallel to the keel line or centerline, and the boat is pulled sideways toward the blade. If applied amidships, the hull slides sideways; if applied at the bow or stern, the boat turns toward the blade.

drop   A steep, sudden change in the level of a river. A waterfall is an extreme drop.

dry bag   A waterproof bag in a canoe or kayak, used to hold gear that should be kept dry.

ebb   A receding or falling tide.

eddy line   The demarcation between a main current and the counter-flowing current in an eddy.

eddy turn   Using the current differential between the main current and the eddy current to make a quick turn into the shelter of the eddy.

eddy   A relatively calmer area just down-current of a rock or other obstruction, with a current flowing counter to the main current.

edging   Tilting a canoe or kayak to one side.

ender   Standing a canoe or kayak vertically (or nearly so) on end, using underwater hydraulics to hold your balance.

Eskimo roll   The combination of paddle stroke, brace, and body movement that enables a paddler to turn a capsized canoe or kayak right side up.

estuary   The zone along a coastline where freshwater systems meet with saltwater.

esturine waters   Tidal habitats and tidal wetlands that are usually partially enclosed by land but have access to the ocean, and are at least occasionally diluted by freshwater runoff.

exit   The end of a paddle stroke, where the paddle leaves the water. Also refers to getting out of a canoe or kayak. A wet exit refers to getting out of a capsized or swamped boat.

fathom   Six feet.

feather   To rotate a canoe or kayak paddle blade so that the blade proceeds edge-forward through the air from exit to catch to reduce air resistance.

feathered   A kayak paddle with blades set at an angle to each other.

ferry   To paddle into a current at an angle, allowing the canoe or kayak to crab sideways so as to cross the current without being pushed down-current.

flare   A hull design in which the boat becomes progressively wider from the waterline to the gunwale.

flat water   Water without rapids, such as a slow-moving river, a lake or a sheltered bay. Sometimes referred to as flatwater.

flood   An incoming or rising tide.

flotation   Buoyant material (including air in an airtight bag) placed in a canoe or kayak, allowing the boat to float if swamped or capsized.

flotation bags   Flexible bags inflated with air, secured within a canoe or kayak to provide extra flotation in the event of a swamping or capsize. Also called float bags.

footbrace   A support against which a paddler braces his or her feet, adding to the effectiveness of a paddle stroke and dynamically securing the paddler to the canoe or kayak.

forward   Toward the bow of a canoe or kayak.

freeboard   The distance from the waterline to the lowest portion of the gunwale.

freestyle   A canoeing style in which canoeing maneuvers are performed to music, similar in many ways to ice dancing.

'glass   Short for fiberglass, referring to a fabric woven of fiberglass.

grab loops   Fabric loops at the bow and stern of a kayak, or a decked cane used as handholds.

gradient   Measuring the rate of a river's descent by the number of feet it descends in 1 mile (or meters per kilometer).

grip   The area or place where a paddler grasps a paddle.

gunwale   The top edge of the hull in an open boat; the juncture of the hull and deck in a closed boat.

hatch   The "door" into the sealed waterproof storage compartments in the bow and stern of a touring kayak.

haystack   A large standing wave, often formed in a train of waves.

hip snap   A twitch of your torso and knee motion to change the angle of a canoe or kayak.

hogged   A canoe or kayak with the keel line bending upward from the lowest points at the bow and stern.

hole   The usually turbulent depression in the water formed as a current flows over a submerged rock or other obstacle. Often called a hydraulic.

huli   A Hawaiian term meaning to turn over or to turn upside down.

hull   The main body of a canoe or kayak, from the keel to the gunwales.

hypothermia   Lowering of the body's core temperature to 95° F or lower.

initial stability   The stable feeling you may experience when first boarding a canoe or kayak.

inwale   The interior rail or a gunwale.

J-lean   Tilting or edging your canoe or kayak while keeping your body erect and balanced over the center of your boat; the name refers to the shape of your spine and hips when the lean is done correctly.

J-stroke   A paddle stroke hooked into a slight "J" curve at the end of the stroke by a solo canoe paddler or by the stern paddler in a tandem canoe, to correct the tendency of the bow to swing away from the paddle stroke.

K-   A letter indicating the paddler capacity of a kayak, followed by 1 for a solo kayak, 2 for a tandem, and up to 4 for some racing kayaks.

kanawa   A word adopted by early Spanish visitors to what is now Canada, to describe the native canoe.

keel   A strip running all or part of the length of a canoe's or kayak's underside from bow to stern, providing structural strength and aiding in tracking. Also refers to the direct line along the bottom of a canoe or kayak from bow to stern, whether or not the surface is smooth or a strip is mounted.

keeper   A large hole or hydraulic that can trap a swimmer or boat for an extended period of time.

knot   A rate of speed equal to 1 nautical mile per hour. It is improper to speak of knots per hour, because this would refer to the rate of acceleration rather than speed.

ledge hole   A hole or hydraulic caused by a ledge.

lee   The side away from the direction from which the wind is blowing; also refers to the side of a canoe or kayak sheltered from the wind.

lee helm   Turning stern to the wind.

lee shore   A shore toward which the wind is blowing.

leeward   Located on the side (of a canoe or kayak) toward which the wind is blowing.

leeway   The drift of a canoe or kayak to leeward (or downwind or down-current) from its planned course.

line   A rope; the practice of pulling a canoe or kayak upstream or lowering it downstream by means of a line or rope.

littoral zone   The area on or near the shore of a body of water, especially the sea; the shore zone between high and low watermarks.

lower grip   The place where a paddler holds a canoe paddle nearest the blade.

mystery move   A maneuver in which the kayak and paddler remain submerged for a half minute or more before popping back into view.

neap tide   Tides near the first or third quarter of the moon, when the gravities of the sun and moon don't work in unison, and the tidal range is decreased.

offing   How far you are from shore, usually a touring term.

off-side   The opposite side of a canoe or kayak from a paddle stroke.

on-side   The same side of a canoe or kayak as a paddle stroke.

outwale   The outer rail of a gunwale.

overfalls   Short, usually steep and breaking waves created by a tidal current flowing over an obstruction such as a shoal or bar, or an opposing current.

paddle float   An inflatable bag that may be attached to one kayak paddle blade while the other end of the paddle is secured at the kayak deck at right angles to the hull. It functions as an outrigger to aid re-entry and water removal after an upset or swamping.

painter line(s)   Short lines or ropes attached to the bow and stern of a canoe or kayak. Also called painters.

pear grip   A paddle grip rounded like a somewhat flattened pear, aiding in power stroking.

peel-out   The reverse of an eddy turn, in which the paddler leaves the eddy and turns downstream.

personal flotation device (PFD)   A life jacket or vest.

pillow   A cushion of water formed on the up-current side of a obstacle by a current flowing against the obstacle.

poagies   Special glovelike garment that fit over the hand and seals to the paddle, allowing a bare-handed grasp of the grip while offering protection from wind, weather, and temperature.

port   The left side of a canoe or kayak, facing forward.

portage   The act of carrying a canoe or kayak, or gear, from one paddleable water to another, around an obstruction. Also refers to the path so used. Also called a carry.

pour-over   A bad hole or hydraulic.

power face   The face of a canoe or kayak paddle pressed against the water during a stroke.

power phase   The portion of a paddle stroke in which power is applied to the blade.

pry stroke   A paddle stroke in which the paddle blade is inserted into the water parallel to the keel line at the edge of or even slightly under the side of the canoe or kayak, and is forced away from the hull thus moving the boat away from the paddle.

put-in   The beginning point of a trip, where you put the kayak or canoe into the water.

raft-and-pump   Assisting a swamped kayak by coming alongside and physically balancing it with your hand as the other paddler re-enters and pumps the water out.

recovery   That segment of a paddle stroke during which the paddle is returned from the exit back to the catch. This may be in the air, or may be through the water.

reverse sweep A paddle stroke in which the paddle is inserted near the stern of the boat and is pushed away from the boat in a "C"-shaped arc toward amidships. This turns the bow toward the paddle side. Same as stern sweep.

river basin The area that a river and its assorted tributaries drains.

river left The left side of a river, as seen when looking downstream.

river mouth Where a river ends by flowing into another body of water such as a lake, ocean, or another river.

river right The right side of a river, as seen when looking downstream.

river A natural stream of water.

rocker The profile of the keel of a canoe or kayak from bow to stern. More rocker—a greater curve—increases turning ability; less rocker—a straighter line from bow to stern—enhances tracking ability.

roller A big, curling wave.

safe swimmer The best position for swimming in white water or moving water: on your back, with feet up and pointing downstream. This prevents your feet from being wedged under a rock, and enables you to fend off rocks or obstructions without bashing your head.

scenic river Defined in the national Wild and Scenic Rivers Act as "those rivers or sections of rivers that are free of impoundments, with shorelines or watersheds still largely primitive and shorelines largely undeveloped, but accessible in places by roads."

scout To examine a rapid or route from the shore before paddling through it.

sculling A back-and-forth motion with a paddle blade, like smearing icing on a cake, that can draw you toward the paddle blade or can keep the blade at the surface supporting much of your weight.

sea sock A fabric bag that fits securely over the coaming of a kayak, with the paddler sitting in the bag within the cockpit. The bag limits the amount of water entering the cockpit, should the boat capsize or be swamped.

sea In nautical parlance, waves caused by winds at the time and place of the waves. Swell defines waves caused by winds in some distant place.

shaft The round or ovalized section of a canoe paddle between the grip and the blade, or between the blades of a kayak paddle.

sideslip Moving a canoe or kayak sideways in the water.

slice   Returning the paddle blade from the end of the stroke back to the catch without removing it from the water, usually rotating the blade so that it moves edge-first to reduce water resistance. Normally done with a canoe paddle.

sneak   Finding the easiest-possible route through a rapid.

solo   A canoe or kayak paddled by one person; also, a single paddler in a canoe or kayak.

splash cover   A fabric cover over an open canoe or kayak with openings for the paddler or paddlers, designed to shed water. Similar to a spray deck or spray skirt over the cockpit of a decked canoe or kayak.

spring tide   Tides near the new or full moon, when the tidal range is at its greatest.

stability   The tendency of a canoe or kayak to remain in one position without wiggling or feeling tippy.

standing wave   A stationary wave in a current.

starboard   The right side of a canoe or kayak, facing forward.

stem   The leading edge of a canoe or kayak, formed by the joining of the two sides of the hull.

stern   The back section of a canoe or kayak.

stern line   A short painter or rope attached to the stern of a canoe or kayak.

stern seat   The rear seat or position in a canoe or kayak.

stern sweep   A paddle stroke in which the paddle is inserted near the stern of the boat and is pushed away from the boat in a "C"-shaped arc toward amidships. This turns the bow toward the paddle side. Also called a reverse sweep.

strainer   Trees or branches in a current with the water flowing through. These can catch and pin a canoe or kayak.

stroke   The motion of a paddle to impart energy or direction to a canoe or kayak.

surf   A wave, usually breaking. Also refers to the act of riding the face of a wave.

swamp   To fill a canoe or kayak with water.

sweep   A paddle stroke in which the blade describes a "C"-shaped arc near the surface of the water, the primary turning stroke.

swell   A long wave that moves continuously without breaking.

switch paddling   A style of canoe paddling that features a set number of paddle strokes on one side, followed by a switch to paddle strokes on the other side, rather than using corrective strokes to maintain a desired direction.

symmetrical   A paddle blade in which the left and right halves of the blade are mirror images of each other. In the water, however, the force on each side of the blade is significantly different due to angle and depth of insertion.

T grip   A canoe paddle grip shaped like a "T" that enhances precise control of blade angle.

take-apart   Gear that may be assembled or disassembled. A take-apart paddle can be disconnected into two or more shorter sections for ease in transporting it. A take-apart canoe or kayak may be constructed in several sections that can be joined or separated, or may be constructed with a removable frame capable of being disassembled and a foldable fabric skin.

take-out   The end point of a trip, where you take the kayak or canoe out of the water.

tandem   A canoe or kayak paddled by two people. Also called a double.

throat   The transition from the paddle shaft to the paddle blade.

throw bag   A fabric bag holding up to 60 feet of line, making it easier to throw one end to a person in the water.

thwart   A crosspiece between the gunwales that gives shape to the hull as well as support to a paddler kneeling in a canoe.

tide   The vertical movement of water caused by the gravitation pull of the sun and the moon.

tongue   A smooth vee of fast-moving water, formed as a current flows between two obstacles such as boulders. The apex of the vee points downstream.

top grip   The top of a canoe paddle shaft, opposite from the blade.

torso rotation   Using your powerful torso muscles to power canoe or kayak strokes.

track   To go in a straight line without corrective strokes.

tracking   Pulling a canoe or kayak up-current with a rope or ropes. Also refers to the ability of a canoe or kayak to glide in a straight line without corrective strokes.

trim   The balance of a canoe or kayak and its load for optimum paddling performance.

tumblehome   The inward curve of the hull from its widest point at or near the waterline to the gunwales.

unfeathered   A kayak paddle with both blades parallel, or in the same plane.

upstream vee   Turbulent water created as a current is split by a rock or other obstacle. The apex of the vee points upstream.

watercourse   A natural stream channel that may or may not contain water as the season and conditions permit.

waterline   The line that water reaches on a canoe or kayak hull when the boat is in the water. A heavily loaded boat will sink deeper in the water; a lightly loaded boat will ride higher in the water.

wave train   A series of standing waves.

weathercocking   Turning bow into the wind.

white water   Literally, water that is white and foaming as it cascades through a rapid. Often used to describe turbulent and frothy water.

Wild and Scenic Rivers Act   A 1968 federal law (Public Law 90-542) establishing and setting forth the procedure for including outstanding river segments in a national system of free-flowing, protected rivers.

wild river   Defined in the national Wild and Scenic Rivers Act as "those rivers or sections of rivers that are free of impoundments and generally inaccessible except by trail, with watersheds or shorelines essentially primitive and water unpolluted. These represent vestiges of primitive America."

windward   The direction from which the wind is blowing, as seen from a canoe or kayak.

yoke   A thwart, fixed at the midpoint or fore and aft balance point of a canoe, and shaped to fit over the shoulders and around the neck, used to carry the canoe.

Paddling Resources

Associations and Organizations

American Whitewater Affiliation
1424 Fenwick Lane
Silver Spring, MD, 20910
Phone: 1-866-BOAT4AW
Fax: 301-565-6714
Website: www.americanwhitewater.org

A national not-for-profit whitewater river conservation organization with a membership of individual whitewater boating enthusiats and paddling club affiliates representing over 100,000 paddlers.

American Canoe Association
7432 Alban Station Blvd., Suite B-232
Springfield, VA 22150
Phone: 703-451-0141
Website: www.acanet.org/acanet.htm

The largest U.S.-based membership organization for sanctioning, supporting, and producing paddlesport events. The ACA is a recognized leader in the instruction and education of paddlesports, and works diligently to ensure that recreational paddlers have affordable, accessible information and courses that promote safe paddling skills.

America Outdoors
P.O. Box 10847
Knoxville, TN 37939
Phone: 865-558-3595
Website: www.americaoutdoors.org

America Outdoors is an international organization representing adventure travel outfitters, tour companies, and outdoor educators, providing trips and outdoor recreation services while supporting sustainable use of our natural heritage.

American River Conservancy
8913 Highway 49, P.O. Box 562
Coloma, CA 95613
Phone: 530-621-1224
E-mail: arc@arconservancy.org
Website: www.arconservancy.org

The American River Conservancy conducts conservation, education, and stewardship programs to protect and enhance native fisheries, vanishing plant and animal communities, scenic vistas, cultural heritage and recreational lands within the Cosumnes and American River watersheds in California.

American Rivers
1025 Vermont Ave., N.W. Suite 720
Washington, DC 20005
Phone: 202-347-7550
Fax: 202-347-9240
E-mail: amrivers@amrivers.org
Website: www.amrivers.org

American Rivers is a national nonprofit conservation organization dedicated to protecting and restoring healthy natural rivers across North America.

Canadian Canoe Association
Suite 705
2197 Riverside Drive
Ottawa, Ontario K1H 7X3
Phone: 613-260-1818
Fax: 613-260-5137
Website: www.canoekayak.ca

The Canadian umbrella organization that promotes and sanctions canoe and kayak competition from the local to the international level.

Canadian Recreational Canoeing Association
P.O. Box 398
446 Main St. West
Merrickville, Ontario K0G 1N0
Phone: 613-269-2910 or 1-888-252-6292
Fax: 613-269-2908
Website: paddlingcanada.com

The umbrella organization for sanctioning, supporting, and producing Canadian canoeing and kayaking paddlesport events. It is a recognized leader in instruction, certification, and education in paddlesports, and coordinates the national activities of the 13 provincial canoe and kayak associations.

International Dragon Boat Association
844 Prospect Avenue
Oakland, CA 94610
Phone: 510-452-4272
Fax: 510-465-8181
Website: www.edragons.org

The umbrella organization for all the local organizations involved in the promotion of Dragon Boats, their ceremonies, and competition.

National Association of State Boating Law Administrators
1500 Leestown Road, Suite 330
Lexington, KY 40511
Phone: 859-225-9487
Website: www.nasbla.org

The umbrella organization for those U.S. state and territorial agencies charged with enforcing state boating laws.

National Organization for Rivers
212 W. Cheyenne Mountain Boulevard
Colorado Springs, CO 80906
Phone: 719-579-8759
E-mail: nationalrivers@email.msn.com
Website: www.nationalrivers.org

A national organization for canoeing, kayaking, rafting, and fly fishing, actively involved with national river issues, river access issues, river destinations, river accident analysis, and river restoration and conservation.

National River Cleanup Week
P.O. Box 10847
Knoxville, TN 37939
Phone: 865-558-3595
E-mail: rivercleanup@aol.com
Website: www.americaoutdoors.org/nrcw/natao10.htm

The national effort to preserve, restore, and clean up America's most precious resource, it's rivers, focusing on a week-long showcase program of cleaning the nation's rivers each spring to bring attention of the littered state of the waterways.

North American Water Trails, Inc.
P.O. Box 53329
Washington, DC 20009
Phone: 202-232-8354
E-mail: astaats@his.com
Website: www.watertrails.org

A coalition of organizations and individuals committed to opening recreational access to North America's wealth of waters.

Professional Paddlesports Association
7432 Alban Station Boulevard, Suite B-244
Springfield, VA 22150
Phone: 1-800-789-2202
E-mail: ppa@propaddle.com
Website: www.propaddle.com

The Professional Paddlesports Association is a premier trade association serving the paddle-sports industry, including canoe, kayak and raft rentals, retailers, liveries, outfitters, manu-facturers, and distributors. PPA members help outdoor enthusiasts experience the fun and joy of rafting, canoeing, and kayaking the lakes, rivers, white-water streams, creeks, bays, and coastal waters of the United States and internationally.

River Conservancy
520 SW Sixth Avenue, Suite 1130
Portland, OR 97204-1535
Phone: 503-241-3506
E-mail: info@rivernetwork.org
Website: www.rivernetwork.org

The River Conservancy is a national leader in supporting grassroots river and watershed conservation groups.

Trade Association of Paddlesports
P.O. Box 6353
Olympia, WA 98507
Phone: 1-800-755-5228
E-mail: info@gopaddle.org
Website: www.gopaddle.com

Professional trade association supporting paddling-related manufacturers in North America.

USA Canoe/Kayak
15 Parkside Drive
P.O. BOX 789
Lake Placid, NY 12946
Phone: 518-523-1855
Fax: 518-523-3767

The United States organization charged with promoting and sanctioning the highest levels of canoe and kayak competition, from local events through Olympic Game and World. Championship events.

United States Canoe Association
Website: www.uscanoe.com

The national umbrella organization coordinating the efforts of local organizations to promote or stage marathon canoe and kayak competition, national aluminum canoe and marathon canoe/kayak competition, paddling instruction and instructor certification, all to encourage and recognize paddling as a competitive sport.

Publications

American Whitewater Journal
American Whitewater Affiliation
1424 Fenwick Lane
Silver Spring, MD, 20910
Phone: 866-BOAT4AW
Fax: 301-565-6714
Website: www.americanwhitewater.org

Canoe & Kayak Magazine
P.O. Box 3146
Kirkland, WA 98083
10526 NE 68th, Suite 3
Kirkland, WA 98033

Phone: 425-827-6363
Website: www.canoekayak.com

North America's number one paddlesport resource, with in-depth articles on fabulous destinations, the latest (and for the beginner, the most basic) paddling techniques, competition, conservation, gear and equipment, and the people involved in this growing sport. Special focus annual publications include the Beginner's Guide, Kayak Touring, Canoe Journal, and Whitewater.

Canoe News
United States Canoe Association
Website: www.uscanoe.com

Canoe News *is a bi-monthly magazine focussing on marathon canoe and kayak racing.*

Currents Magazine
The National Organization for Rivers
212 West Cheyenne Mountain Blvd.
Colorado Springs, CO 80906
Phone: 719-579-8759
Fax: 719-576-6238
E-mail: Nationalrivers@email.msn.com
Website: www.nationalrivers.org

Covering national river news, river access issues, river destinations, river accidents, and river restoration and conservation.

Kanawa
P.O. Box 398
446 Main Street West
Merrickville, ON K0G 1N0
Phone: 613-269-2910 or 1-888-252-6292
Fax: 613-269-2908
Website: www.paddlingcanada.com

A quarterly magazine published by the Canadian Recreational Canoeing Association, covering all phases of Canadian paddlesports and activities.

Paddler Magazine
Editorial and Advertising
P.O. Box 775450
Steamboat Springs, CO 80477
Phone: 970-879-1450
Website: www.paddlermagazine.com

Paddler Magazine *covers in depth all phases of paddlesports, from high-level competition to exciting and interesting destinations around the world.*

Sea Kayaker
P.O. Box 17029
Seattle, WA 98107-0729
7001 Seaview Ave NW, Suite 135
Seattle, WA 98117
Phone: 206-789-9536
Website: www.seakayaker.com

The definitive word on all phases of sea kayaking, from destinations to boat reviews, from analysis of accidents to the latest in gear and equipment.

Float Plan

A Float Plan is a simple document that identifies who is going paddling, where, with what, and when they are expected back. Before you head off on a paddling adventure, for a few hours or a few days, take a minute to fill it out and leave it with a responsible friend or relative. If something unforeseen happens, if unexpected weather keeps you beach-bound, or a boat wraps around a rock in a river locking the party into a remote canyon, your float plan will make the job of the search-and-rescue agencies called to help look for you immeasurably easier. When you note your return time, give yourself plenty of time to finish your paddling and to drive home or to the nearest phone.

Most important, remember to tell whoever has your float plan when you have returned. Being searched for when you're not missing is embarrassing at best, and at worst you might get a bill for the cost of the search.

1. Name and telephone numbers of paddlers:

   (1) _____

   (2) _____

   (3) _____

   (4) _____

2. Medical conditions of any of the paddlers: _____

_____

3. Descriptions of boats (deck color, hull color, length, whether open or decked):

      Boat 1 _____

      Boat 2 _____

      Boat 3 _____

      Boat 4 _____

4. In states or provinces where canoe and kayak registration is required, registration numbers:

      Boat 1 _____

      Boat 2 _____

      Boat 3 _____

      Boat 4 _____

5. Colors of expected paddling clothes, if available: _____

_____

6. Trip Plan:

      Put-In _____

      Take-Out _____

  Planned route _____

_____

      For overnight trips, planned campsites:

      Day 1 _____

      Day 2 _____

      Day 3 _____

      Return date and time (anticipated) _____

7. Contact information:

    Cell-phone numbers _____

    Radios and frequencies _____

    EPIRB _____

8. Tent(s) color, style, and number (for multiday trips):

    Tent 1 _____

    Tent 2 _____

9. In case of emergency or if overdue:

    Contact person _____

    Contact telephone _____

    Cars and licenses _____

        At put-in

            Car 1 _____

            Car 2 _____

        At take-out

            Car 1 _____

            Car 2 _____

        At other locations

            Car 1 _____

            Car 2 _____

For an obscure route, attach map or chart marked with put-in, take-out, and route.

If you need more space, use the back side of your float plan for additional names or information.

Index

N

Q-R

W

X-Y-Z